Praise for *The Human Experience*!

"I read these chapters with eagerness and gratitude. Like the author, I sense that the whole *rhythm* of
our existence is ignored and not understood, so that
there is no 'gathering' (of scattered human forces,
fragmented efforts of a society of alienation). Reminds
me of Desmond Tutu: 'I'm too busy to pray for less
than two hours a day.'

As McNamara says, deep humanness requires
ample time, splendid leisure and attentive silliness.
'We love because he first loved us'—could we say also,
'We live because he first lived us'? This is a vision that
a two-dimensional Church and a one-dimensional
world are so hungry for."

—Rowan Williams, Archbishop of Canterbury

"To read this book is to drink cold, clear water that
both quenches your thirst and shows you how thirsty
you have actually been—for deep spiritual passion. An
ecstatically insightful and joyously troubling book!"

—Jacob Needleman, author of *Why Can't We Be Good?*

The Human Experience

Published in the United States by
Beckham Publications Group, Inc.
P.O. Box 4066, Silver Spring, MD 20914

ISBN: 978-0-9841991-2-9
0-9841991-2-8
Library of Congress Cataloging in Publication:
2010902832

The Human Experience
A Divine Madness

William McNamara

THE Beckham
PUBLICATIONS GROUP, INC.
Silver Spring

It has never been my ambition to please everyone. I am always prepared to take the criticism along with the praise, and on the whole think that the former is more stimulating. It keeps me in a state of healthy irritation rather than of complacent satisfaction.

— Ogden Mills

Every truth is a reflection; behind the reflection, and giving it value, is the Light. Every being is a witness; every fact is a divine secret; beyond them is the object of the revelation, the hero witnessed to. Everything true stands out against the Infinite as against its background; it is related to it, belongs to it.

— A. G. Sertillanges, O.P

Clergymen short of a simile sometimes upbraid the heedless by likening their behavior to that of the beasts. They flatter us: hippopotamuses don't teleview, pigs don't read the comics and cats don't memorize smut to tell to other cats.

— Bruce Marshall, *Thoughts of My Cats*

Contents

Preface

inherited from my parents and siblings (I am the baby) a way of life suffused with grace, the transforming life of the spirit. I will call this ontological tenderness and affectionate kindness. This mode of existence, free of violence, vulgarity, and impurity, permeated our whole family—its domesticity, hospitality, and congeniality, its joyful discipline and wonder-filled worship, its unselfconsciousness and courageous acceptance of hardship; and in particular, one stunning achievement: the preservation of elegant and reverent language—no small accomplishment in this age when language is everywhere humiliated and left in a shambles.

And yet—and this thrills me to pieces—there was no snobbery, no prudishness. Our sense of home and holiness was not rectitude but amplitude, sheer grace co-acted by parental wisdom. Even I, the family rascal, became imbued with this good infection. The word that seemed to capture for me this family vitality, this community of love, was *purity*. In the humdrum questionnaires I have filled out since childhood, when asked, "What is your favorite virtue?" I answered, "Purity."

Now at the end of my life it is for the sake of purity—genuine, vivacious, embattled purity—that I am

focusing so intensely on *eros*, that basic divinized sexual energy in us that seeks the pure intuition of God
born of love: union with all, care of all, compassion for
all. Whoever remains unloving and un-contemplative,
arrogantly separate, can do no good. All the therapy
in the world won't help if we do not love boundlessly and unconditionally. Therapists, and the cowards
they pander to, love boundaries—always something
safe and secure, a good hiding place. Jesus, the whole
man, pulverized them by His presence, His consuming fire.

Jesus prayed that His compelling spirit would restore in us the likeness of God, and that we in turn
would ignite it in the whole natural world, glorifying
everything—"give to them the glory you gave to me"—
thus accentuating the interdependent non-duality of
the universe, and making it pellucidly, clear that we
are relational, and authentic to the extent that we recognize this intrinsic constitutional fact, a fundamental given of existence. Consequently, what is required
of us, whether we be mystical or scientific, is compassion, indeed, empathy, for all of creation. We must
take good care of the Earth. We must struggle for justice and peace, for environmental holiness.

I know it is dangerous, at this time when pandemic
fear has skewered the minds of a vast segment of civilization. Tenderness and compassion, in fact all of the
unifying forces that once established our glory, are
now suspect, including perseverance and fidelity—
and not just fidelity to a spouse but, even especially,
fidelity to a friend or to a cat, a dog, or a hairy-nosed
wombat. The judgmental windbags will call it inappropriate. What do they know? Only you know. So do
it anyway. Otherwise you sell out. And the plangent
howl of the crucified-risen Christ is even more shattering than the one we heard on Calvary.

Human life really lived is always an adventure and a discovery. If we are not breaking through, attaining deeper levels of being, becoming more and more human, i.e., radiating God exquisitely, then we stagnate. We lose our original glory. We think we are highly advanced, superbly sophisticated, and yet the 20th century is the most murderous in human history. The horrible thing is that our barbarism is more sophisticated. The Holy Traditions, depositories of wisdom, highlight this fact and represent in word and deed what a humanizing, divinized breakthrough is really like.

In the traditions of East and West, positive, transforming breakthroughs are often described as the glorious effect of a mighty lion.

"As for the lion which you saw coming from the forest, roused from sleep and roaring...this is the Messiah whom the Most High has kept back until the end," claimed the priest-scribe Esdras in an apocryphal writing only a few hundred years before the birth of Christ. "He will be merciful to those of my people that remain...; he will set them free and give them gladness" (2 Esdras 12:31-34). In more recent times, Swami Vivekananda speaks in the same terms in *The Complete Works of Swami Vivekananda*:

> A lioness in search of prey came upon a flock of sheep, and as she jumped at one of them, she gave birth to a cub and died on the spot. The young lion was brought up like a sheep, and it never knew that it was a lion. One day a lion came across the flock and was astonished to see in it a huge lion eating grass and bleating like a sheep. At his sight the flock fled and the lion-sheep with them. But the lion watched his opportunity and one day he found the lion-sheep asleep. He woke him up and said, "You are a lion." The other said, "No," and began to bleat like a sheep. But the stranger lion took him to a lake and asked him to look in the water at his own image and see if

*it did not resemble him, the stranger lion. He looked
and acknowledged that it did. Then the stranger lion
began to roar and asked him to do the same. The
lion-sheep tried his voice and soon was roaring as
grandly as the other. And he was a sheep no longer.*

THE LION STORY

The Lion Story is another version of the Bible story. It's the story of the Exodus, the Passover, the de-
liverance of the people of God from the enslavement
of Egypt. It took a wild, "wanted," passionate man,
seized by the fury of God, to free the Israelites from
the Egyptian slavery to which they had grown accustomed. Once liberated they fell into other forms of disgraceful bondage so that other prophets of the same
indomitable spirit of Moses had to rise up and reform
the people of God, lest they lose their image and likeness of the deity and become, by the force of sheer
habit, immutable slaves once again.

Out of this resolute race came one who was more
than a prophet. He was a special kind of man. Jesus
became the Christ, the free man, the God-man, and
therefore, the liberator, the divinizer, the pontiff: the
bridge to freedom and the way to deification. The Lion
Story is above all the story of Christ who recognized
that he was no sheep and could roar like a lion! When
he perceived the divinity within him, our pristine unfettered humanness was restored; in fact, it was infinitely improved. Christ came "that we might have life
and have it more abundantly" (John 10:10). He insti-
tuted what we call the Church (a pack of lions) to keep
this wild, exuberant, and divine vitality alive in the
world forever.

After the Ascension, however, the baby lions Christ
left behind were overwhelmed by the huge number of
sheep compared with the paucity of lions. Impressed
by the fact that sheep are protected in safe, lush
places and fed regularly, even though eventually led

to slaughter, they crept back into the sheepfolds. By the fourth century there were only a few wild, roaring lions left, and with some exceptions they survived only in the wilderness. You could hardly tell the difference between the average, nice, tame lion and the sheep of the flock with which he merged.

When intimate communion with the deity began to fade and the loving awareness of the ultimate ceased to be the formative principle in human consciousness, then human diminishment became prominent. It happened not calamitously but clandestinely—a pretty poison seeping into our nicest people, our best institution. Lions became sheep without knowing it. The "common man" became all too common.

THE COMMON DENOMINATOR

There ought to be a great deal of devotion, solicitude, and reverence for the common man—but for his manhood, not his commonness. Today, instead of demanding only that the common man be given the opportunity to become as uncommon and superior as possible, we make this commonness a virtue, an obligation, an end in itself.

Mr. Joseph W. Krutch has written an excellent and revealing article in the *Saturday Review of Literature*, where he gallantly endeavors, and partly succeeds to answer the pertinent question: "Is the Common Man too Common?" Of all the influences which Mr. Krutch lists as unfavorable, and, in fact, injurious to our society, the most serious, he says, is the tendency to confuse the Common Denominator with a standard of excellence. This tendency is glaringly exemplified by radio and television, which produce what the greatest number of people seem to want. The mechanical and economical facts which tend to give the purveyors of mediocrity a monopoly may possibly be changed by new developments. But to confuse the best with what

is most widely and most generally acceptable is to reveal a spiritual confusion which is as fundamental
as it is subtle and insidious. It could readily bring to
naught any solution of the mechanical and economical problems created by the age of mass production.

The common denominator is being exalted, unfortunately, not only by the common man himself and
his exploiters, but also by those who are supposed
to be educators and intellectual leaders. They seek to
know not what a good education essentially and necessarily involves but what *most* college students *want*.
Instead of using books that are wisest, best and most
appropriate, they use books that have been proved by
the polls to be the most read with least pain.

"Examination papers are marked, not in accordance with any fixed standard, but in accordance
with a usual level of achievement; the amount of work
required is fixed by the amount the average student
does, and even the words with which the average student is not familiar are edited out of the books he is
given to read." Courses are planned for and built up
around the median, the middle of the class. The good
student is unchallenged, bored. The loafer receives
his passing grade. This lack of outstanding students
and high standards passes for democracy.

In the meantime, we are eminently in danger of
losing what Seymore St. John calls "our Fifth Freedom"—*the freedom to be one's best*, the opportunity of
each person to develop to his highest power.

This is the kind of freedom I mean to highlight in
this book. It is necessarily so because of our vocation:
to appeal to the elite, not to cater obsequiously—with
cruel pity—to the crowd; and because of our terrible
responsibility: to be society's leaven rather than its
tool. It is our task to sharpen the spirit, to cultivate
taste, to develop personality, to save souls for glory,
for splendor, for God—not by shaping our efforts to

[margin notes: Roots of mediocrity; Where's pursuit of Excellence; Challenge to a higher aspiration; non-Conformity]

their apathy, but to their highest aspiration; not by
highlighting the lowest common denominator, but by
emphasizing the highest.

PERILS OF CONFORMITY

Many of the nation's wise men stake the health of
our society upon consistent adjustment of individuals
to the consensus of the group. This is not simply an
unwitting yen for conformity, but a philosophy of otherwise reasonable men. It is a damaging philosophy. It
clips the burgeoning brilliance of our youth. It chokes
enthusiasm. It destroys genius. It impedes holiness.
We have no one with a gift for mockery, no one on fire
with holy indignation, no one with capacity for Olympian laughter, no great tranquil rebels like Christ, no
saints who refuse, like uncompromising Gibraltars, to
adjust to the capricious temper of the times.

The ideal of the schools, churches, clinics and societies are all the same: *Conformity* by means of adjustment. *Normalcy* has almost completely replaced
excellence as an ideal. It has cast dubious shadows
over such terms as *righteousness, integrity, truth.* The
question is no longer how one ought to act, but how do
most people act. Or, as David Reisman sums it up in
his brilliant work called *The Lonely Crowd,* the American who used to be conspicuously "inner-directed" is
now conspicuously "outer-directed."

A biological axiom explains that progress is made
only through differences. The breeders of race horses
would have little success if some animals were not
born different from the ordinary. The same is true
of tulips, or tomatoes—or thinkers. If we all tend to
think, or appear to think, the same way, under compulsion or out of laziness, the laws broadly determin-
ing intellectual development cease to operate.

Must we adjust ourselves to the aims of our present-
day culture, which are avowedly ease and material

Charles Malik spoke at my graduation ND.

US weakening of our moral fibre

well-being? Or are we required to spend ourselves untiringly in an unremitting effort to challenge the best that is in our people and evoke a consequent response? The answer is obvious. But it is not, in reality, evident. Small wonder that Charles Malik, former Lebanese delegate of the UN writes: "There is in the West (in the United States) a general weakening of moral fibre. (Our) leadership does not seem to be adequate to the unprecedented challenges of the age."

freedom through self-discipline mainstream

We owe to our people—to our readers—the most demanding and challenging reading that is within their capabilities. Abraham Lincoln did not achieve his enviously high and noble stature by doodling. Mendelssohn did not compose masterpieces in his ?youth as a result of spending his days passively in front of a TV set. Like St. Pope Pius X and St. Therese, like Joan of Arc and Helen Keller, they responded to the challenge of their lives with a disciplined training: and they gained a new freedom.

PEOPLE ARE UNDERESTIMATED

On the other hand, people are getting much less than they can take, much worse than what they want. We underestimate the people. John Stuart Mill wrote a century ago: "Capacity for the nobler feeling is in most natures a very tender plant. . .Men lose their high aspirations as they lose their intellectual tastes, because they have not time or opportunity for indulging in them; and they addict themselves to inferior pleasures, not because they deliberately prefer them but because they are either the only ones to which they have access, or the only ones which they are any longer capable of enjoying."

Joseph Krutch reminds us that "at a time when the two major networks were offering daytime serials all day long and protesting that women wouldn't listen to anything else, 78 percent of all women in such a

Joseph Krutch?,

city as Boston were simply not listening; within a few years it was discovered that women would listen to many other kinds of programs." The success of Bishop Sheen is just another example of how erroneous we can be in our estimation of what people like and want.

One learns from this book "that people at every level of education, in significant numbers, imply dissatisfaction with the radio programs they are getting, and among these are 10,000,000 not habitual book readers, not college graduates, who consistently ask for programs of a higher intellectual content. Book readers and college graduates make the same request twice as often but are numerically less important."

Mr. Krutch lays bare the blatancies of radio, TV and press management in committing the irreparably harmful fallacy of gauging the common man's capacity too low. This is an error which the Catholic Press has not entirely repulsed; to which it has, in part, succumbed—to our own loss and shame. From further compromise and secular influence, O Lord, deliver us!

"WE JUST WANT THE FACTS"

That is, unfortunately, what the majority of people probably say. That is why we are constrained to take St. Augustine's advice: "not to write for the majority of men." Why not? Because "most men have learned to read to serve a paltry convenience, as they have learned to cipher in order to keep accounts and not be cheated in trade; but of reading as a noble intellectual exercise they know little or nothing; yet this only is reading, in a high sense, not that which lulls us as a luxury and suffers the nobler faculties to sleep the while, but what we have to stand on tiptoe to read and devote our most alert and wakeful hours to. . . The result is dullness of sight, a stagnation of the vital circulations, and a general deliquium and sloughing off of all the intellectual faculties. This sort of gingerbread is baked daily and more sedulously than pure wheat or rye—and—Indian in almost every oven, and finds a surer market. . . . We are a race of titmen, and soar but little higher in our intellectual fights than the columns of the daily paper." Augustine? Sounds more like Thoreau.

Not everyone will read books like this. If we can reach an elite, whether it be among family people, workers, students, engineers, soldiers, farmers (and the more specialized the group, the more intensive our message can be), then that elite will lead their brothers.

Shakespeare's Cassius says: "Upon what meat doth this our Caesar feed that he has grown so great!" Upon what meat does the soul of modern man feed that it has grown so puny? A man can't sustain his soul in maturity with spiritual baby food. This is not a new idea. It stems from St. Paul's familiar text about milk for babes, meat for men. We who write ought to strike out boldly in a gallant effort to wean men away from pap, gruel, spiritual sweetmeats.

✓ Trouble is, according to Oscar Wilde: "Great Literature is the only thing readable; and Journalism is the only thing read."

But men can't live on facts. Facts are nothing. There is nothing older than yesterday's newspaper. What a man needs is truth, the profound mystery of being that lies beyond every fact; truth—to stimulate his mind so that he can see beyond the gaze of his eyes and aim infinitely higher than the reach of his arms; to dilate his heart so he can break through his conventional, parochial circle of narrow interests and petty concerns.

While we live in the world as citizens, we must, to some extent, be interested in facts, somewhat impressed too; but we may, respectably, be tired of facts raw, unpondered, unalchemized. One may not weary of truth, though one may of news.

The eternal truths are not pillows on which to go to sleep. Nothing is easier as life goes on than to sink back into well-worn grooves of thought, prejudice—and even dogmas—from which there is no emergence, to become set in an intellectual immobility, a kind of hardening of the psychological arteries.

Dogma is not dead; nor is it static. Without change, it develops; it unfolds itself. The Church is not a rock. It is built on a rock. That is why it can grow mightily, straining for perfection and ultimate triumph with reckless abandon, with divine freedom. It can apply its most ancient principles to the most modern needs with perfect adequacy and calm immunity. It can reach out with its saving power to the dimensions of the universe: the Church is built on a rock—it has no fear of tumbling.

We cling like green lichen to the rock of the Church; but reach out like bursting clouds to embrace the parched earth.

Inattention!

THE DECLINE IN READING

One recent poll indicated 18 percent of Americans were reading a book. In England, 55 percent. In Australia and Canada, 34 percent. Only 28 percent of Americans with college education were reading a book.

It seems evident that there are more radical reasons for this decline, both then and now, than the growth of TV. Dissipation of attention is by no means a minor factor in the staggering statistics. Two things have happened in the decline of attention during the past hundred years or so. There has been a *displacement* of attention, as Wordsworth pointed out so cogently in his *Lyrical Ballads*: "For a multitude of causes unknown to former times are now acting with a combined force to blur the discriminating powers of the mind, and unfitting it for all voluntary exertion, to, reduce it to a state of almost savage torpor. The most effective of these causes are the great national events which are daily taking place, and the unceasing accumulation of men in cities, where the uniformity of their occupations produces a craving for extraordinary incident which the rapid communication of intelligence hourly gratifies."

Fifty years later, Henry James writes not merely of displacement, but *paralysis*. In a letter to William Dean Howells he wrote: "The *faculty of attention* has utterly vanished from the general Anglo-Saxon mind; extinguished at its source by the big blatant Boyadere of Journalism, of the newspaper and the picture (above all) magazine; who keeps screaming, 'Look at me, I am the thing, and I only, the thing that will keep you in relation with me all the time without your having to attend one minute of the time. . . . Illustrations, loud simplifications and grossissements . . . the prose that is careful to be in the tone of, and with the distinction of a newspaper of bill-poster advertisement—these, and these only, meseems, stand a chance.

Editors and publishers have found success capitalizing on the debilitated, dissipated attention of their readers who, they know, want to be well informed, not induced to reflect; to be attracted by what they see, not engaged by what they read. And so have the digests, the pulps, the picture magazines, the weekly news catalogues, the sensational mammoth monthlies, and all the other soft ottomans of print.

This book will not displace these others, we know. But if we do our job vigorously and prayerfully; if Catholics take their Christian vocations seriously, and fulfill their duties faithfully—with respect to reading; then this book should make an impression, and subsequently have some kind of impact on the world around us. We think it will. Shall the inheritors of the skies be satisfied with the husks of material satiety? Shall sharers of the Divine life, partakers of the Eucharist, go on nibbling the paltry morsels of a puny, slanted press? "To whom shall w go? You have a message of eternal life; we fully believe and are firmly convinced that you are the Holy One of God!"

It is a dreadful thing to wait; to tarry on the wrong road, to dally with signs and samples, and miss the substance, the reality. It is a terrible thing not to have lived. This book is coming into print for the same reasons that the Word was made flesh: "that you may have life, and have it more abundantly." It will quicken one's pace, enliven his pulse, stimulate thought, dilate his heart and drive him to action. He will be alive.

ABILITY

It would be egregious folly for us to comment with complacency upon our skill and ability. We will never feel adequately equipped to cope satisfactorily with our towering objectives. We do know though, like Leon Bloy, "that it is indisputable that Truth should appear in Glory, and that splendor of style is not a luxury; it is a necessity."

But our singular advantage lies not in the excellence of our brains, but in the strength of our principles.

Arthur Macken, an English essayist, writes succinctly on this point: "Unless you digest and assimilate dogmas, the eternal truths, you cannot write literature, however clever and amusing you may be. . . . From a literary standpoint, Catholic dogma is merely the witness, under a special symbolism of the enduring facts of human nature and the universe; it is merely the voice which tells us distinctly that man is *not* the creature of the drawing room and the Stock Exchange, but a lonely, awful soul confronted by the Source of all souls, and you will realize that to make literature it is necessary to be, at all events subconsciously, catholic."

Religious —
reflect revelation of the
and tradition of the
Church !

We are religious; and because we are, in blood and bone and sinew, in body and mind we bear the revelation, the tradition, the earthly experience and the accumulated wisdom of the religion.

If we, as writers, hope to forestall the grotesque aberrations that beset our civilization, we have got to be more than tools of its blind, unsavory growth; more than mirrors of its violence, and disintegration. We, through our own efforts charged with God's grace, have got to regain the initiative for the human person and the forces of life, chaining up the demons we have allowed to run loose, and reintroducing the angels and ministers of grace we have sinfully and shamefully imprisoned.

The writer is, above all, a creator, a maker; not merely an informer, a recorder of fact. It is his job to arouse thought, to break down barriers of vision, and open up new horizons, to interpret vast and lofty possibilities. His intuitions of the future may give substance to a better world, and help steer our civilization into a fresh cycle of adventure and effort. The writer of our time must strive for wholeness in a disorganized and divided society. He must be capable of interpreting life in its manifold dimensions, especially on levels woefully neglected by the past half century; restoring reason to the irrational, purpose to the defeatists and drifters, value to the nihilists, truth to the pragmatists and hope to those caught in the plague of mass desperation.

We who dare write need to be chided by you the way that French intellectual giant, François Mauriac, did years ago:

> "I would like to be assured that they are not too much affected by what is 'of the day,' they from whom we ask the words of eternity.... I confess that it does not interest me in the least to know what my friends in Orders think about the

Marshall Plan, the revolution in technics, or the crisis of French cinema....The purpose of these Religious in the (world) of today is to maintain a guide-post, is to say over and over again untiringly in the name of their Master: 'I am there; I am always there....' How ill-adapted they are to this world whose language they do their utmost to speak! How one would like to cry out to them – but most certainly not as an affront – on the contrary, as praise "attend to what concerns you, to Him who concerns you, to Him whom you concern; initiate yourself into the secret of contemplation....Oh! how avidly I would listen to them, if they spoke to me of the Son of man, not as theologians, not as sociologists, but as those who see, who touch the resurrected Christ!"

I have witnessed and experienced many tragedies in my life. Though wrapped in banalities of everyday, commonplace calamities, the one almost fated to be potentially disastrous is the fall from grace into the psyche, from mystique into technique. Two contemporary striking examples of such abhorrent pitfalls are ubiquitous cell phones and illusory therapy. Granted, a few lives have been saved but millions have been alienated from the Truth, the self and Ultimate Love. Unfortunately this is all part of the Western World's tendency today to be twee.

Like the lion in the sheepfold, we are captive and de-lionized, but satisfied enough in a tweely sort of way. We live on pills and paltriness—a diet of pretty poison. Whether we are Protestant or Catholic, our sheepfold is *subverted Christianity*. We eat grass and bleat like sheep. We need to be liberated. We need to be radically transformed to look into the eyes of the Lion King, the Christ, and to hear him roar with the bellowing cry of the universe, and then to lift our heads up high and roar the naked Truth, embody the boundless

Love and be a sheep no longer. We must remember, though, that the gracious, infinitely attractive Lion we follow is not a tame lion.

Still, no need to be psychologically afraid, but rather ontologically awed, drawn by humble wonderment away from the moralism of domesticated Christianity into the moral audacity and spiritual grandeur of a Christ-man or Christ-woman. Jesus didn't want rhapsodic fans, but intrepid, inventive followers. To be content with subverted Christianity is to be a coward.

A while ago I encountered a fervent band of Christ-followers who often performed classical Christ-myths, sang warrior songs and even introduced a large, heavy, magnificent sword to play with in their impressive rituals. But when they were really challenged by life itself they sought sheep pens and ran perfidiously into safe, gated places. Piety is easily and often inflated. What we do need always and everywhere is wisdom, kindness and courage.

Our task is to become exquisitely human, to develop a capacity for morality, for participating in the creative act of Infinite Being. We are eminently in danger of losing the deepest aspect of our feeble freedom: the urge to become one's best self, the opportunity of each person to reach the pinnacle of divine humanness, i.e. the loving awareness of the intimate Realness of Existence. This is the kind of sheer, undiluted—unsubverted—Christianity that ignites and cultivates.

Boundless gratitude to my editors: Michael Witt, former editor of Cowley Publishers and Barry Beckham, publisher of this book. What a joy to work with such men—so personal, so present and so good at their jobs!

Wm. McNamara

"Every man needs a little bit of madness; otherwise he will never cut the rope and be free."

—Zorba the Greek

Cry of the Heart

The basic human instinct is to pray. Stifle prayer, your passionate longing for communication with the Ultimate, and your existence within, your personality, shrinks and your demeanor turns into a stuffy semblance of something human. This remote resemblance to humanness issues in mannequin men and women.

So I begin this book with a chapter on prayer, and I'm sure I will return to this humanizing act toward the book's end. In between I will eschew pietism, moralism, and narcissism, hoping all along that your consciousness and mine will be heightened and that our humanity will be divinized, or, as the brilliant church fathers put it more daringly and truly, that we will be deified.

Enlightenment is what we seek. What does that mean? Existentially, it means this: that I relish all the gifts that God bestows upon me to make life more and more livable, that both the pleasures of the flesh and the delights of the spirit are, to some degree, the presence of God felt, and that every joy, sacred and profane, lures me into the plenitude of the Ineffable.

And this too: that the loss of health, home, friends, and reputation, the pain of aloneness, poverty, and reflection, the suffering caused by mendacity and the absolute horror of perfidy—that these sad events enable me to bear the pain of Christ and the kiss of God and thus to offer God a pure heart.

CHRISTIAN HUMANISM

all inclusive under God.

Christian Humanism is a worldwide perspective that is neither liberal nor conservative, neither relative nor absolute, neither fixed securely in lapidary dogmas nor floating lackadaisically in far-flung fantasies. Though steeped in science and sustained by the arts, Christian Humanism is larger than both; though inspired by the Christian experience and enlightened by other reliable religious traditions, it exceeds them, while integrating them seriously and creatively, acknowledging their value with pungency and enthusiasm. A humanism that is merely secular is hardly a genuine humanism.

Any ideology that divides the human race into *us* and *them* is not an authentic humanism. A belief system that regards a select segment of humanity as either chosen or superhuman is not humanistic, nor is ethnocentrism, chauvinism, anti-Semitism, radical feminism, or homophobia. If we are actively convinced of our interfused relationships to all creatures on Earth, and nothing is foreign to or independent of our love and care, then our spirituality may be called cosmic or planetary, and our lifestyle a fulgent instance of Christian Humanism.

"Christian" does not introduce an exclusive note, but rather a universal principle, a unifying presence. The world belongs to God, not us. We are responsible stewards or, if you will, high priests of creation. If we love God, we love God's world. Christ is the embodiment of this love—of the Infinite, the Ineffable. "He who sees me," Jesus said, "sees the Father," the Origin, the Source, the Erotic Energy, the Unifying One who is always there. And the ravishing marvel is that the Holy Other is there, here, everywhere—infinitely distinct, super-personal, but utterly, unspeakably intimate.

In the rhythm of life and its revolution at the center of the cosmos, in the hurly-burly of the world, there is the eternal Creative Act, the Cosmotheandric Presence whose heart beats always with the fierce and fiery energy of eros and pathos.

We have finally come to realize that the Ultimate, the Absolute is not static. In a sense He (She if you like) is the Unmoved Mover; in a larger sense, the most Moved Mover. His spirit, stirring up the mass of the universe, is ultimately there—in the sunset, in the music, in the cancer. When we rejoice, His joy is more, when we suffer, His pain is more.

I cannot think of The Source, The Ground of Being, The One as way up or out there. No one is more intimate, nothing more ubiquitous. To think of Him as an object is almost to blaspheme. He is that super-personal *moreness* that haunts every human being. Is Michelangelo enough? Dante? Beethoven? Shakespeare? Is Marilyn Monroe? No. Is Beyonce Knowles? Well...Well...Hmm... No!

Our infinite, eternal lover did not once create and then stop. It goes on intensely and boundlessly. To love is to love without measure; and this is true of Deity and Humanity. Bind love, restrain it, categorize it and you stifle it. We need an interior sense of things, a universal perspective. Zorba the Greek was right: "Every man needs a little bit of madness; otherwise he will never cut the rope and be free."

Free to love and to love freely. Categorize love either psychologically or theologically and you stifle it. The greatest lovers in the world were condemned because their love had no boundaries and fit no categories. They were not bold, brazen outlaws. Neither were they conformists, cogs in the system, routinized robots. They were themselves. Jesus was unique because he was normal. He respected the standards of his Jewish culture while being astutely and faithfully docile to the transforming Spirit. In those depths he "lived and moved and had his being." His mission was to convince us we must do the same. Like St. Paul and all the enlightened mystics, we must evolve until we can say: "I live now not I but Christ lives within me." Becoming human means becoming the contemporary Christ. A bloated ego is the basic human disability. A highly developed eros is our vital force.

This erotic-spirited energy is what fuels the whole human adventure, enabling us to relate with awe and reverence to every creature and to the One who Shepherds all of being toward fulfillment. The highest human act is communion, reaching an ultimate state of glory in the love between a man and a woman and the ultimate glory in union with God.

When a man loves a woman passionately, astonished by her beauty that lures him into her mystery, all his quotidian trivia, his petty preoccupations, and his soporific lusts are eclipsed. She reveals God, manifests Him and conveys the real world for him, and yet she is not the center of the world.

The plangent cry that rises up from the innermost depth of our being is indeed a howling search for the other, not for an equal to cherish, not another human to comfort us. What we long for is a God to adore.

There is nothing like the Incarnation of God to shake us out of our humdrum everydayness. Our contemporary problem is banality, a bland, boring disorder that can be vanquished by only one thing: carnality infused with spirit. Teilhard de Chardin, a religious scientist, mystic, and audacious human lover, protects devotion to the Sacred Heart from pietistic claptrap and sentimental schlock. The reincarnate spirituality of divinized matter and flesh, of hallowed heaven and Earth, of crucified love, of sheer loyalty—this is real Christianity, and it keeps the world from falling apart.

The most popular of all religious devotions calls this dynamic central force, this diffusive energy, the Sacred Heart. Unfortunately, like so many popular devotions, it tends to be presented in sentimental, often spurious, even Pecksniffian terms. But in His scientific work, such as *The Phenomenon of Man*, Chardin, one of my favorite human beings, captures the fascinating, thrilling, and shocking reality of the Sacred Heart. Christ's heart became for him the powerful image of God's outpouring love and life pulsating through the whole of creation. That small, fleshy human heart embodied a fire animating the whole world.

Jesus was passionately pure and purely passionate. He was led by the Spirit directly to the end, to the Other; so following him means risking our lives for the other. Genuine otherness evokes from the *yearning* lover three riveting, reverent acts of contemplation: aspiration, appreciation, and adoration. *Aspiration* drives us beyond satisfaction to something that endures faithfully and permeates deeply. *Appreciation* is so delightful; it pleases and gratifies us forever. *Adoration* catapults us out of our separate existence into union with the other.

One caveat: The words *passionate* and *wildness* will pervade this book, necessarily so, because they describe and qualify a vital existence and a significantly human adventure. I am so firmly convinced that we are not erotic enough that I feel compelled to highlight being human as personal, passionate presence—sharing with God His wildness, a state of being in which there are no stingy motions of envy, just sheer generosity.

But beware: There is nothing giddy or grandiose about a passionate life—nothing perfervid or pietistic. The intensity is interior and completely devoid of histrionics. Let me share with you a funny example of a wild, passionate meeting between a man and a woman. Traveling through Boston I needed a haircut. I phoned and arranged one for the following day, a cutting-edge rendezvous between "Anna" and "William." At 11 a.m. I opened the salon door and entered. A vision of beauty, splendor, and serenity approached me. Clothed in a long, luminous, and colorful dress—very Russian, I think—she shimmered in loveliness. And then she spoke: "Are you William?"

Stuttering with astonishment, I said "yes."

"I'm Anna. Come, William, follow me." I followed her with awe-filled alacrity. I sat, silent and surrendered. While she immersed herself in her craft we remained wrapped in mutual silence. Occasionally, I'd open my eyes and behold this gorgeous woman floating gracefully around the chair, smiling all the time, blessing my head with her perfect hands, cutting, snipping as if enveloped in art, in worship, in love. And, in fact, she was. And so was I.

The silence was never broken and contemplation was sustained to the end. I rose from my chair, reached for my wallet, and she spoke: "There is no charge." We embraced. I departed. I have lived on a higher level of consciousness ever since. That silent "cry of the heart" still resonates through my whole body-person.

This is what Jesus taught His friends when, out of a felt need, they asked Him how to pray. Prayer is a cry of the heart, ultimately the cry of the sacred heart of Christ. Think of the whole world crying out of an immense sea of sorrow or out of Olympian joy, the universal cry of the deer, the wolf, the coyote, the lion, the dog and cat, the donkey, the horse, the seal, and the loon; think of old men and young girls, of lonely individuals and mindless crowds, of refugees and prisoners, of triumphant athletes and multitudes of the sick, the halt, and the insane. Think of soldiers in battle all over the world. Then think of the Representative Man, the High Priest of creation, who hangs on the cross, gathers up all these tiny fragments of prayer, the cries of the heart, and unites them with His own infinite and ultimate cry: "My God, my God, why have you forsaken me?" (Matt. 27:46).

This terrible, tormented scream from the cross was followed by the most triumphant human howl in the history of the world: "It is done!" What exactly was accomplished? His glorious passion; His passionate life, lustrous and radiant, culminating in His tortured way of the cross on Calvary, fulfilled in His stunning victory over death. After His donkey kicked the stone away from the tomb, the Representative Man, the God Man, rose and rode, gleaming with divine dignity, smiting His beloved, Magdalena, with unbearable, untouchable love, and gathering His feckless, fearful disciples into an unflinching commitment and unfailing solidarity. His cry became their cry and the panting, sweating, soaring Church came into existence and to this day, though beaten and ashamed, remains indomitable. How come? Because the Spirit, Eros, enlivens and dynamizes the worldly saints and the touched sinners. And that one salvific cry of the Sacred Heart sanctifies us all despite how oppressed we are by absurdity, banality, and ignorance. Sanctify us? Well, yes, if we resemble him in our own unique way as faithful lovers. Jesus did not want fans. He wanted robust followers.

Christ's cry of the heart is called the Our Father, and that's what he taught the disciples. The concept of God as "Our Father" was already prevalent in Jewish piety centuries before Christ. Jesus simply intensified this central concept. In the Jewish tradition, God is the father of a family, a people in covenant with God, a covenant of obedience to God's will. In the Gospels, the disciples of Jesus are the family, the people with whom God makes a new covenant. The word father is full of love and affection. But the New Testament is unique and revolutionary when it uses "Our Father" as a personal address to God. Never before was the Holy One called *Abba*. Modern exegetes have made the most of this newfound "Daddy" tenderness in the Deity. A plethora of the populace has turned the Ineffable into a soft and indulgent God who is infinite sweetness to them, offering comfort and solace in all circumstances. So the Christian challenge is gone and with it, the loss of awe, wonder, holy fear, and radical astonishment.

Jesus' own understanding of Abba, Father, was quite different: absolute love, truly intimate and involved, but transcendent and unbearable except for grace. When we pray we enter into the cave of a lion, all right, and we do not know if we will come out alive. We must go in, otherwise there is no intimacy, ecstasy, or fecundity; but we go in appropriately only if we are ontologically fearful—that is, reverent, humble, repentant, and ready for total ego-annihilation.

Jewish culture influenced the Gospel concept of the father-son relationship. The son had no life or even existence of His own; all was the father's. The son owed him complete, unconditional obedience. Jesus was the perfect example of this. He claimed nothing for himself. He came from the Father and was returning to the Father.

In the meantime, Jesus had only one criterion for everything: Father's will. Our following Christ means identifying with His living for the Father. It means being nourished for that carefree, God-centered life by the same wellsprings that fed Jesus. When we are nourished on this food, we rarely, if ever, need psychotherapy, Jesus does not come to coo but to share with us His vision, His passionate dedication to the Father's will. He inspires, instills pluck, ignites fervor, and braces us for crucial situations and life's momentous tasks.

OUR FATHER

All this is contained in the Our Father. If we really pray it mindfully, absorbingly, then we think like God by putting on the mind of Christ. But this seldom happens. We hardly know what we are saving and what we mean when we recite the prayer mindlessly. No matter how gravid with spirit a prayer is, when we repeat it as often as we do the Our Father, it is liable to become rote, recited with no deep conviction, no inspiration, no uplifting worship, and no religious experience.

Therefore, a suggestion: Pray the Our Father backwards—not word by word, but petition after petition from the end to the beginning. It seems to make more sense that way, at least existentially. When I do it, the experience unfolds differently each time but essentially in the following manner.

The first petition from the back end is *Deliver us from evil.* We desperately need to be liberated, to be rescued, to be transformed. We need a redeemer. We are stuck in evil, so subtly submerged in it that we hardly recognize our situation. We let too many things happen. We get used to living insouciantly in a calamitous and decadent situation. I am not referring to outrageous, appalling deeds of a criminal nature. I mean *pretty poison*, the respectable kind of evil that killed Christ. Big bad men didn't do it. Pretty poison did. Pretty poison is the kind of infection that seeps unnoticeably into our nicest people and our best institutions. It permeates our culture. The poison is potent precisely because it is so pretty.

The Aramaic Scriptures were translated into Greek. Three different words were used to indicate three particular kinds of evil. The one used in the Our Father was *poneros*, conveying a very specific evil. It means "hard labor" with no significance—the kind to which criminals are condemned. Little rocks are made out of big rocks simply to pass the time, without purpose or meaning. We don't need to go to prison to experience this. Most lives, and the jobs that fill them, are equally meaningless. It is from this we beg to be delivered.

Lead us not into temptation, the next petition, is not a request to be spared all temptation. That would make our lives dull and bland. We need to be tempted, challenged, and provoked. So we pray to be delivered from those temptations we don't need in order to confront with focused energy the very temptations we cannot live without.

Forgive us our trespasses as we forgive those who trespass against us. This is a crucial petition. It's like crossing the Red Sea. What a responsible prayer! We are not simply seeking forgiveness; we want pardon only to the extent that we forgive others. Forgiveness is freedom. We get rid of all the baggage that clutters the interior and makes us sluggish and lethargic. The trick is to take God so seriously that we take ourselves and our little world lightheartedly. There is no hardness of heart in a God-centered, lighthearted person.

Give us today the bread of tomorrow. This petition was not understood until a century ago. No one (not even Origen and St. Jerome, who were pioneer Scripture scholars) knew what the Greek word *epiousios* meant. This word appears nowhere else in literature. Only recently did new archaeological digs, new discoveries, and hard exegetical work shed light on the word and, therefore, on the meaning of the petition. We are praying for *epiousios* bread, symbolic bread, the bread of tomorrow. We are praying for the *eschaton*, that personal, direct encounter with Christ, knowing once that happens, we will never be the same again. We were created and are graced for that momentous experience.

There is a tendency in us to deal with God indirectly, to pose, to fabricate, to postpone and hide like Adam and Eve. We want to be warmed by the fire who is Christ but never consumed. Yet we are aware of our restless hearts, our loneliness, our dissatisfaction, the absence of ultimate, intimate presence, of spousal union. God invites us again and again into this final communion. The no's we come up with are uncanny: polite, respectable, polished, and imaginative. But they are a sham and worse than a sham: our pretty, poisonous way of saying "Crucify him, crucify him!" The invitation persists, and so does the fierce ontological ache of our shriveled existence.

To experience the *eschaton* is to look into the eyes and heart of the Divine Lover, Infinite Eros, and, as in a mirror, to behold ourselves, as we are now and as we were meant to be. This encounter is not way off, way out there, at the end of our lives. If is here and now, so we pray that it happens today. Only then can we really mean the next prayer.

Thy will be done on Earth as it is in heaven. Who can say this prayer and mean it? We need lots of *espiousios* bread. We need trust and courage. We need authenticity. But if enough ardent souls really prayed this petition, we could change the world.

Thy Kingdom come. The Our Father is a genuine cry of the heart, utterly existential, and therefore magnificent and magnanimous. And it cannot be thus without being significantly political-mystical. "Thy Kingdom come." That's all that matters. Oh Thou!

Forget the I, the me, the my, and the mine. All I want is you, not a version of you, a theology, a prayer, a spiritual path, or a worldview. I want you, and, therefore, your Kingdom. Establish your reign in the world. Let there be justice and peace and, above all, love. Whatever of me or mine impedes your reign, take from me. If I myself am obtrusive or preoccupied with something other than your Kingdom, your perfect love, then slay me.

Hallowed be thy name. There is hardly anything sacred in this secular world. Times and places have been flattened and made to serve our utilitarian purposes. But the Name of God is so intrinsically holy, so immutably good, that nothing can extinguish it. Be hallowed. Be holy. Be God in our Godless society. Be a luminous, refulgent presence in our dark, dull midst. Be pure passion and pathos in our apathetic, frantic business. Be a harbor of stillness in the midst of our media-madness. Save the disgraceful shambles of our language, profaned, humiliated, and vulgarized, by the rumbling thunder of your Word.

Thou who art in heaven. We are almost ready to pronounce the two words that alone constitute the essence of prayer. But we must not botch it, so we set the stage and refine our disposition, branding our worship with awe, alterity, and adoration.

Our God is not a nice or comfy thing to be possessed, amused, palliated, or manipulated. God is not a mascot, an uncle, or a teddy bear. God is an earthquake. God does not fit into our pocket, our mind, or our Earth. Though deliciously immanent, God is in heaven—transcendent. He is Wholly Other. God designs our destiny and enables us to achieve it. We become miserable—and the infection spreads—when we try to control our own lives and be our own captain. How silly to expect God to be the kind of God we want. We cannot pave a way for ourselves; the Spirit must lead us. Choosing our own path conveniently is always egregious folly.

"In heaven" means that God transcends our natural boundaries. It is up to God to reveal himself. Jesus proves the trustworthiness of God. He lives out of one basic conviction: God is love. This love is a force, a fire, a father, a mother, a spouse. God makes high proposals of love and devastating demands.

We need to be irrevocably committed to Jesus. We need to remain faithful. If we break the bond, we break His heart and body on Earth. We need to base our lives on His dark knowledge of the Father. There is no other way. Some try to drag Jesus onto a path made garish by natural human lights. We absurdly try to dictate to God providence. We are actually with God in heaven. We see the tip of the iceberg on Earth. There, too, we see the tip of human consciousness. The deeper and more real self is hidden "in heaven" with Christ, where everything is related directly and immediately to the Father. Apart from His exquisitely tender, fierce love, nothing makes sense.

Now the mental stage is set. Having prayed the other prayers from the bottom to top, we are now carefully disposed and ready to say the perfect prayer with an informed and enchanted sense of the Holy: *Our Father.*

Becoming Human

The art of being human is the art of being whole: wholly related to the whole of reality. The word for this exquisitely human response to the manifold in the One is *holiness*. Far from a diminution or restriction of the human, holiness is an enlargement, an expansion, and, in fact, a divinization of human life.

The purpose of life is life. Until we experience the fullness of life, we are in passionate pursuit of it. Human happiness is being full of life and spreading that good infection gracefully, generously, and unself-consciously. Sanity, sanctity, functional families, education, the Mystical Body of Christ, the body politic, the military-industrial complex, and social justice all depend upon this quality of life. So do the felicitous futures of the Boston Red Sox, the San Diego Chargers, and the All-Ireland Soccer Team, of Alicia Keys and Jennifer Lopez, George W. Bush and Tony Blair, Sean Connery, and Brad Pitt.

Human beings cannot live without science. Nor can we live with science alone. In the same way, we cannot live without reason, but we cannot live with reason alone. Enlightened Man is as much a myth as Economic Man. No one emphasized this more than Carl Jung, one of the most towering intellects in human history. Jung insisted that the personality has not one function but four: not reason alone, but feeling, sensation, and intuition as well. This whole response to the whole of reality enables the mindful person not only to communicate something about reality but also to enjoy communion with reality. The reporter conveys cold facts *about* an event. The contemplative lives *in* that event. As contemplatives, with head and heart united, we do more than observe rationally; we participate lovingly. Reality reveals itself only to lovers.

Real power, that which saves, redeems, and transforms, is for the lover. That is why it is idle to hope or work for a new world or united nations unless we are ready, or at least trying to be ready, to kiss the vagabond, to meet, greet, and enjoy Christ in His most disreputable form. Not the priest or the Levite, but only the Samaritan can build a new world (see Luke 10:29-37).

THE PERSIAN LOVE STORY

Nothing sheds more light on this central human quality than the Persian Love Story. The lover knocked at the door of the Beloved, and a voice replied from within: "Who is there?"

"It is I," he said.

And the voice replied: "There is no room for thee and me in this house," and the door remained shut. Then the lover returned to the desert, fasted, and prayed in solitude. After a year he came back and knocked once more at the door. Once more the voice asked: "Who is there?"

He replied, "It is thyself." And the door opened to him.

Wholeness opened the door and wholeness entered in; and into more wholeness the lovers grew together.

Learning this is terrifyingly difficult. Loving the whole requires soulful, unflagging effort and sheer, self-abnegating attentiveness.

Selective love is a stolen luxury. Loving this and that attractive thing may be a lotus flower enticing us away from the ugly and dull aspects of reality. So often what we love does not mirror Infinite Love and Beauty but only ourselves. I myself must not ignore the racing rapacity, lightning speed, and thunderous violence lurking beneath the graceful façade of our monastery's ravishing cat, Neri. He is a tender, loving creature but also ferocious.

Disciplined wild lovers, authentic human beings, *learn* to say in truth that is as deep as it is dazzling: "It is thyself." This is the same drive that enables us to be our real selves, neither independent nor codependent but interdependent. If I am regularly overwhelmed by thyself, chances are I can then say, "I am myself." I become "Thou" not by losing my real self but by finding it.

This is the stuff to humanity: the art of being whole, holy, and human. To everything in its particularity—from Halle Berry to cherry cheesecake, from Saddam Hussein to a single Great Dane, and to him who is all in All—we shall have learned to say, "It is thyself."

BECOMING HUMAN

We find the real purpose of life revealed in the Word of God. When we read the Gospels, we notice that whenever Jesus speaks of this purpose, it is never in terms of "getting" anything: moral improvement, perfection, or enlightenment. It is always in terms of giving—giving honor and glory to God. This is our true purpose in life. The by-product of zest and zeal for God's glory is wholeness, holiness, and harmony with the universe. Jesus meant exactly this when he said that we must lose our lives in order to save them, that we must seek first the kingdom, and everything else would unfold inevitably and graciously.

We must be so concerned about God and His kingdom, glory, and will that we come very close to forgetting about ourselves. We must be so taken up with our Father's business that we never think of setting up a pokey little business of our own. And so our petty little problems get swallowed up in the unrelenting, consuming pursuit of God's honor and glory: ultimate and intimate communion with the engaging Particular and the mysterious All.

Giving honor and glory to God is the purpose of all life, vegetable and animal as well as human. At the heart of the universe is a creative force, a divine energy. The best and oldest word for this universal and unifying power is *eros*. Eros personified, the Beloved, is the one to whom we refer when we speak of God. This Holy One, our Source, our Ground, our Eros, is glorified by trees being good trees, by dogs being as doggy as possible, and by humans becoming distinctively human.

PEOPLEY PEOPLE

One day many years ago I finished a retreat for the cloistered Trappist monks in Dubuque, Iowa. Then I had to shift gears radically because on the same day I was scheduled to open a retreat for young students in California. I was a bit apprehensive. Could I gracefully segue from adult discussions on anthropology, scriptural exegesis, and the *eschaton* to the questions and aspirations of youth? It was worse than I anticipated. My retreatants were not young adults but children—seventy of them. While talking to the nun in charge, I noticed a jubilant parade of tiny little girls pass by. I said, "Sister, those wee girls aren't the retreatants, are they?"

"Yes, Father," she answered, as she tried to comfort me in my panic. She said, "Girls in California mature much more quickly." And they do, but not that quickly! So I ran to my room, tried to recall significant stories and fairy tales, and dressed up in *full* Carmelite attire, white mantle and all. Needing all the props I could find, I put the hood up, took seven deep breaths, and entered the conference room where the lovely little nippers awaited me.

Once they caught sight of the flying mantle and the brown hood, the excited voice of a lovely little girl piped up: "Are you Zorro?"

"Yes," I said, and that saved my life.

I quickly resorted to my "saint" theme: "What does a saint look like?" They came up with a panoply of saintly images: caricatures of Patrick, Francis, Joan of Arc, and many others. So I urged them to concentrate on the here and now. "What would a live saint in our midst here today look like, sound like, and behave like?" Their response was illuminating and graphic but unreal. It was my turn. I began to develop my "art of being human" theme something like this: Becoming a saint is becoming human. We are not born human. We are born only with the basic amorphous stuff. To become really, truly, shockingly human we need to play, work, study, pray, and find better ways to love and make others happy. Becoming human is an adventure, a lifetime game that draws us into deeper love and joy. We suffer, too, but hardly notice it because life is so full.

A saint is uproariously happy, taking God so seriously that lightheartedness characterizes all of life, a life full of care, concern, compassion, and deep sorrow in the face of evil, but nevertheless an enduring delight because God is love. All life is a gift from the Holy One who guides us safely through dangers, surprises us hilariously, and transforms us into God's own image and likeness. It's not easy to become a saint, but it's simple. I mean an unofficial, uncanonized saint. We simply need to do what we are doing with all our might out of love. That kind of realness, "just-thisness," self-giving presence, helping others can make a saint out of anyone. It puts us in touch with the Living God; and because God is not separate but at the heart of everything, God enables us to climb inside of everything and feel the Mystery, feeding us with all the gifts that make life so livable. That is why the saint gets more pleasure out of one glass of beer than an unholy imp gets out of a tankful. So becoming a saint is becoming our best and truest selves. Only the real person can give glory to God. Again, trees give glory to God by being good trees, dogs by being doggy, cats by being as catty as possible. How do we do it?

This is what I asked the children. One of them, Maureen Allen, who has remained a close friend all these years and still makes retreats at our hermitage in Crestone, Colorado, was waving her hand, bursting with the right answer. "By being peopley," she said. I was thinking "human," but "peopley" was better. A saint is a peopley person! A saint trusts God, falls in love with God, and with hope and passion for the possible, follows an open way into a unique and unrepeatable existence, a singular destiny that transfigures all the scabrously raw matter of the world.

THE FREEDOM OF FIDELITY

So good and true in one way—the way being emphasized here—the "be yourself" maxim can be distorted and used nefariously for selfish purposes; one very popular purpose today, in this notoriously hungover "me" generation, is the sophisticated but solipsistic flight from fidelity. The tragic nature of this meretricious ruse becomes shockingly evident when we honestly face the heinous ultimacy of infidelity, an aspect of our dehumanized condition that I reflect on elsewhere in this book.

Right now let's highlight a sad and significant feature of our human decadence and our cultural decline. Here's the nub of it: Over the last forty years we have suffered an egregious loss of the meaning of vocation, a sense of being called, and simultaneously developed a raging salacity that has led to caducity; in other words, we became cowards incapable of fidelity. Alterity withered, bonds were broken, eros became a blob of glup, and all the energy of mankind was squandered in what Walker Percy called the "long suck of self."

Only the courageous one who says "yes" to God becomes himself. God's call is not imperious but it is pungently persistent. It has an absolutely alluring and Orphean quality. To resist it is to court disaster. The *only* "way" issues from God's call. The norms and the meaning of the "way" or the "path" are fixed and maintained by divine decree by Infinite Eros.

Our selfism has turned everything upside down. We make our plans, choose our own way, do our own thing, and then, being as nice as we are and quite religious, we invite God in, begging God to bless our secular pursuits. But there is no place for God in our plans. God *is* the place and the plan. Unless God draws us into His Mystery we remain mired in our misery. None of our own "paths" leads to freedom and oneness. We remain alien and estranged. Inevitably, then, the slogan "be yourself, be faithful to yourself" is ambiguous; we slip into a climate where fidelity to a higher duty is distorted and reduced to a pseudo-fidelity to a personal fulfillment such as is determined by our nonpurified spontaneity. I call this fidelity *pseudo* because it is so contrived and fragile. If a shallow person so lightly committed is challenged, the bond is broken. Halfhearted followers of Christ would rather defect than convert. Transformation into Christ requires one conversion after another to become free of egotistic addictions, fixations, compulsions, and disguised idolatries. Great lovers carry this cross bravely, longing for a pure heart and divine union. Others—the groovy, soft multitude—simply break their conjugal or celibate promises and prolong their mediocre, uninspired existence.

In their sophisticated effort to excuse themselves they become exceedingly smarmy: "I am not the same person I was a year or twenty years ago, and I must be true to myself, finding a path that suits this fluid 'is-mess' that is the Real Me at this time." This slick mendacity allows traitors to live at peace with themselves. Such petty souls seek their own individual fulfillment at any cost. No bond, no covenant, no commitment to another—not even to God—must stand in the way.

Live souls, on the other hand, know their shining vitality comes from faithful relatedness to others and ultimately to the Wholly Other who comes to woo us eternally, not to woo momentarily. So the one who is committed unconditionally to a solemn promise or profession will be steeped and renewed in that vocation even more deeply twenty years later on. I am assuming, of course, that the promise or profession really functions as a frontier line: Everything is left behind us because of the One who invites us and whom we love.

A life without restraints? Right, that can be a terrible tease. But as lover and monk I refuse to identify myself with this desire or this transitory "treat." What I must do is integrate those very energies that might have led to betrayal into the faithful movement of love, which will then be deeper and more confident than ever.

In the face of God's promise we tend to be so cowardly and stingy. Why not risk all for Christ? "He who leaves all for my sake will receive a hundred-fold now in this present time" (Mark 10:29-30, paraphrased). The presence of the Lord is felt as peace that the world cannot give (John 14:27), as a joy that no one shall take from us (John 16:22).

There is no adventure as dynamic, liberating, and rewarding as fidelity through love. It is *God's* desire, God's designs of love for us that give progressive meaning to our lives. The more perfect our commitment is, the more joyful our lives are. Fidelity is an in-depth disposition of being, way below the passing states of soul that may afflict us or delight us on the surface.

It is at the Spirit-level of being—the spiritual life—that the call of God is heard. Whatever is authentic issues from this deep seat of the soul. Whatever we do externally must be the fruit of this profound communion with the Beloved at the center of our being. Lose touch with the creative Spirit at the center and there is nothing left but legalism, formalism, and a deadly moralism. What we need, and only fidelity assures, is a new springing up of life.

RIPE, RICH, AND ROLLICKING

The human vocation is so unique. The great world religions make that plain. "Something more" calls us into eternal being. Mystery haunts us. The Tao beckons. Shiva teases us into more and more spaciousness. Buddha strips us of all our illusions. Jesus invites and challenges us into a unifying relatedness with the "Beyond-in-our-midst." No skin-encapsulated ego can survive true religion. When religion is realized, there is intimacy and no alienation; there is ecstasy and no stuckness in dead space; there is fecundity and no satisfaction with production, only the ripeness of fruit and the richness of One in all and all in One.

What a rollicking, riveting vocation the human adventure is! It takes boldness, courage, and daring to embark upon it. The human adventure is not for cowards. It may be "the little way," as St. Thërîse put it, but even that way is for disciplined wild ones, not wimps. Little Thërîse, the French Carmelite nun, was not comforted or cosseted in her cloistered convent a hundred years ago. She was hurtled by the exigencies of that concentrated, contemplative existence into the cauldron of God's love. Her consciousness was altered, her being transformed. A paradigmatic shift toward the ultimate took place. Her life was utterly simplified. She discovered *in depth* her own vocation: to love. This was no bromide. It was a brutal as well as little way for this wild, madcap creature of God.

Remember Zorba the Greek from the novel by Nikos Kazantzakis, made into both a stage musical and a movie with Anthony Quinn? Zorba said: "Everyone needs a little bit of madness; otherwise we will never cut the rope and be free." The big St. Teresa, the felicitous scourge of Avila, said that we are meant to strive and strive and strive. Without striving against the odds (and the oddballs), we shrink. So we need pain, trouble, opposition, worry, and some failure if we are going to be humanized and so simplified that we are fit for divine union, ready to be deified.

In the last act of his play, *A Sleep of Prisoners*, Christopher Fry looked at the frenzied turbulence of our age. Far from being bamboozled by it, because of it he was able to point out with pungent clarity our most urgent vocation:

> *Dark and cold we may be, but this*
> *Is no winter now. The frozen misery*
> *Of centuries breaks, cracks, begins to move;*
> *The thunder is the thunder of the floes,*
> *The thaw, the flood, the upstart Spring.*
> *Thank God our time is now when*

Wrong comes up to face us everywhere,
Never to leave us till we take
The longest stride of soul men ever took.
Affairs are now soul size.
The enterprise
Is exploration into God.

On that day when we become as perfectly human as we can in this world, then we shall be saints: live saints, not dead saints; human saints, not odd, inhuman saints. As St. Teresa prayed, "Oh God, deliver us from sour-faced saints!" If here and now we are not saints, it is only because we are not human enough. A saint gets up after every fall and still chooses to follow Christ. A saint is determined to become whole; and wholeness is almost synonymous with holiness. Almost! No need to be a handsome, healthy hunk or a light, lissome lovely diva. Simply *being there* is enough, personally, passionately present or, in the stunning instances of heroic humanity, painfully, haltingly present.

ENLIGHTENMENT OF MIND, ENLARGEMENT OF HEART

What distinguishes us from every other animal in the world and really makes us human? Our spiritual powers of knowing and loving. When these powers are fully exercised, then we are completely humanized. But God alone can fully satisfy our human hunger for knowledge and love. Therefore, loving knowledge of God and creation makes a saint, not flight from the world, a multiplication of spiritual practices, or even moral rectitude.

The sanctifying process is a humanizing process: a progressive enlightenment of the mind and enlargement of the heart. We come to know God so well that we fall in love with him. Once we get to know God, we've got to love Him because He is so infinitely lovable. This positive, outgoing, unselfish love drives us to avoid evil and practice virtue. But above all, it makes us human; kind, joyous, enthusiastic, adventurous, uproariously happy, generously serving.

To emphasize the human element is not to ignore the divine; to value the creature is not to lose the infinitely greater value of the Creator as though the *other* created by God were *apart* from him, as though God had to compete with other forces and therefore demand that we love nothing but Him. This false "either-or" principle crops up frequently in spiritual writings. To hold creatures cheap slights divine power. We must frown on nothing except our sinfulness.

Love is not merely the soul's response to the breath of the Spirit. It is a response of the *whole person* to the touch of God that we call grace. We are called into lasting friendship with God. If we are merely God's instruments and not lovers in our own right, this diminishes the dignity of charity. Grace does not work best when everything congenial to us has been pumped out. Nature abhors a vacuum, and so does supernature. Grace does not dwell like a lonely, lofty light in the attic of personality. It is not even limited to the technically "spiritual." Grace permeates and transfigures the whole person. The virtues of fortitude and temperance are not qualities of our higher selves or habits of willpower but transfigurations of emotion: Fortitude is temper restrained or fired according to circumstances; temperance is passion and pleasure controlled but unmitigated.

We are fundamentally created and conserved by divine power. Our actions are motivated and energized by that same power which wells up in us like a living, superabundant fountain of life, divinizing us at every level and expanding organically through every facet of our personality.

DIVINIZATION

This merging of the natural and supernatural brings us to another crucial affirmation: *We cannot become perfectly human until we are partly divine.* The humanizing process is from beginning to end a divinizing process, a suffering of divine things, a life dominated by the indwelling Spirit. This is the mystical life. The whole person, then, must be mystical. A mystic is one who knows God by experience.

All twelve of Jesus' apostles were mystics. St. John the Evangelist opens up his first Epistle with a clear, outspoken admission of this essential fact:

Perfectly human — we become partly Divine — finally God by we know God by Experience Experience!

> What was from the beginning,
> what we have heard,
> what we have seen without eyes,
> what we looked upon
> and touched with out hands
> concerns the Word of life
> for the life was made visible;
> we have seen it and testify to it
> and proclaim to you the eternal life
> that was with the Father and was made
> visible to us—what we have seen and heard
> we proclaim now to you,
> so that you too may have fellowship with us;
> for our fellowship is with the Father
> and with His Son, Jesus Christ.
> We are writing this so that our joy may be
> complete

(1 John 1:1-4)

John, the beloved disciple, has given His witness. What he once touched and tasted, he declares unto us. He and the Twelve had discovered the shining epiphany of God the Father, tabernacled close at their side in the body of Christ. "We saw His Glory, the glory as of God himself" (John 1:14).

John's first encounter was the day he saw Jesus coming toward him and a wonderful word broke from John the Baptist: "Behold, the Lamb of God" (John 1:36). This proclamation fascinated and haunted him. On the following day, when the Baptist uttered them again, John and two of His companions could not rest; their hearts burned to know more.

Andrew and John, the beloved, who tells the story, followed the stranger. When Jesus discovered them following him, he turned and spoke. For the first time He gazed at them with that look which again and again had the power to draw tortured souls out of the darkness of night into eternal light of day. John and Andrew heard His voice, the voice whose cry could raise the dead. "Whom do you seek?" He asked. That was all. They hardly knew how to reply. But they knew they had to go with Him, so they stammered: "Rabbi, where do you live?" And Jesus said: "Come and see" (John 1:38-39). They went and saw. John's memory of that personal encounter is so intense that he can never forget they very hour of the day. It was just ten o'clock when they got to the house. They stayed with Jesus long enough to know by experience who He was.

MYSTICAL EXPERIENCE

This religious experience of the apostles is a basic form of what we call mysticism. The mystic has firsthand experience and knowledge of God through love. This is quite different from knowledge by hearsay or cold, detached study. It is what breathes eternal life into every form of abstract knowledge. "And this is eternal life, that you may know God, and Jesus Christ whom He has sent" (John 17:3).

We are prone to limit the modes of God's action in us to familiar forms, so we tend to restrict unduly the number of contemplatives. There is a different texture not only for each great contemplative, but for each person, even the most ordinary. The experience of God may come in many ways and under many symbolic disguises. It may be steady or fleeting, dim or intense, but insofar as it is direct and intuitive, it is always a mystical experience.

Experience is a difficult term to describe or define. The word that seems to get closest to the heart of it is *awareness*: a subjective response to some objective reality that is perceived in some way by the subject. This awareness can be conscious or unconscious, and that is what differentiates saints who are mystics from those who aren't. Mystics are conscious of their experience. Ordinary saints are not, but the awareness of God is genuinely mystical in both cases.

This awareness is not simply an intellectual recognition of some object of thought but an awareness in which the whole person is engaged, involving, and normally causing some sensation. It is a body-soul response to a mystical reality, an encounter with the divine. The experience cannot be reduced to emotional feelings, but the spiritual response of mind and will often has some subsequent effect on the emotions.

Sacred history is the history of mystical experience: God intervening in human affairs, revealing Himself, inviting and readying each of us to reach the pinnacle of all human experiences, a personal encounter with the Living God. The cosmic and Mosaic revelations represent stages of growth in our knowledge of God. In Jesus Christ the hidden God is magnificently revealed. God has expressed His fullness in Jesus.

The Incarnation of Jesus, the Word made flesh, is the unique high point of the whole divine-human encounter. And the Church is the prolongation of the incarnation. The code and cult of the Church are meaningless apart from mystical experience. The code—the doctrine or teaching—is a conceptual interpretation of mystical experience. The cult—the ←

Church is the prolongation of the incarnation — code & cult.

liturgy or ritual—is the external, cultural embodiment of mystical experience. Anything unrelated to this spiritual center is ecclesiastical materialism. In light of this, it seems that our religious revival today is defective. Most of us spend our time and energy running around the circumference, forgetting the center that is mystical experience.

We have shied away from the term *mystical experience* due to the disastrous forms it sometimes takes. Shall we discard mystical experience because we have read or heard about aberrations of the experience? Do we condemn sex because we know of perversions that abound in the sexual sphere? It is unreasonable to reject mystical religious experience as subjective illusion when in power, satisfaction, and delight, and in its intellectual and spiritual value, it incalculably exceeds any other form of human experience.

What, then, is mystical theology? It is the theology of the fullness of Christian life lived in union with Christ and the whole Christ, the Church, and lived in such a way that it is experienced as well as understood. Mystical theology is bound up with what Christians for centuries have called "the mystery," the living mystery of Christ on Earth being born, living, redeeming the times, dying day by day, and rising again in the life of individual Christians who can say with St. Paul: "I live, no longer I, but Christ lives in me" (Gal. 2:20).

Any deep spiritual life is mystical life. If we define the mystical life as life dominated by the direct action of God through the gifts of the Holy Spirit, we cannot conceive the possibility of living the spiritual life in any other way. Extraordinary favors and thrilling experiences are not an essential part of the mystical life. The life of St. Thomas Aquinas, and even the lives of Mary and Joseph, show us that the highest mystical life may be, and often is, without any appearance of dramatic mystical phenomena.

Mysticism is our passionate longing for God, the Unseen Reality, loved and adored for himself alone. Genuine mystics are not those who engage in unusual forms of prayer, but those whose lives are ruled by this thirst. Genuine mystics feel and respond to the overwhelming attraction of God. They need not be great religious personalities, but they must be servants of the Word. They may not vibrate to the presence of Christ, but they can know and cleave to him nonetheless.

EXUBERANT LIFE

We are enriched today by our refined programs of spirituality and scientific studies of religion; by our advanced education and psychological discoveries; by spiritual writings, retreats, meditations, and rituals. And yet, with all this at our disposal and plentiful evidence of goodwill, we do not find many convincing Christians among us. Why? Because we are afraid to live fully and exuberantly. We are not human enough. Out of an utterly false notion of spirituality, we dare not let ourselves become human beings.

A human being is made, not born. But we do not become fully human by our own effort alone. Christ came to divinize us, to make us like God and enrich us with divine life, life that never diminishes or dulls with age or boredom. The Church, the contemporary Christ, has the same purpose. So does grace, the gift of divine life, super-vitality. It is a mistake to think that the only purpose of grace is to help us keep the commandments, to make us better, improved human beings with nicer manners. This attitude misses the whole point of what Jesus means by being reborn, of all that St. Paul writes about "newness of life," being "alive to God," and "all aglow with the Spirit." The purpose of grace is to make us richly, exuberantly alive.

But grace needs deep, healthy, natural ground if it is to take root and bear fruit; otherwise the supernatural becomes unnatural, a phantom without strength or lifeblood. We all need a passionate hunger and thirst, a spontaneous zest for life. Whom does Jesus take special pains to commend? The Roman centurion, the woman of the streets. Who is the only man in the world to whom Jesus promised heaven? A thief. And the heroes of His favorite parables are the prodigal son and the outcast Samaritan. He denounces the scribes and Pharisees with their strict but heartless fidelity to the law. He calls them "whited sepulchres" because they were closed and opposed to lighthearted joy and mirth, to love, freedom, and the good fellowship that characterize the children of God.

The real saint is therefore the man or woman who lives life to the hilt and does so with lilt. We are not saints because we are afraid of our own weaknesses and the difficulties of life. Instead of giving ourselves enthusiastically to life, we approach it halfheartedly. By impoverishing the life of the spirit, we heighten the temptation of what is traditionally called "the world, the flesh, and the devil." To paraphrase St. Thomas Aquinas, "No one can live without delight. When we are deprived of spiritual joy, we resort to carnal pleasures."

We don't begin to live once we've solved our problems. We solve our problems by living. That's what Jesus meant when He spoke of losing one's life in order to save it. In other words, we mustn't try to save our life by guarding and hoarding it carefully and fretfully, but by living it, spending it rightfully, bravely, and unstintingly. As French novelist and playwright George Bernanos so aptly wrote: "Won't damnation be the tardy discovery, the discovery much too late, after death, of a soul absolutely unused, still carefully folded together, and spoiled, the way precious silks are spoiled when not used?"

POVERTY OF SPIRIT AND SELF-DENIAL

If the Christian life is vital, positive, and affirmative, then why do we emphasize self-denial, mortification, and detachment? The desire of every Christian is a full life and great love. Clearly, we are faced here with paradox. We are to love and yet remain nonattached; the Earth is dark and tempting, yet it is God's gift to us, and ceaselessly it gives Him glory; we are to be mortified and treat earthly things lightly, yet we are to love the lilies of the field, to reverence the hallowed mystery of human love, to delight in the wine that "rejoices our hearts," as we pray in the Psalms.

What is the answer to this paradox? It is based on a very sound principle: Two contraries cannot exist in the same subject at the same time. I cannot move north and south at the same time. I cannot serve two masters. My affections cannot be absorbed by distractions and by God.

The word *detachment* has a negative ring to it, and for this reason it seems wise to use the term *poverty of spirit* instead. It seems easier to see "poverty" as positive: unattached, but full of concern and deep love. Not that it is necessary or even desirable to rule out negation for the sake of accentuating the positive. This isn't even possible. We must not cater to an unrealistic, unbalanced humanism, acting as if grace were an injection that by itself turned our natural lives into a most pleasing service of God without our constant, heroic effort to live full lives of Christian virtue. We cannot become full unless we are empty. We cannot receive a gift unless we make space to receive it. Supernatural life is a gift from God. We receive it by becoming empty, open, and receptive, by making room for God's onrush.

The first step toward exuberant fullness, the first aspect of detachment or poverty of spirit, is emptiness. Not a destructive, meaningless void, but a constructive emptiness, like the hollow in a reed, a space to receive and form the piper's breath and express the song in His heart; like the emptiness of a chalice; above all, like the emptiness of our Lady Mary's virginity. There was nothing more positive than our Lady's emptiness, for out of it God became man.

It takes courage and trust to empty ourselves and wait for the advent of Christ. Remember the story of the Dutch boy who put His finger into a hole in the dike and prevented the water from flooding Holland. That is unfortunately what we do when we spoil our emptiness by allowing even a single attachment to prevent the ocean of God's love from flooding our souls.

We all need the experience of denial, negation, and mortification. What happens when a boy meets a girl who catches his eye and captivates his heart? He makes sacrifices. A sacrifice is a living expression of preference. The boy denies himself the time he used to spend so fondly at the gym because he prefers to be with His love. He denies himself certain luxuries and pleasures because he prefers to spend His money for her. This is what inevitably happens when we get to know Christ. When we really begin to love Him, the real meaning of sacrifice helps us avoid fatal misunderstandings in our popular versions of spirituality.

Self-denial leads to self-mastery. We lost self-mastery and integrity with the mysterious "fall" of our first parents, Adam and Eve. Integrity did not return to us through Christ's redemption. We received instead something better: the gift of unique graces "tailored" to each moment of our lives and each need of our personalities. By the aid of grace and our own effort, we are meant to restore balance and harmony to our humanity. We gain mastery not by renouncing

[handwritten margin note: we are willing to sacrifice once we experience love!]

human nature, but by renouncing anarchy. Becoming deliberately human is extremely difficult. Renouncing the inhuman or subhuman in our lives is more painful than a lifetime of hair shirts and fasting. But there is a more valuable point to sacrifice. Sacrifice is giving something to God, something treasured and fine, given with joy and liberality.

We sometimes believe it is the pain and loss sustained in giving that are the most important features, as if it were self-inflicted misery that pleases God. This is dreadfully wrong. We don't give in order to hurt ourselves; we give to please the receiver. The pain accompanying the gift is at most the price of our precious right to give. We do not haggle or complain about it, nor are we proud of it. The giving simply is.

DEATH AND REBIRTH

There is another cogent reason for mortification: It stresses the positive and affirms the good found in creation. All spiritual emotions and high resolves die unless we nourish them. We are sometimes surprised and chagrined at our own loss of zeal and piety and at our inability to pray as we once did. One day, like the startled bridesmaids of the Gospel (cf. Matt. 25:1-13), we wake up and see smoking wicks instead of brilliant flames. The snuffed flame is a result of our doing nothing, luxuriating in the status quo, stagnating and sleeping, like the bridesmaids. Most lives are not ruined through wickedness but through the gradual gathering of grease and scum when not stirred by sacrifice.

It is therefore understandable that the bright, vivid life theme of the Gospels also includes a strong undercurrent theme of death. Rebirth implies death. Grass must die in order to enjoy the higher life of a cow; the cow must undergo death before it can take part in the higher life of man or woman; we must die in order to live in Christ.

Even Jesus followed this principle of loss and gain. The purpose of Calvary was not the death of Christ but the resurrection. The purpose of renunciation is not to annihilate life but to enhance it. The rightness of renunciation must be judged by the intensity of life that results from it, by the openhearted attitude of acceptance that ensues. Life means choice and renunciation. To choose what is human, to live at all worthily, is to renounce what is inhuman. Life without choice is not worth living.

Like the saints, we must not be afraid to live. We must choose our mortifications in view of greater life until we become more magnificently alive with supernatural life. Neither must we be afraid to love. Detachment does not mean that we love nothing but God; it means that we love everything in God; it does not mean that we love creatures less and less; it means that we love them more and more, but it means loving them in God, not apart from God.

THE DRAGON OF SELFISHNESS

In our efforts to become detached, we must never destroy our love for anyone or anything. We are only permitted to kill the one thing that spoils our love: selfishness. This is the function of mortification: to kill all forms of selfishness, thus liberating us from enslavement to any creature and empowering us with intense and universal love. This love is no longer limited, imperfect, sin-ridden, and possessive, but the healing love of Christ.

How do we detect selfishness? When we find we are using people and things not for God's honor and glory but for our own, seizing upon them for our own pride, profit, or pleasure, then we are selfish. When we find we are reaching and grabbing instead of standing with reverence before the sacredness of being, then we are selfish. When we allow a creature to compete with God for the possession of our hearts, when our love is divided between God and something else, then we are selfish.

How do we kill the multi-headed dragon of selfishness and put order into love? By mortification: not a wholesale program of mortification but exactly the right one that will remedy our particular kind of disordered love, and for as long as it takes to bring order out of chaos. Suppose the time you spend in front of the television prevents study, prayer, and sufficient rest. Then this is what you mortify: cut your TV time down to a minimum. Suppose your business consumes so much of your life that you have little energy left for your family or a leisurely celebration of Sunday; then this is what you mortify. If you find that your most frequent distraction in prayer is the tendency to daydream; then you mortify this.

We cannot use created things for the glory of God unless we are masters of ourselves. We cannot master ourselves if we are under the power of our desires, appetites, and passions. We cannot give ourselves to God if we do not belong to ourselves. And we do not belong to ourselves if we belong to creatures. The real function of renunciation, then, is to liberate us from desires that debase and enslave us to creatures. The real purpose of self-denial is to turn ourselves over to the Holy Spirit so that we may become masterpieces of transformation.

On the other hand, as great lovers, free and detached, we are high priests of creation. Our human vocation is to take good care of the Earth and all its inhabitants.

Because of the supernal goal of all human striving, our humanization depends upon our divinization, and the divine influence depends upon God. It is up to us to immerse ourselves in a wholly human way in whatever human task God requires of us. God is always there and we are always in some way being deified.

One of our chief tasks today is to liberate the Earth. Until now we have been destroying our environment by a global system that seriously jeopardizes our survival in the twenty-first century. Scientists warn us of our unprecedented predicament. All in all, life on this Earth is under threat. The human race can become extinct, like the dinosaurs millions of years ago.

To liberate the Earth we need to understand one thing, and that is that all things are interrelated. The life of the whole continues because all give themselves to it by giving themselves to each other. The dynamic interconnections sustain all participants. To grasp this is to enjoy ecological awareness, that is, awareness of the basic interrelatedness of all beings. Our love of one another needs an erosphere: a field of love toward all living beings, toward all things. *Our* life is certainly a matter of indefinitely expanded sharings through the Earth community. This is how we do it: all of us living for one another. There is no greater love than this, according to St. John (John 15:13).

Ecological morality is urgently incumbent upon us all today. Our moral practice will be vitally virtuous if we simply remember: Everything in the universe is alive; and we are all relatives.

we all live for the whole — live for one another!

The Human Climate

HOLY LEISURE

One of the greatest blessings of modern technology and our productive economic system is the new leisure they have given us. Golden hours have been added to our lives. But the ironic, even tragic, part of this boon is that few of us have learned how to use the new leisure. Many of us are uneasy when we try to relax. The very qualities indispensable for creating our standard of living become a formidable handicap when we seek to enjoy our hard-won leisure.

Restlessness, boredom, and a frantic search for diversion are the common reactions to an hour or day of quiet. The modern Cleopatra in T.S. Eliot's poem "The Waste Land" desperately asks: "What shall I do?... What shall we do tomorrow? What shall we ever do?" She expresses one of our most pathetic contemporary problems. Publishers of pornography and pap, producers of endless third-rate movies and television programs have made their fortunes providing a false but lucrative answer. Our entertainment industries are based on the assumption that modern society

Challenge of good use of leisure time.

is so poor in personal resources that we must be entertained at the turn of a switch twenty-four hours a day. Amusement is indispensable for those who do not or cannot think.

Challenge of Communication

Communication obsesses us and kills the art of communion by which we are enriched and ennobled. Communication starts by being a good convenience. It grows and grows—like a tree if we like it, like a cancer if we don't. It ends up a way of life. The transmission and reception of information, almost devoid of meaning, become an activity fascinating in itself. It can be quite satisfying, though never fulfilling, especially perhaps for those whose temperaments are outgoing, social, manipulative, present-minded. But information yields its last measure of satisfaction only if pushed to its last degree of development. This involves an assault on privacy or, rather, a common, unconscious willingness to be assaulted.

Key ? quest.

We also suffer from a compulsion to keep on the move. What would happen to us on vacation if we were to linger somewhere long enough to open up the possibility of perceiving and understanding? What keep us "on the go" are emptiness and an incapacity to fill a pause in the day's occupation with anything worth doing: a fear of leisure time.

Work has its) place.

Our lives revolve around our work, in what Henry David Thoreau called "quiet desperation." This is killing us. We become inhuman when we are fettered to our work. Anyone whose life is completely filled by work shrinks inwardly and contracts. As a result, few of us can act significantly outside work and perhaps are no longer even able to conceive of such freedom.

The problem begins early and at home through enforced leisure. When we make our children stay alone as punishment, they develop a distaste for aloneness that may last a lifetime. The child who whines, "I've got no one to play with" or "There's nothing to do," must learn delight from a parent's joyous example: "I've got a whole hour, or a whole day; how wonderful!" If children see their parents hiding from themselves in bustling activities, always finding ways to while away the time through television, golf, the Internet, or idle chatter, children, too, lose the depths of their being and live only on the surface.

THE FREEDOM OF IMPRISONMENT

A child favorably impressed with leisure may indeed reap precious fruit from even enforced solitary confinement later in life. Prophets and philosophers, saints and revolutionaries, have achieved wonders in jail. It is always a mistake for the enemies of dynamic men and women to lock them up or confine them in any way. According to the first prime minister of India, Jawaharlal Nehru: "Prison gives us enforced leisure to read and think—the sources of real power." These sources are valid for saints and scoundrels alike. Would it not be wiser for their enemies to leave them at large to work off their steam in a life of action than to put them in jail where they concentrate on manufacturing intellectual time bombs?

Humanity seldom looks more foolish than it does through acts of persecution. Take Boethius. Awaiting execution in prison at Pavia in 524 C.E., he wrote *The Consolations of Philosophy*, which made him schoolmaster to Europe for centuries. Miguel de Cervantes wrote *Don Quixote* in jail, so charmingly conveyed in the contemporary musical *Man of La Mancha*. John Bunyan lay in the dungeon of Bedford Gaol when he could have had his liberty at any time if he had promised to give up preaching. As a consequence, *Pilgrim's Progress* goes on preaching hundreds of years later to people of all nations, races, and religions. The *Spiritual Canticle*, one of the greatest pieces of religious poetry in the world, was written by St. John of the Cross, most of it inspired in prison.

The list of masterpieces written in jail is exceeded only by those written in exile. Mohammed fled for his life from Mecca and in desert wandering dictated the Qur'an. Athens banished one of her generals, Thucydides, for his failure in an expeditionary campaign, and he wrote his incomparable *History*. Euripides went into voluntary exile in Macedonia, where he wrote his most poetic tragedy, the *Bacchae*. While the Florentines sought Dante to burn him alive, he wrote the *Divine Comedy* in exile. More contemporary examples include Martin Luther King, Alexander Solzhenitsyn, Desmond Tutu, Vaclav Havel, and Adam Michnik, one of the founders of the Solidarity Movement in Poland.

So beware of the dynamic, thoughtful man or woman in exile or in jail! In prison, exiled, solitary thinkers are free to rip through social pretenses and write out of their own raw experience of reality. "Liberty means responsibility," said a famous philosopher. "That is why most of us dread it." Dreading liberty, persecutors try to deny it to others. But this is shortsighted. Persecution may be an immediate success, only to destroy for centuries the present good or bad condition of the nation, the community, the leader that encourages it.

SCHOOL, OR *SKOLE*

Our school system is partly responsible for our incapacity for leisure. The original Greek word, *skole*, means "leisure," but leisure has been squeezed out of school. The hallmark of education is attention. Who can be attentive without leisure? Without leisurely intervals between classes, students cannot absorb and assimilate what they learn (or at least hear) in class. The next lesson eradicates memory traces framed in the last session. Retroactive inhibition sets in. As Barliman Butterbur puts it in *The Lord of the Rings*, "One thing drives out another."

Without interims of leisure, contemplative space, and reflective moments, education becomes a rat race on an info-highway at best; and students become robots on a treadmill, not enjoying contemplative insights and learning in depth, but leading half-lives, half-heartedly, with only one half of their minds actively engaged in direct contact with the universe around them. This seems odd to say about a generation that has learned more about the universe in a shorter time and used that knowledge more efficiently than any generation before it. But the unwise and uncontemplative nature of this achievement has in itself helped create the climate of our malaise. Our astonishing work to attain this technological end is the very half-life we have led so brilliantly. In His bracing book, *The Decline of Pleasure*, theatre critic Walter Kerr reaches the following conclusion about our unleisurely work:

> *The disappointment and distress we feel in the face of our accomplishment is the result of its having engaged only one-half of our faculties, while the other half of our instincts, affections and energies was permitted to atrophy. It is as though we had used our right hands exclusively for a great many years, so exclusively and for so long that our left hands had withered; and we now wanted to play the piano.*

In differing degrees, we are all born with the same potentialities. When we who enjoyed painting in kindergarten grow up, nothing has happened to deny us the same satisfaction, though not necessarily the same excellence, that Pablo Picasso, Marc Chagall, and Georgia O'Keefe got at an easel—nothing except that we have allowed the faculty to atrophy from disuse.

As children we also enjoyed dancing and singing, but as we continued through school, we learned that nothing was worth learning unless it had pragmatic value and advanced our specialization. Education has increased our will to professionalize and specialize even our sports and games, leaving us incurious about any intellectual or sensuous experience that a specialist cannot put to use. If our schools provided leisure, we would be less specialized but more original, creative, and versatile. Fewer of us would be pros and more of us amateurs. But we would be ourselves; and we would be whole, happy, and really alive, making a greater contribution to the world.

Our basic indisposition for leisure is tragic because the basis of human wholeness is free time. We are now liberated from the practical, workaday world, from the welter of ordinary, undistinguished existence, from our puritan-inherited concept of morality that enshrines work as the highest virtue: "Idleness is the devil's workshop"; "Hard work is our salvation." Now that we are free, are we going to fritter away our heritage playing computer games, reading the comics, or wasting time in some equally childish manner? Science has led us to the pinnacle of human possibilities but has not added a single cubit of wisdom to our lives. Wisdom is our inescapable responsibility. It poses, in fact, the biggest problem of the modern age, perhaps even bigger than war: what to do with ourselves. As we cease to be creatures of endless toil, we are likely to find ourselves liberated into a vacuum. Our leisure time can become more of a curse than the plagues of old.

What, then, must education do? What is its biggest responsibility in an age of leisure? The making of a new humanity—men and women who have confidence in the limitless possibilities of their own development, men and women who are not intimidated by the prospect of an open hour, men and women who are aware that science may be able to make an easier world, but only a mindful person can make a better one.

CONTEMPLATION AND CELEBRATION

What will save us from whiling away our time and make leisure the most fruitful experience we have yet known? Contemplation. Leisure is not merely the interim between the acts of our working life but an intense activity of a different kind. True leisure or repose cannot be enjoyed without some recognition of its spiritual dimension, for the first purpose of repose is contemplation of the good.

"God saw all that he had made and found it very good" (Gen. 1:31). Such contemplation of our work is natural for us as well, wherever we are engaged in a creative task. We must, like a fine painter, take time to stand back from our work and be still, to see "what's what." We cannot act virtuously unless we see what's what, so we need time to contemplate. True repose is standing back to survey our daily activities. Repose allows us to contemplate the little things we do in relation to the vast picture that alone gives them meaning. Repose gives us time for an intensely active and creative contemplation of divine things from which we arise refreshed.

In leisure genuinely understood, we rise above the level of things to be used. We enter the realm where we can be at home with our deepest human potentialities. There, with no disdain for doing, no neglect of the immediate, the particular, and the practical, we can above all simply contemplate, attend to the love of wisdom. We can begin to lead truly human lives.

Plato, in his *Laws*, said it this way: "But the gods, taking pity on mankind, born to work, laid down the succession of recurring feasts to restore them from their fatigue...so that nourishing themselves in festive companionship with the gods, they should again stand upright, and erect." The nature of leisure is thus basically united to contemplation, the great tradition of Western culture, and both are dependent on a real awareness of the transcendent and the divine.

The soul of leisure is celebration. When a day is too good to be used, we make it a feast-day and celebrate it. British writer G. K. Chesterton said, "When we give God a holy day, God gives us a holiday." Since God is too good to be used, we celebrate God's goodness. This is divine worship, which ultimately makes leisure possible and justifiable. Divine worship relates to time as the temple relates to space. The temple is a particular space of ground or a specific building withdrawn from utilitarian purposes and dedicated exclusively to the presence and purposes of God. Similarly, in divine worship, a definite space of time is set aside from working hours and days, specially marked off and not used for any utilitarian ends.

In this atmosphere of worshipful leisure, we overstep the frontier of the everyday, workaday world, not in external effort and strain, but lifted above it as though in ecstasy. This is the meaning of the word *sacrament:* a visible sign of a deeper, unseen reality. A sacrament should lift us out of ourselves so that we are rapt to the heavens. This is not a private or romantic interpretation. The Church has pointed to the meaning of the incarnation of Jesus, the Word made flesh, in the same words: "May we be rapt into love of the invisible reality through the visibility of that first and ultimate sacrament, the Incarnation." It is, therefore, through this kind of leisure, holy repose, this kind of divine worship and celebration of the liturgy, that we, "born to work," are drawn out of ourselves, out of the toil and moil of every day into the sphere of unending holiday, drawn out of the confined sphere of work and labor into the heart and center of creation.

Cut off from worship of the divine, leisure becomes laziness and work inhuman. Leisure embraces everything that is not merely useful but an essential part of full human existence. The deepest source of leisure is the celebration of divine worship by which it is fed and continues to be vital. Through the Mass, sacraments, and a liturgical cycle of fasts and feasts, the Church invites us to that leisure and contemplation where we can again "stand upright and erect." The Church helps provide one of the last remaining refuges from a busy, restless world, as do the Jewish celebration of the Sabbath and the innumerable colorful festivals celebrated by the Hindu tradition.

SOLITUDE AND SILENCE

The contemplative spirit, born and nurtured in the sacramental life of the Church and the spiritual traditions of the great world religions, needs for its full growth copious supplies of solitude and silence, which are absolutely indispensable ingredients of leisure. Much more is involved than simple withdrawal from society and the cessation of speech.

Solitude means being full of God. Although this sometimes means absolute aloneness, at other times it simply means self-possession, the sense of God's presence on busy streets and during the most crowded moments of life. But we seem to be capable of the latter only after we have resorted deliberately and frequently enough to periods of absolute aloneness.

In all ages, God has formed the contemplatives and instruments of His great works in solitary places. Moses went into the desert alone where God manifested Himself and made Moses leader of the Hebrew people. After walking forty days into the desert, Elijah heard a gentle whisper that revealed the divine Presence on the desolate mountain of Horeb. John the Baptist was drawn into the desert by the weight of a singular grace received on the day of the Visitation of our Lady (Luke 1:39-45). He did not leave the desert until the age of thirty, filled with the spirit of God and ready to accomplish his mission as precursor of Christ.

Mary Magdalene was smitten by Jesus and espoused by God. She hastened to the desert so that she could cope in holy leisure with the raging ramifications of such total love. After his conversion, St. Paul retired into the solitude of the Arabian desert. There, under the direct action of the Holy Spirit, he prepared for his special mission to the Gentiles. Out of desert solitude came the great leaders of the first centuries who built our Christian civilization. Later, in the sixteenth century, St. Ignatius of Loyola spent a year of solitude at Manresa and received inspiration that permitted him to write the *Spiritual Exercises* and organize the Society of Jesus. And the order of Carmel, which has given the Church her great mystical doctor, St. Teresa of Avila, St. John of the Cross, and St. Thërîse of Lisieux, had its birth in the desert and there returns continually for the atmosphere that alone provides the essence of its life. And so it is in solitude that we most readily and frequently encounter God and become divinely empowered to become His apostles and servants.

But even from the purely natural point of view we need solitude. Without it our natural life suffers serious vitamin deficiency. The shallowness that stultifies so much of our existence comes from a lack of quiet solitude. Solitude is the nurse of full-grown human persons. The human person consists of three living components: body, mind, and soul. Each must be sustained, each must be given food, exercise, and pleasure. In order to learn how to provide the necessities of life for our three components, we must learn the secret of constructive solitude. To go into solitude is not to void the mind but to rest it. As Isaac D'Israeli, father of British statesman Benjamin Disraeli pointed out, the mind truly at rest is "the nurse of enthusiasm, and enthusiasm is the true parent of genius. In all ages solitude has been called for and flown to."

The German word *sammlung* has no explicit single word translation in English. It means a collecting or marshalling of forces. *Sammlung* could be the label for that gathering of forces, that time of solitude and mind-rest when a great writer, leader, or mystic shuts out everything but the mood at hand. In self-integration of this sort, we do not negate the world around us. We get ourselves and the world into focus. Out of the scrap basket of a day's small frazzlements we put together a time of containment and a time of strength.

Solitude, then, is as necessary for human sanctity and sanity as human fellowship. But it is much harder to acquire. In contemporary living, the mind at rest in solitude is a discipline exercised by fewer and fewer people. Our physical and material surroundings do not encourage solitude. The architecture of our homes provides an almost automatic short circuit to contemplation. The private den has become the public TV room. The dining room is an open area. Kitchens are no longer cozy but efficient; gone is the comfortable chair that once invited reflection while dinner bubbled softly on the stove. In most contemporary houses there are no hidden rooms upstairs far away from the noise downstairs. We are subjected to the hustle and bustle of ordinary, leveling "togetherness." We even eliminate doors between the rooms of our houses, and with them has gone the last slamming refuge of an outraged child and the easiest means for ensuring a time of repose to "repair our nature," as Shakespeare put it. Missed most of all is the screened-in front porch, open to the neighbor, always admirably conducive to either family fun or solitary contemplation. My own family was formed on such a porch on Cass Street in Providence, Rhode Island.

We must fight for solitude, for the right to be alone, to be still and know God, to be quiet and thoughtful and see things as they really are. Toward this end we must construct each day, live it, refuse to be inundated or dehumanized by it in any way. In the budget of hours, whether a lifetime or a day, there is room for whatever we want to create, but we must be creative about the means at hand and work with them. Every day can have its contemplative peak, as the German poet Goethe reminded us: "On every mountain height is rest."

INTERIOR SILENCE

Besides the positive cultivation of solitude within the realm of leisure, we need to develop interior silence. Serious-minded, magnanimous people are necessarily silent. What kept the Mother of God silent most of her life? Something in her so sacred, so magnificent and compelling left no room for much verbiage. Mary was filled with the Word of God. All she could do was listen. She spent her days pondering the meaning of the words of her divine Son. She was the "woman wrapped in silence," absorbed and captivated by the power and glory of the Word made flesh.

What happened to John the Baptist when Christ appeared on the scene? John was the last towering figure of the old world. He was a mighty defender of the rights of God, rugged and thoroughly masculine. His voice was strong and relentless, crying in the wilderness: "Make straight the way of the Lord" (Matt. 3:3). And his voice was heard; it made a universal and ineluctable impression. But when Christ came, John ceased to raise his voice and kept silent. Why? Because John was a stouthearted man, a man apart, a man with a single eye. He wanted only one single joy, one unique pleasure: the incomparable joy and pleasure of hearing the voice of His Beloved. John gave up everything else for that. He became silent in order to listen with all his might to the voice of Christ.

Even Jesus' enemies claimed He spoke like no other: "And no man ever spoke like this man" (Luke 4:22).

On a purely natural level, why do we sometimes find it difficult to speak? Because we are deeply engaged; our minds are absorbed; our hearts are full. For the same reason we find it impossible to do two important things at once. We cannot solve intricate mathematical problems and play tennis at the same time.

When we are preoccupied with God, we are bound to be silent. God invades the secrecy of our souls and imaginations, our intellects and wills, and compels us to be silent. Silence is not a negation but an absorption, a recollection, an inwardness: being drawn deeper and deeper into the ground of the soul where we are confronted with ultimate reality, with God. God has spoken. Silence is listening with all our might to that Word made flesh.

PRAYING AND PLAYING

Praying and playing are primary examples of leisure. These two acts are properly called leisure when they are expressions of wonder in the presence of the Numinous, when they spring from the deepest level of human vitality, when they are true and pure, unspoiled by utilitarian motives. The inherent qualities of leisurely prayer and play are mindfulness, relatedness, and trust. These interior attitudes erupt in festivity: a wild and wonderful spirit of abandonment, a frame of mind that is always awesome, reverent, and open to the transcendent.

Genuine leisure, therefore, is a far cry from the so-called "leisure activities" offered by hotels, vacation packages, and "leisure centers." Such activities are fine, but they lack one or another of the inherent qualities that characterize leisure. Do you want to pray or make a deal with the Deity? Do you want to play just because it is good, for instance, to run? Or do you want to lose weight or pump up the heart, so you decide, with grumpy rectitude, to jog? Do you want to enjoy the highest act of leisure and enter into your spousal love chamber and celebrate love? Or do you merely want to "have sex"?

LEISURELY MIND AND MEANING

Becoming human requires a leisurely mind. To sustain this mental capacity we need concentrated days and hours of leisure. No matter how secularized our society becomes, therefore, retreat houses and hermitages will always be pertinent and popular. A human being who has not a single hour of his or her own every day is not a human being. What is the most important thing for us to do? Just this: that is, whatever we are doing here and now—cooking, shaving, driving—whatever, as long as it is done with grateful awareness, alive to God and the glory of His gifts.

When we compartmentalize religion, we lose our sense of the sacredness of life and the holiness of creatures, both in their natural state and manufactured. We should approach a friend the way we approach God. That exquisite man of both work and leisure, Henry David Thoreau, refers trenchantly to the central form our dehumanization takes: "Unless we meet religiously, we profane one another."

We need structured leisure until we develop the habit of contemplative thinking and action. Then the active life itself becomes leisurely. That's the ideal. Once achieved, however, the active life still needs specially sacred places and times for doing nothing gainful. According to the central revelation of the Eastern *Vedas*, "Only the wise know the action of inaction and the inaction of action." Lao Tzu, from the Taoist tradition, adds: "The most important thing to do is to be." The psalmist of the Western tradition agrees: "Be still and see that I am God" (Ps. 46:10).

We need another term here to express active receptivity. That term is *sustained attention.* If you want to see the lovely patch of earth along the Charles River in Boston full of walking automatons, then let Harvard fail to evoke sustained attention. Without sustained attention, the academic world can transmit no wisdom, only heaps of information. A university without structured leisure is a monstrosity. Churches without ecstasy, the experience of being beside ourselves with awe, wonder, and radical amazement, and the leisure that sets the stage for it, are in the same predicament. Churches, of course, cannot provide enough leisure for everyone. People who restrict their religious practice to church duties deprive themselves of human growth spiritual life, and substantial religious experience. Going to church no more makes us Christian than going to a garage makes us a Toyota.

The only alternative to leisurely life is driven life. Sooner or later, drivenness leads to boredom and loneliness. Boredom is the shriek of unused talent, unactivated potential. Loneliness is the scourge of undeveloped faith. All of our human deformities of spirit can be summed up in one word: lovelessness, or, to be more specific and decisive, morbid self-love.

Joseph Pieper, one of the last great classical philosopher-theologians of today's world, wrote a book called *Leisure: The Basis of Culture*, one of the twentieth century's seminal books and a personal favorite. With trenchant arguments and pellucid clarity, Pieper asserts that there is no culture without leisure and no leisure without worship. In leisure we have time to wonder, a primordial human act without which there is no genuine philosophy, theology, or prayer. Without wonder there is no insight, no sense of the ultimate, no communion with the Absolute, no communion with anything. And if there's no communion, there's no meaning. Isn't this our tragic plight today? How much meaning is there in our alienated, derivative existence? We can be as purposeful as we want, but without meaning, despair and insanity will increasingly characterize our whole society: "Without vision the people perish" (Prov. 29:18).

Victor Frankl, the logotherapist and former inmate of Nazi prison camps, wrote a salvific book entitled *Man's Search for Meaning.* Frankl observed that prisoners who were able to cling tenaciously to meaning endured; the others perished. Meaning has proved to be one of the best cures for our schizoid society.

Dag Hammarskjold, former Secretary-General of the United Nations, discovered in one momentous occasion how shockingly wonderful the personal experience of meaning is. His felicitous expression of it, as he wrote in *Markings* has become one of our literary treasures: "For all that has been—Thanks! For all that shall be—Yes!...And from that hour I was certain that existence is meaningful and that, therefore, my life, in self-surrender, had a goal."

Without this contemplative meaning, action goes berserk and becomes frantic, even violent. We become like Pyrrhus, king of ancient Epirus, who decided to invade Italy. He sent for Cineas, a philosopher and friend, and sought his counsel. Cineas asked him why he wanted to invade Italy.

He said, "To conquer it."

"And what will you do when you have conquered it?" asked Cineas.

"Go into France," said the king, "and conquer that."

"And what will you do when you have conquered France?"

"Conquer Germany."

"And what then?" queried the philosopher.

"Conquer Spain."

"I perceive," said Cineas, "that you would conquer

the whole world. What will you do when you have conquered it all?"

"Why then," said the king, "we will return and enjoy ourselves at quiet in our own land."

"So you may now," said the philosopher, "without all this ado."

PENETRATING THE INNER MOMENT

Leisure means penetrating every moment with deep inwardness. The inner moment, with permanent reverberations, is the vital principle or culmination of existence. For lasting effect and communal sharing, this vivifying moment needs penetration, expansion, and expression. Institutional solidity and solidarity depend on its socio-political embodiment. If religion is to be substantially reliable as well as veritable and vivacious, it needs to celebrate the inner moment ritually. Culture must reiterate the inner moment with original and creative artistry. Interiority and reflection constitute, along with Scripture and tradition, the very heart of contemplative living.

Why are people, especially the young, leaving the Church in droves? No meaning grabs them. Nothing about the Church inspires or excites them. Did Christ initiate a dull religious program? Or did He invite and challenge us into a dynamic enterprise, a dangerous exploration, an uproariously happy but perilous pilgrimage into the abyss, into the fullness of life? Our major task is to rediscover the questions for which religion is the answer. Philosopher Alfred North Whitehead said that religion is the answer to the question of what each one of us does with out solitariness. If that question remains unanswered, if we remain secularly acute but religiously mute, then we become victims of loneliness and alienation. We become so boring and bored that craziness seems our only option.

The live ones, nurtured in leisure, are the contemplatives who, like fish jumping out of the water, push back their boundaries. As Alfred North Whitehead says, contemplatives resist the repetitive mechanism of the universe. We love Loren Eiseley, the gifted anthropologist, for his perceptive appreciation of the irreducibility of the wild, "the dearest freshness deep down things" (Gerard Manley Hopkins, "God's Grandeur"), that gives them their unique angularity. In a lecture to scientists, Eiseley said: "Perhaps, after all, a world so created has something still wild and unpredictable lurking behind its most sober manifestations." I believe that this is true, and that the rare freedom of the particle to do what most particles never do is duplicated in the solitary universe of the human mind. By stripping the veil of the familiarity of things, contemplatives see things as they really are. Those corybantic particles just need to be caught in the act! The terpsichorean display of nature, the glory of God in "dappled things," is available to all who contemplate. There is only one requirement: leisure. As Brother David Steindl-Rast, O.S.B., says, "Leisure is not the privilege of those who have time but the virtue of those who take time." If we do not enjoy the leisure barely possible today, we will never know the leisure postponed until tomorrow.

It is in lavish, spacious moments of leisure that I am often most joyously entertained. On a recent walk up lovely Lady's Brae at our Holy Hill Hermitage in Skreen, County Sligo, Ireland, I watched an enterprising, playful lamb gather seven others, mark off a good section of the hill, and start a race. Our big black Newfoundland dog, Duende, not only howls at the prayer bell but weeps over human departures. Celebrating Mass once in Malibu, California, my altar boy got sick. His perfect dog took his place, sat attentively on the step left vacant by his master, barked a response to every "The Lord be with you," stood like a Swiss Guard at Holy Communion, and at the end led me solemnly through the church and out the door.

Things like this happen all the time, but we miss them because we are half-awake, driven workaholics whose unlived lives are encumbered by the dingy detritus of derivative existence. Direct contact with the Earth is salvific. We need to share G. K. Chesterton's Christian amplitude. Ever since Jesus' birth at Bethlehem, everything earthy reminded Chesterton of God and bound him to Christ, as he expressed in a letter to His fiancëe: "I do not think there is anyone who takes quite such fierce pleasure in things being themselves as I do. The startling wetness of water excites and intoxicates me; the fieriness of fire, the steeliness of steel, the unutterable muddiness of mud." Prodigious leisurely time, full of useless acts, poetic gestures, stillness, and deep human communion, is salutary for every human spirit.

We must learn to use the leisure with which we are already blessed. And we must make a colossal effort to introduce more and more holy repose into our lives. As St. Thomas Aquinas said, in an inspired effort to express in a simple, limpid way the very heart of the human climate: Contemplation is holy leisure.

Meeting

ON THE EDGE

Why is society so dehumanized? Why do so many of our children fail, unable to enjoy their human existence? These are some of the questions thirty-three research scientists raised in a project sponsored by Dartmouth Medical School, the YMCA, and the Institute of American Values. Their conclusion, found in a report titled "Hardwired to Connect," is a deficit in human connectedness. So many of us remain unrelated to other persons and institutions that satisfy our mutual need for moral and spiritual meaning. The basic expression of this need is religious yearning: a lively openness to the transcendent and a desire to be one with the Holy, the Ineffable, the One who loves us. This need is natural, arising from "our basic biology and how our brains develop." Meaning is revealed in our attachments. So Victor Frankl was right to stake so much health and healing on degrees of meaning, which he elaborates on so magnificently in his logotherapy.

The report goes on to explain how social environments that meet—or defeat—this need "affect gene transcription and the development of brain circuitry." Psychiatric disorders can be traced back to a child's "relational context," which leaves encoded in the right brain the exact propensities for such an unfortunate eventuality. Parents' love life and love making also affect the child's brain and does, in fact, reduce a future tendency toward violence and sexual promiscuity. And so we have—as George Will says in his column commenting on this report—biology buttressing important moral conventions.

To overcome the vacuity of our social connectedness we need to recover, enliven, and expand the family unit and to revive and improve all other authoritative institutions, especially religious communities. I'm not thinking of some nice patchwork. I'm suggesting a radical upheaval resulting in a radical renewal where connectedness becomes attractive, transforming, and fruitful on both individual and social levels. Otherwise, the inherent longing for such communities—for love, challenge, and beauty—among adolescents will continue to take the form of gang membership.

What the world needs is a plethora of communities of love—a love, braced and laced by discipline, self-denial, and self-oblivion; a love that expects no comfort or consolation, nothing or nobody to rely on forever; and finally, no satisfaction except the unsatisfied one of being there, to help if you can. And in all this denudation the lover experiences a carefreeness as wild as the wind and a joy as pervasive as the sun.

Over forty years ago I had the graced opportunity to form such a community of love to which I attached the clumsy title "Spiritual Life Institute of America," and under its secular aegis, "The Religious Order of the Apostolic Hermits." The men and women of this community, though silent and solitary so often (or, I

should say, precisely because of that), relate mindfully and heartfully to each other and to the retreatants
and guests who spend time with us. "See how they
love one another" is overheard so often among our
visitors. The common knowledge is that this attractive
and infectious love was engendered by the deep palpable love of the founders. That is my own conviction
as well. However, in our fortieth year we were drawn
into a "Dark Night" composed by a divine, inflowing
presence and human folly. Very often we create our
own paltry, painful existence by egotistic intrusion
and foolishly call it a "Dark Night" as if God caused or
wanted this misfortune of missing the target.

Why are we so obtusely addicted to what is pretty, trivial, and banal? Why do we clutter our minds
and impede the truth? Why do we live on the surface
when God invites us to dwell in the sublime depths?
Why do we want a quick fix from therapy when we
can be transfigured by a theophany? Why do we fuss
so much and prattle so much when the Word longs to
become our flesh? We cannot grasp God by our words
but we can enflesh Him. Come Holy Spirit, transfigure
all the matter of the world.

Technological society has provided immense possibilities for human growth but in reality has hampered humanness. Ironically, it has separated us from
direct and immediate contact with real things and live
people. We gaze at things through a screen—television, movies, computer, windshields, and tinted glass.
Having watched from our safe, soft, sybaritic enclo-
sures, cruelty and tragedy are observed without empathy. Nothing keeps us awake or makes us pray or
repent. Beauty no longer stirs us. We are jaded.

Technological society spawns a culture of
alienation by depriving us of communion, of the
crowning act of presence. No one is "there" anymore,
no one is living on the spot where they are, instead

missing the revelation of here and now. Even when with friends, they are talking to others a thousand miles away. This plugged-in age has robbed us of the capacity to observe, judge, and act, and serious human diminishment has been the result. We can no longer live on the spot where we are. We are careless about the person, place, and event that confront us. We refuse revelation to satisfy our restlessness. We squander profound, personal communication for the sake of shallow, mindless communication.

Christian humanism does not dictate a program or subscribe to a system, but, in a language new enough for the creative task, indicates what we must do to make and keep us human. Humanizing Christianness makes a decision to become a free subject. As such, we are free to repudiate the inhuman of the present, stretching our consciousness toward the unfinished character of our world, naming the things injuriously absent, and making our negative critique and our positive hope historical through action. It is our transcendence that brings one day to an end and generates a new one. This is the only way to leave untruth behind while moving with alacrity toward truth. Transcendence thus takes shape historically. Transcending history we are able to create a new history throbbing with life. Eros empowers and engages transcendence, charging it with pathos and compelling it—alluring and freely—into the future, into a new tomorrow: a far cry from the "ups" and "outs" of the worn-out language of transcendence that has led so many inevitably into nihilism. Separated from God we felt doomed: worms instead of glow-worms; bums but no longer burnished bums; sinners, a dreadful thing unless touched sinners—a divine thing. The old language did not understand transcendence as a reality in the midst of life that creates history. The unfortunate result was an unreal, deadening separation between time and eternity, heaven and Earth, transcendence and history.

Transcendence longs for immanence, which depends upon us. But what have we done? Entrapped it in religion, guaranteeing that it remain stable and fixed amid the historical process. Christopher Marlowe's perception, from *Dr. Faustus*, seems so foreign to us: "See, see, where the Christ's blood streams in the firmament! One drop would save my soul, half a drop. Ah, my Christ!"

Transcendence is just another word for God's humanity. From all eternity God spoke one word; that word reached its fullness in Christ. Nothing remains to be said, but it will take us forever to carefully absorb, significantly grasp, and personally respond to His erotic disclosure. Until then, there is no revelation. To respond is as crucial as to be addressed. In revelation we are responsible partners. We are so inescapably relational that wherever we go and whatever we do, we end up meeting, jack-sawing between the magnificent and the messy. Go to work or play and you meet. Go to church or the theatre and you meet. Go away, even into the wilderness, and you meet. You meet people, animals, natural things, artistic things, the cosmos, and, ultimately, where all things have been drawn and lifted up, you meet Christ.

Meeting explodes into transcendence and ignites immanence, culminating into such intimate union with God that enlightened love ensues. This peak human experience occurs when we go beyond ourselves and receive the divine spirit into our hearts, that is, into the center of our being. Only here, at the fine point of the soul, is life renewed and the fire Jesus yearned for set blazing. This is the meeting point between our spirit and the spirit of God. Often *spirit* is used ambiguously either in reference to a human being or to a cosmic, theandric person. It doesn't matter. They are united in the Spirit. In order to be centered here, to be focused and united, we meditate. This alone disposes us for prayer and social action.

Skip this fundamental human act and humanity on both an individual and a collective level is so enormously diminished that divine disclosures, allergic to a vacuum, become severely restricted. We all tend to be cowards, afraid of being called, chosen, and sent; frightened of risk, of God's inappropriate behavior, and, ultimately, of eros. Jesus, disarmed, "overcame the world." He met and met with no power except the fierce, erotic Spirit that made Him the bravest man ever and the supreme lover.

How silly our own petty pursuits seem in the face of Jesus' titanic passion, His zest for life, His acute sense of humor, and His noble bearing of pain and rejection. Human evolution is delayed immeasurably while we dally perfidiously with fatuous inanities and feverish activities that we think will, somehow or other, fabricate our makeshift identities. How foolish! Straw men are made by fools like me but only God can make us free. Freedom means being able to make a promise and keep it. In other words: endure.

THE HUMAN ACT

If we are erotic enough, moving with awe and wonder into a boundless awareness of the Ineffable; if we actively respond to our own unique call and the lure of every opening way; if we live leisurely enough; if we protect and develop a lively language full of theophanous enchantment and fashioned by a matrix of silence—then perhaps we will become mindful enough for the quintessential human act: *meeting*. All the other transformative aspects of life, in the marketplace or the cloister, are meant to dispose us for the deep encounter of total communion. I mean the deep encounters of every day, so I use the word *meeting*.

Martin Buber's insight into the "I-Thou relationship" is a perfect reference to this divine-human encounter, the unitive experience of all in one and one in all, this heightened state of consciousness. Ultimately all living is meeting. Every genuine life-stance is made up of meetings—not business meetings but theophanous meetings, contemplative interactions full of revelation, which, of course, should happen at work and play.

This is comparable to the difference between *feelings*, which are not important, and *feeling*, which is a mystical experience: the presence of God *felt*. We feel the presence of God through our whole being and our whole life, not in sporadic, isolated happenings, but in the ongoing experiential trek through the desert into the Holy of Holies, through the night into the Numinous. There we are struck by the mystery: the *mysterium tremendum* and *mysterium fascinans*. *Mysterium tremendum* evokes dread; *mysterium fascinans* evokes delight, together constituting the full range of human drama.

One man goes to work, another to play, and another to church, all for the same purpose: to meet. One woman goes to graduate school, another goes on retreat, and another into the bedroom, all for the same purpose: to meet. The meeting we all want is a deep, personal exchange where we interrupt routine habits of thinking and make free, deliberate choices, so that new ways of living open up for us. In such concrete situations of altruistic relatedness, transformation occurs and a more real self emerges.

This way, without undue introspection, we come to find by surprise who we are. That is why Jesus said, "Unless you lose your life you cannot find it" (Matt. 16:24). In losing our life in the other, we find it. When we find this life, we find life itself, we find God. And we find ourselves in true perspective: not in terms of projections, compulsions, and social conventions, but our pure, naked self, the true self we never knew. We must be disabused of the self we falsely identify with because this is not the true self. Neither is "the other" the one we think he or she is; nor is God the God we think He is. I often wonder how much there is of the "he" in the deity. He certainly is not *my* God. According to the famous German mystic Meister Eckhart, if we have a God, then we are not poor enough. If we are not poor enough, then God cannot reveal His true self to us. Only the poor man, the poor woman, comes to know God. Poverty is openness, and where is an opening way, reality reveals itself because there is nothing to impede the onslaught of God's love.

When we really meet, when we truly and vulnerably encounter another—a person, a tree, a cat, a dog—then, in a sense, we fathom the unfathomable, darkly, but directly and immediately. We "ef" the Ineffable, but unself-consciously and self-forgetfully.

People are surprised and subsequently pleased to learn that in our own community of apostolic hermits we base our life on persons even more than prayer. We lived over thirty years together before we dared write our Rule because our life is based on persons moving steadfastly, mindfully, away from problems into the Mystery. We deliberately, freely choose to enter the Mystery and be mystified, to live in wonder. We cannot package truth. We cannot take a series of sacred propositions and put them in our pocket and walk away, safe and sane. If we forget this, a likely misfortune, we face monastic chaos.

God loves to surprise us. When we let too many common, ordinary things happen, the surprise, gets lost in jejune solemnity. If we get into functional little ruts, the surprise never happens. We need to startle others by really meeting them in the mysterious depths, receptive and open to the transcendent, to the

Transcendent One who is sheer love, and therefore always a surprise.

This is why meeting strangers is so important: We don't know what to expect or even how to approach. I once went to visit some distant relatives in Detroit. We had a delightful encounter full of startling revelations. After three hours and high tea it dawned on us that we were not related at all; we were, in fact, total strangers. I had gone to the wrong house. Yet that visit was one of the most pleasant of my life.

James Agee writes in *A Death in the Family*: "I believe that every human being is potentially capable within his limits of fully realizing his potentiality, that this, his being cheated and choked of it, is infinitely the ghastliest, the commonest, and the most inclusive of all the crimes of which the human world can accuse itself....I know only that murder is being done against nearly every individual on the planet." That really says it, but it has to be properly understood.

The concept of self-realization has philosophical roots in Aristotle's concept of *entelechy*, whose root is *telos*, which means "end." *Entelechy* is the existential process of becoming yourself. Based on Aristotle, our emphasis on self-realization has produced one "ism" after another: humanism, vitalism, feminism, pragmatism, existentialism, psychologism. Each of these has a good component as well as errant exaggerations. Self-realization has been the focus of philosophers such as Jean-Paul Sartre, Martin Heidegger, and John Dewey, and psychologists such as Rollo May, Carl Rogers, Medard Boss, Erich Fromm, Karen Horney, and Abraham Maslow.

I myself am indebted to all these outstanding thinkers. But notice how they all assume there is in us a given, real self. Can we define ourselves or our potentialities apart from the direction we give them, apart from what we become in relation to others? Prior to the direction we take, there is no potential and no real self. Only when we become engaged and immerse ourselves in a contextual situation do we discover our true potentiality and our real self. Take the risk and bear the incalculable disclosures of the newness and realness of life.

The marvelous Viennese logotherapist Victor Frankl has always been my favorite psychologist. He emphasizes meaning in his seminal book *Man's Search for Meaning*. We must find the self. The self is not already given, lying dormant in the cellar of being. The self emerges as we engage in a pilgrimage, seeking and searching, to find meaning. Frankl said that all neuroses are due to a lack of meaning.

The real self, real human potentiality, is discovered, not invented. God did not invent them and neither do we. Potentialities are evoked by what life specifically demands today and tomorrow and tomorrow. The more intense life is, the more capacious we become. We develop a *capax Dei*, a capacity for God, for all things all at once. Concrete life situations tear up old possibilities and tease us into new ones. That's why a difficult life where the cross is central is so marvelous. Life is urgently inviting and challenging, and as we respond to each surprising address, we find our true potentialities in the daily drama. The Holy Spirit lures us into the fullness of life, into new being, the Christ-man, the Christ-woman, the real self we'd never dreamed of. So we must not get stuck en route into the Numinous, into the blazing truth that lights up the inner reality of every human being, every tree, and every shee. We must never make self-realization the end. We pursue the Holy, the Numinous, and in that self-oblivious pursuit, because we are totally engaged and can't squint back at ourselves to see how we are doing, we become our real selves. As we pour ourselves into this altruistic, erotic, existence, we begin to live with wild, wondrous recklessness: reckless because we are mad about God, and wreck-less because we are rooted in God. Honoring that sacred bond, "riding for that brand" (as every cowboy rides for a brand!), we persevere in our commitment and find the bond, the covenant, our overwhelming contentment.

All our troubles, our cowardly compromises, come from loosening the bond, an equivocation of that brand, as we seek comfort and solace outside the heart of God. We let ourselves be carried along by the lethargy of nondecision and routine practice, making no free choices, no radical commitments, never living deliberately. Only responsibility and maturity enable us to choose our potentiality.

We need to scan the horizon, learn the territory, and recognize the possibilities. Then, intuiting the choices we must make because God is calling us, luring us into our own existence, we overcome our fears, out lackadaisical tendencies, respond to the divine enchantment, and follow that inspired hunch into more life, more love, into spiritual matrimony with God.

Not the God of the World Trade Center, by whom, however indirectly, we are startled and staggered momentarily into fearful wonder, but the high and haunting Holy One who dangles dailiness over the eternal abyss of love and evokes from our quotidian quasi-existence heroic acts of moral grandeur and spiritual audacity. We don't really live unless we are coaxed, teased, or torn out of the comfort zone. Divine dynamism does this better than terrorism. We cannot wait for extraordinary events. But neither can life be packaged or managed. We've got to go wild. Boundaries, of course, must be faced, but with boundless love.

Becoming human is becoming more intimately engaged in the act of God. Every human vocation is a summons into divine activity; the terrifying, ravishing, and worldly love life of the Trinity. God's suasive summons is more compelling than a draconian command. And a refusal on our part is more perilous. "Come follow me" has an incomparable urgency. Not to follow is disastrous. Life without meaning is unbearable. Without the consciousness of a vocation— being called out of the enclosed self into divine action— there is no meaning. Deafness to that call accounts for the emptiness of contemporary society.

We respond to God's challenge and invitation by our own personal commitment to another, a few others, a cat, a dog. A story from the Hindu epic *The Mahabharata* is instructive here. The great god Indra confronts Yudhishthira: "You are now ready. Leave everything and come abide with me. But first get rid of the dog."

Yudhishthira responds, "No. I will not get rid of the dog."

Indra says, "You foolish man, I've given you everything. Fulfillment is yours. You've reached the pinnacle of all human striving. Come now to heaven. But get rid of the dog."

"No, I won't get rid of the dog."

"Oh, silly man! You enjoy enlightened harmony with the universe, why not get rid of the dog?"

"But Indra," explains Yudhishthira, "This dog has been faithful to me all my life. It is said that to renounce one who is loyal to you is an infinite evil. I will not get rid of the dog." Indra finally agrees.

At that, the god Dharma spoke up: "Because you said 'This dog is loyal and loves me and renounced thereby the Godly chariot,' there is no one in heaven who equals you. And so you will attain to imperishable worlds in your own body and tread the divine way than which there is none higher."

So we must not cave in to the God we think is God, to the God we think is saying, "Get rid of the dog." We know the dog is real, but we can't be sure the God we think we know is real. So stick to the dog!

It's the unconfronted God we don't know; and bereft of God's intimate love, we are frightened. We keep our distance and live a derivative existence. Despite dutifulness and religiosity, the Spirit withers in us and joy eludes us. Grooving on the spiritualities and path hopping does not help.

Our human plight reminds me of a person who comes close to sneezing a million times in one bland life, but never experiences the explosive abandoned relief of "AAAH-CHOOO!" This is like organized religion without religious experience, liturgical fidget and devotional fuss without mystical life, or churchy setups and services without meeting or personal, passionate presence.

We tend to identify with the untrue and unreal rather than moving dangerously and daringly into the real and the true. Living as we do in the suburbs of reality, we prefer to pray by proxy: let the choir, the soloist, and the guitarist do it; let the priest, the minister, or the rabbi do it. But unless we ourselves enter into communion as intimately and directly as possible, another event simply takes the place of genuine religious experience and we lose the overwhelming sense of presence.

After William Johnston, S.J., celebrated Mass at a Christian-Buddhist conference, an enlightened Buddhist asked, "Why did you sing after Communion?"

Father Johnston said, "It's something we picked up from the Protestants."

The Buddhist said, "You're shooting yourself in the foot. Why sing together then of all times? Why act communally and use someone else's words, hear someone else's noises when you have just been given God by God? You have just been drawn into the deepest possible spousal moment of your life in Holy Communion!"

Sometimes that will erupt in song, but not often. A better practice is silence.

When I was a silly child, I used the "power" of physical communion with the living God unusually. As I walked home from grammar school, I had to face my enemies at the railroad tracks. They knew I had to cross the tracks to get home, so they were always there. When I went to Mass, I left after Communion so that Presence would still be in me. Then I'd run like mad to the railroad tracks to meet the enemy and disperse them. It didn't work. I came out alive, but it never happened the way I thought it would. But I was on to something: a presence, an incomparable and infinite divine energy in me, an energetic presence connected to the bread I'd just received, bread that is not merely a symbol but an incarnational embodiment of the Wholly Other. An event from a few years ago highlights this eucharistic presence in a spectacular way.

After a visit in America Pope John Paul II was heading for the airport. On the way he came upon a church that struck him as particularly beautiful. He announced his desire to visit it. His security men objected. He insisted. The men demanded a quick inspection; so in they went with their fantastic dogs. The dogs checked out every nook and corner with greater severity—until they came to the Tabernacle. There they took a stand, dug in, and barked furiously, indicating that someone was in the Tabernacle. No wonder St. Alphonsus said, "the barking of dogs can give more glory to God than the chanting of monks."

A person is by definition one who is always in search of another. Another incident illustrates this: Father Murphy was eager to get in touch with Dr. Henry Sully so he phoned him at home. His son, Tommy, about ten years old, answered the phone.

"Tommy, is your dad there?"

"Yes, but he's very busy."

"Your Mom home?"

"She's busy as well."

"Anyone else?"

"Uncle Pat, but he's cranky and busy, Father. You don't want him."

"Well, anyone else then?"

"Yes, the police."

"Oh my, put one on."

"I can't, Father. They are so busy it's scary."

"All right, Tommy. I'm a fool, but I'm asking one more time. Anyone else there?"

"Yes, the firemen."

"Yeah, yeah, I know, Tommy. They are all frightfully busy. Tell me one more thing: what the heck are they all doing?"

"Father, they are looking for me."

Sexual integration is a lifetime process. We don't need moralistic lists of what cannot be done in human encounters. I began to do this in the fifties during retreats for high schools and colleges, but quickly abandoned such tripe as I felt exorbitant silliness of such shallow treatment of the glorious mystery of sexuality.

What we need is character, depth and an inner moral sense of things. The human task is to become originally, exquisitely human, to become capable of high moral acts. We are bound to make mistakes along the way—not impure, reckless mistakes but simple oddities of behavior that are either funny or grotesque. Moving beyond stuckness and sterility, away from the baby food of love into an adorable attachment and adamant commitment to one another, and in these transcend depths to express the perfect love of God.

What most often prevents this from happening is our bad education, our superficial friends and the embarrassing preaching of the churches. So we turn the pinnacle peak of our lives, the supreme pleasure into a sordid aberration. We then crawl back into the cozy, safe, but miserable mediocrity of the crowd. Feckless in the foothills, distaining the mountain top, we plod along in the shallows. *Technique* possesses us. We are its impersonal, dispassionate, routinized slaves. We've lost mystique—no more glee, joy, surprise, enlightenment, no more intimacy, ecstasy, and fecundity, no more overwhelming pleasure. And no one can live without pleasure.

We must not aim at self-realization but at the altruism of the Holy Trinity. All three persons eternally become themselves by being altruistically related to the others. Since we are the image and likeness of God, we must imitate God. We do that by being altruistic, by giving and giving and giving in healthy and happy ways. Then community arises, giving to one another over and over again, ultimately giving to the Ultimate Other, is ultimate communion: the contemplative life. Being altruistic means being mindfully involved in work, doing things, making things, making love; that is, in meeting. Called out of the protected ego, out of routine and convention, into the battle, into the drama, into our own terrifying destiny—this is what it means to live. It is beyond our human limits. So St. Paul said: "I live now, not I, but Christ lives within me."

We all work for a living. Meeting is the heart and soul of work. Without awestruck, in-depth meeting, work becomes trivial, pedantic, and monotonous. Meeting turns it into an adventure. In fact, work done leisurely and mindfully *is* the contemplative life. Only if we work leisurely can we meet.

Recognition of this maxim does not align me with those popular contemporary authors who minimize prayer. Moments of prayer here and there, they say, are enough. But traditional wisdom and quotidian experience contradict this. Though prayerful at its best, work is not prayer. The most useful thing in the world is work; the most useless is prayer. A utilitarian mind helps work but spoils prayer. Meaningful, reverent work sets the stage for prayer, for awareness of the Ineffable. In prayer we attend to God directly. Christ promised to refresh us in prayer. Prayer and work are different but closely connected. Work without prayer becomes pompous; prayer without work withers.

My own shaky contemplative life has suffered enormously from a reduction in physical work because of illness and infirmity. When I used to dig, fetch water, and deliver oil with an old tractor, I was a better contemplative. Work gives shape and form to love and thus reduces ego inflation and enhances the glory of God. I work as hard as ever, but am physically less employed. The lack of good physical exertion such as gardening, playing volleyball, and running has made my contemplative life more difficult. Let me emphasize running, a holy, happy, unself-conscious act. Running is so different from jogging. Running is playful, spontaneous, and free. Jogging is so often a grim determination to achieve a utilitarian end. Pigs and ponies don't jog, nor do children! Jogging, it seems, is an unhealthy form of exhibitionism.

MEETING TESSA

How wondrously exciting and uplifting she was and different from all the other thousands of college students I had been meeting while leading retreats in the '60s. She was vivacious, intelligent, happy, and deeply committed to Christ and whatever pertained to Him. She had true values and broad interests. The reconciled polarity of sexuality and purity invested her with extraordinary focus and exhilarating enthusiasm. Her attractive purity was due to her undispersed energy. What a perfect candidate for monastic life based on vitality! What an unmistakable vocation! Thus began our community of Carmelite-Celtic Hermits—not formed because of apostolic need or ecclesiastical rule but out of love.

All future vocations were equally erotic. By that I mean enamored of life. They wanted more life; attracted to the monks they wanted to be connected, infected by community love. They wanted to live in that particular erosphere. Love calls and love responds. If the love is pure and faithful, monks ripen and become astonishingly fecund. This kind of monastic fecundity touches our guests and retreatants so effectively. "See how they love one another," we hear over and over, or "What an erotic atmosphere their life in Christ creates. It's absolutely contagious." This love expresses itself principally in three ways: care, playfulness, and prayerfulness.

No wonder Pope John Paul II was so concerned to build a community of love. On all levels there is no greater need in the world today. One genuine lover is worth hundreds of apathetic twits. Yet our life is so challenging, I believe it's tougher than the Marines. Egotistic softies never make it.

This world-wild love agony is a reality caught so trenchantly by James Baldwin and quoted by Robert A. Raines in *Creative Brooding*:

> *The joint, as Fats Waller would have said, was jumping...and during the last set, the saxophone player took off on a terrific solo. He was a kid from some insane place like Jersey City or Syracuse. But somewhere along the line he had discovered he could say it with a saxophone. He stood there, widelegged, humping the air, filling His narrow chest, shivering in the rags of His twenty-odd years, and screaming through the horn, "Do you love me? Do you love me? Do you love me?" and again, "Do you love me?" the same phrase unbearable, endlessly and variously repeated with all the force the kid had...the question*

was terrible and real. The boy was blowing with His lungs and guts out of His own short past; and somewhere in the past in gutters and gang fights...in the acrid room, behind marijuana or the needles, under the smell in the precinct basement, he had received a blow from which he would never recover, and this no one wanted to believe. Do you love me? Do you love me? Do you love me? The men on the stand stayed with him cool and at a little distance, adding and questioning...but each man knew that the boy was blowing for every one of them.

"Do you love me?" Everyone exists to answer that question, especially monks. Prayer is a cry of the heart. The heart cries above all for love. Ultimately the cry is a yearning for God, for divine union. Yearning keeps the world from falling apart. When we cease to yearn we are dead. Yet we shrink from communion and thrive on camaraderie. In that case, despite all our other efforts, true humanism eludes us. Communion is the exquisitely distinctive human act. In so many cases what prevents communion is shallow communication, a flatulent fluvial of words, words, words. Real words, live and lustrous works that do indeed commune, grow out of silence. They are suffused with wisdom and steeped in stillness. The one woman we boast of as human, Mary the mother of Jesus, was the "woman wrapped in silence," dazzled in stillness and full of wisdom.

Fifty times a day, yearning for communion. I pray these words I learned in grammar school: "Most pure heart of the Most Holy Virgin Mary, obtain for me from Jesus, purity and humility of heart." Humility directs my yearning; purity unifies and magnifies it. Detached from pounds and pounds of pettiness I participate in the Trinitarian love life of the universe. My horripilating and humiliating pitfalls, ego intrusions, and evil urges are not necessarily impediments but an unskippable part of the human struggles toward divine union: enlightened harmony with the universe.

And now I wonder, "Do you love me?" Is that really and truly, absolutely, the basic cry of the human heart? Maybe not. It is certainly not mine. Seems more like a curse than a blessing. And to be extolled is abhorrent. Craving to be loved is a disease. All my life I've said I'd rather be understood than loved. Understanding fosters fidelity and fun along the merry way. Love tends to be fickle, fatal, and dreadfully sad beneath the jolly surface. Eros, however, reconciles opposites. Eros fosters heroes, while the men and women are so divinely disciplined that they "care" passionately— and forever.

Still, there is no understanding or enlightenment without love, but it's assumed with subtle efficiency and suffused with unpretentious wholesomeness. Craving and raving are not conducive dispositions. Self-oblivion and other-centeredness are.

After all, Cupid shoots his arrows at random. So does God. The results are remarkable: Mary Magdalene and Jesus, Mary of Nazareth and the apostle John, Hëloise and Abelard, Clare and Francis, Winston Churchill, John and Abigail Adams, Pope John XXIII, Maximilian Kolbe, and Saints Teresa and John of the Cross, Thërîse of Lisieux, the Little Flower, and Josephine Baker, the big banana—a few off the top of my head. I skipped a few friends and a few giants such as the last lion-king of Ireland—Boru—and, oh dear, Moses, Elisha, Jeremiah, Isaiah—all the prophets!

Moses was shot by Love's arrow. He balked initially and objected very reasonably; but in the end, he accepted responsibility for the momentous task God had chosen for him. Moses shows us how prophets bear the awful presence of the Holy and, despite reasonable objections ("the dark night"), commit themselves with tenacity and fidelity. "Here I am," says Isaiah, "send me."

God does not want a merger but a union. He does not want to absorb and replace our otherness but to ignite and enflame it. He wants the highly selfed other to penetrate the Mystery, to participate in it and preach it; that is, be a living witness of it. The Mystery? What is it? The early Church Fathers called it *eros*: that ultimate longing at the heart of the universe for interrelated oneness. The deepest desire of every human being is to be alone with God. To be *alone* is to be *all-one*. This is the very heart of the Mystery.

We need the best possible condition for breathing: atmosphere. We need the best possible condition for eros: erosphere. But we are not erotic enough. No wonder God's summons always calls us to become more and more erotic. When the Holy Spirit called me out of a conventional parish-monastery and led me into the desert, the only thing I was certain about was my requirement to build an erosphere, based on persons young men and women striving to become heroic lovers. We had to let the Spirit transform our personal horrors into holiness, and our world of chaos into cosmos. To achieve this end we had to become monks in the deepest, purest sense of the word *monos,* which means "one." We had to immerse ourselves in what Jesus called "the one thing necessary"; shun the erosphere and you shrivel the spirit. You stifle love. Without God's presence and glory, our lives make no sense.

Vocation is the only key to authentic existence, the only way to discover meaning, the one life-stance full of joy and peace. The sense of vocation, of being called by name to fulfill a particular destiny, does not preclude pain and sorrow but increases it. So what, as long as we are called! Meaning sets us free, even if we are hanging on the cross.

The physical penetration that sometimes occurs when lovers meet is, however exhilarating, merely a symbol of the enraptured spirit of I-Thou in total congress. Meaning is revealed through deep, adoring penetration that is both cognitive and spiritual. It takes a lifetime of mutual caring and mounting eros. The casual, mindless sex so prevalent today, especially among the young, is destructive and dehumanizing, without meaning. The awesome beauty and transcendent glory of God in the flesh are not an "affair." Stunted spirituality is often due to runty sexuality. Ubiquitous unhappiness and therapy will continue to be paramount in our dying culture as long as sexuality remains unintegrated. Erotic lovers are in search of meaning and intimate reverent communion. There is no liberation from our waist-high culture until we realize that the chief sexual organ is the brain. What we most want subconsciously and desperately need is penetration of the truth. Toward this magnificently human end, condom-caparisoned organs play a small part. The unifying action cementing an I-Thou relationship is not taking, shoving, or humping, but contemplating: being overwhelmed by the ravishing sacredness of the other. This act not only unites, it liberates. Human freedom is the capacity to make a promise and keep it. Freedom can be maintained only by reliability and fidelity. "I love you." What a promise that is! What responsibility! And how rare! Why so foreign to our postmodern age? The answer is simple: We do not live in an erosphere but in an inflated egosphere, so we are prone to be selfish, unrelated, and alienated. The inevitable consequences of selfism are isolation and loneliness.

Even a robust community of monastic contemplatives can, after years of disciplined dedication, give up love and cease to follow Christ. Some trivial matter can suddenly turn them into vipers. The Christian revolution is softened and subverted. The ritual goes on, a vapid kind of democratic fellowship endures, but a satanic venom permeates the center. Passionate purity is replaced by pretty poison. Dead men and women say their prayers and do their work but the fiery charism, the fierce spirit, has soured.

How watchful we need to be! Not grim and solemn but alert and attentive, on the edge, quickening the evolutionary process, the resurrected order of being. To overcome our apathy, out complacence, we need to do the Christ-thing: conquer un-love.

We need to respect tradition and be steeped—not stuck—in it. Why can't we improve on formulas that are hundreds of years old? And new ideas and symbols? Even a new way of being religious? If we could make the church happen out of our own raw experience, then it wouldn't be a boring repetition of events, but an experience. The church happens when Christ is personally encountered, and then a lively effort is made to share this infinitely attractive person with others. A presentation based on Empire versus Kingdom would be interesting; in fact, very gripping and satisfying. The Empire subsists on mediocrity, manipulation, and mendacity. It would take a whole course or book to unpack that. The Kingdom can be identified by wisdom, kindness, and courage.

The old lists—virtues, vows, gifts, and capital sins—don't mean much to most people. Whoever heard of perfidy? And yet that's the big sin. And envy, the original one? Who knows the difference between deliberate, righteous anger and the corked volcano of vulgar, self-pitying wrath? Why do most people choose to be spiritually gelded lackeys when they could be saints? What's the difference between a divine summons and a fit of narcissism? What we need from beginning to end is great expectations, reaching and yearning for the pinnacle of human experience with, as G. K. Chesterton put it, "The firm feet of humility that grasp the ground like trees."

God calls us out of this dead place and longs to make us whole (holy) and uproariously happy (blessed). On the other hand, God weeps over our refusal to be what He created us and graces us to be: His own image and likeness. God is Trinity. God does not *have* community life but *is* community life. The persons of the Trinity become who they are eternally by being altruistically related to the others. Since we are God's image and likeness our lives should follow suit. I regret that St. Augustine has such an excessive influence on us. He was on target in many things, but not everything. In his crucial and sometimes bitter debate with the brilliant Irish theologian Pelagius, he was misguided: he saw God's image only in the soul of the individual person.

We know that the Kingdom of God is between us, that the image of God is found in the interrelatedness that links us all together, and not only with our fellow humans but with the Earth. We do not find God only by withdrawing inward but by going out to meet the divine in concrete situations in the hurly-burly of the world. God is not hidden in the *I* but in the *Thou*. He is reflected in the whole person, body and soul; the whole community embodies him. In solitude we prepare to meet God and reflect on having met or we are taken by surprise and in agony or ecstasy we experience, however briefly, a more direct and immediate presence. One way or another, we need to waste time with the Beloved. The spiritual life is equally outward and inward.

Real meeting is communion. Without communion we over-communicate. Over-communication leads to mismeeting and misunderstanding and blocks the opening way to the fundamental human act of meeting.

I must confess that not so long ago I grew so weary of so much maudlin mania and chirpy chatter (the Irish call it "crac") that I developed a peccant response, which was almost no response at all. This was shoddy irresponsibility on my part. I lost my contact with the otherness of the Other. Whatever my companion feels significant enough to share with me, or with a group of us, I must respond sincerely and uniquely. Sometimes a nod, a yes, is not good enough; a respectful, tentative *no* often deepens and enlivens the conversation. Give and take that is genuine and pleasant, despite the edge, sets the stage for revelation. If I am nothing more than an objective observer and a good listener, I can contribute nothing to the dialogue. Once I enter an exchange personally and vibrantly, something new and beyond the original intention of any of us emerges from our mutual presence. The word becomes flesh. What a responsibility: to fashion words so mindfully and honestly that enfleshment follows and the original word proclaims—This is my body. A few humble words and a divine enfleshment.

What a dramatic difference from the dismal distance I had established to cope with my displeasure over "table talk." My token effort to make a little voyage to the other and come back safe and sane was a failure. And I was a fool. No matter where I am, even in seventh heaven, I must respond from there, entering willy-nilly into the dialogue. If the events and images that envelop me at the moment cannot be quantifiably defined or clearly articulated, it is enough to point. It is imperative that I point. Some of humanity's greatest art, literature, music, and philosophy are the fruit of such "pointing." Remember the legendary founder of Zen Buddhism: he understood when the silent Buddha held up a flower.

Only mystics really meet deeply enough to enjoy the ultimacy of communion. You may lament, "Well, that leaves me out; I'm no mystic." Perhaps we should give up the words *mystic* and *mystical*. Maurice Friedman felt compelled to move beyond mysticism into what he calls "basic trust." The great Spanish mystic and Doctor of the Church St. John of the Cross said that the only direct and immediate means of union with God is faith. And faith is trust.

One of the most enlightened men in history, Fyodor Dostoyevsky, portrayed the great Russian *staretz,* or holy man, Father Zossima, not so much as a mystic but as a humble lover. And that, in turn, is what Father Zossima teaches: not mysticism but humble love. These striking paragraphs from *The Brothers Karamozov* convey His style:

> At some thoughts one stands perplexed, especially at the sight of men's sin, and wonders whether one should use force or humble love. Always decide to use humble love. If you resolve on that once and for all, you may subdue the whole world. Loving humility is marvelously strong, the strongest of all things, and there is nothing else like it....
>
> Have no fear of men's sin. Love a man even in His sin, for that is the semblance of Divine Love and is the highest love on Earth. Love all God's creation, the whole and every grain of sand in it. Love every leaf, every ray of God's light. Love the animals, love the plants, love everything. If you love everything, you will perceive the divine mystery in things. Once you perceive it, you will begin to comprehend it better every day. And you will come at last to love the whole world with an all-embracing love....My brother asked the birds to forgive him; that sounds senseless, but it is right; for all is like an ocean, all is flowing and blending; a touch in one place sets up movement at the other end of the Earth.

DISCIPLINED WILD MAN

The temptation is not, I want this exquisite pleasure, this drunken delight, this ecstatic surrender. No, that seems trivial compared to the unspeakable thing waiting to be seized in this searing transport of unbounded mutual affection. And that "thing"—the *haecitas or quiddity* of eros—through a long, slow, deep, cognitive penetration of the mysterious other, erupts and explodes into a sacred seizure, a divine abyss of luminous glory. And the glory is the bonding. And the bonding is permanent.

The lovers become de-egotized, even un-selfed, because they are reborn, Christened, divinized. They know now that their basic being is neither individual nor community, but something entailing individual and community stuff yet also way beyond—call it, if you will, transpersonal and transerotic.

So what's my temptation? In what way would intercourse attract me? It would attract me—and the idea once seemed compelling—whenever I assumed that nothing but utterly intimate sexual expressions of love would overcome the fragile, feeble, and short-lived nature of a relationship. That was a mental question answered negatively by noting how very often and very quickly the most ardent and intense lovers, superbly experienced at love-making, not only separate but despise each other. Though I find the phenomenon abhorrent, I recognize its sad objectivity and respond accordingly. If we accept the responsibility of sexual integration and real love of one another, then we must face all kinds of intellectual questions and resist enslavement to a systematic, preconceived outline of canned answers. The Church has discovered basic principles and does shed some light on the sanctity of sexual behavior, but the adventure goes on. So do revelation and evolution. We have hardly reached the depths and we cannot without openness, change, and risk. Have Soloviev, Dostoyevsky, Shakespeare or even Augustine, John of the Cross, and Teresa of Avila exhausted the subject? Have Freud and Jung discovered all? By no means. Divine revelation requires human partners. We must explore.

Learning sexual integration, I have made intellectual mistakes but have been spared sexual ones. On that level, thank God, I have enjoyed and shared profound joy, peace, and spiritual growth. Watching others enjoy liberation and divine union is an incomparable delight. A sad note must be added: Unless the newly liberated person abides long enough with the mature and stable friend and imbibes a rich erosphere, fear develops, doubts occur, the old stuff—what Scripture condemns so often and so ferociously—the old Adam is reasserted and the new man gets suppressed. What a tragedy, a sickness! A stiff rectitude based on childish rigmarole expels moral beauty—so fresh and new and vibrant—and besmirches a pure heart. It is this lazy, lumbering, narcissistic atmosphere that turns little ones into victims and all too often the chief accomplices are uninspired, shallow therapists.

The bonding is a permanent seal on one unique relationship. The sexual genital act, without the glory of bonding and permanence, can issue, at it often does (but not always), in calamity.

The same glorious end—and intoxicating union—can be achieved or, rather, given in ways other than sexual intercourse. Celibacy, for instance, is a superb way or condition in which the celibate is a disciplined wild man, carefully educated, with highly developed sexual energy integrated into his personal life and his or her major project of existence.

There is nothing worse than a family or a religious community that is unsexual and erotically squeamish. Appalling is the strident hoopla over common, everyday expressions and gestures of love. Stiffness and stuffiness replace ardent, warm-hearted compassion. A goofy, comfy camaraderie takes the place of deep concern, tenderness, and intimacy. Laws lacerate love. Moralism excludes and condemns as inappropriate behavior the deep, deifying gifts of eroticism. Vivacious, sexy men and women whom God has chosen for that reason are, through sex mania and bad theology, reduced to robots and mannequins. Do not be deceived by the brash bravado, the loopy gaiety; that happy style is a cover-up for celibate cowardice. A shallow celibacy makes fun and cool possible, but not intimacy. Among sterile, impeccable celibates communication can be impressive, but there is no communion. And without the union enlightened love provides, we all perish.

Some time ago I spoke to a renowned psychoanalyst in Boston, a man who worked with religious orders for many years. We were discussing the prominence of mental breakdowns among people seeking perfection. I suggested that scruples made nervous wrecks of them. No, he said, scruples are not part of the disaster. The cause is clearly the horrible fact that religious do not take honest-to-goodness, down-to-earth care of one another. Exactly—not erotic enough. Erotic behavior should be such an acceptable, admirable, and normal kind of quotidian demeanor that it's hardly noticeable—and certainly, for mentally healthy people, sexually integrated persons, commendable.

This kind of behavior most appropriate for every unique occasion depends on common sense and docility to the Spirit. An overall orientation is governed by rules. Explicit acts are dictated by the objective situation and inspired by subjective virtuosity. This is how God's will is done, not in some automatic, moralistic sort of way—a way that can be rigidly prescribed ahead of time by an organized system. Morals maketh the man—true. But morals are mindfully developed as we respond soulfully, that is, totally and skillfully, to each contextual situation. Any other response, however lawful, is bound to be not only shallow and superficial, but blatantly phony. There are no good consequences of such vapid behavior. After a brief showy semblance of order, chaos follows inevitably.

Since religious people, monks and nuns certainly, are usually quite educated, they abhor a vacuum and invent clever devices to cover up the erotic vacuity. Typical modes of deception are corny humor, loud laughter, brazen banter, flimsy flirtations, and, in general, a goofy kind of pleasantness. The flimflam works publicly but is privately devastating, personally demeaning.

There are other, more subtle ways of killing love and poisoning the erosphere. First among these aberrations is, it seems to me, a heavy, humdrum consciousness of being "in a relationship." This leads to anxious, selfish strategies that segue into constraints of such rigidity that spontaneity and receptivity are lost—and so is the potential loving, joyful friendship.

Thank heavens for Freud, who discovered the unconscious—well, he published it; I think the Bushmen and the Native Americans and the old Celtics discovered it. We need to come to terms with the unconscious but still not mess with it. There's a plethora of stuff buried there and we can cope with only one bit at a time. Think of it this way: The unconscious is what we can't and shouldn't be attending to right now. In fact, may not the unconscious simply be the body? Peering into it constantly would be like staring at the body all the time. Yikes!

The wise man said, "See and pass on." Take God alone with ultimate seriousness, everything else with reverent lightheartedness. So, incorporate sexuality and move on. No sex on the brain. Let it empower you, not distract you.

And if you err sexually—who doesn't?—repent and regroup; that is, get your fractured act together again and love more than ever. There are no victims in real lovers' lives. Love does not victimize, manipulate, or obstruct. Silly therapists and ignorant twits torture and terrorize faltering lovers by calling them victims. And they disgrace themselves and their profession by such reprehensible tripe and flagrant sciolism.

I know a religious community that suspected one member might be guilty of "inappropriate behavior." They panicked, pooled their fears and fantasies, and transmorphed into a vicious mob. To see this happen in the Wild West, in burgeoning belligerent nations and unfortunate families, in the street gangs and among lubricious lovers, is shocking and shaming enough, but to see it gentrified and demoralized under the cover of religious respectability is mind-boggling. It's a pretty poison that seeps unnoticeably, surreptitiously into our nicest people and the best institutions and eradicates alterity and authenticity.

In all communities there is a wise and judicious way to deal with questionable behavior. This subject needs to be explicated more comprehensively, which I have attempted to do elsewhere. Criminal activity, for example, demands trained attention, a focus of its own. But in this case, I want to address the way religious communities can overreact to small mistakes, provoking brouhaha over trivia. In the case I discuss above, it was the unbecoming brouhaha of the religious community, not the trivial behavior of the individual member (or, rather, suspicions of that person's behavior) that constituted the scandal.

Take Thomas Merton as an example. While in the hospital, Merton fell in love with his nurse (don't we all?). A monastic quisling overheard a phone call of Merton's. He reported the call to the Abbot. What if the Abbot had announced this discovery to the whole community, called in the Bishop, arranged an extremely dramatic, doomsday intervention, and then wrote inflammatory letters to all Cistercian friends? This would have obviously been an excessive, gormless reaction with monstrous consequences for the monks, the church, and the world—and, of course, for Merton himself. Merton was a holy, fulgent man and a unique and powerful influence on the leaders of the world and on a society yearning and searching for ultimate communion with God and peace on Earth. Overreaction to his error would have had far-reaching, damaging consequences.

So, how to cope with what seems at the moment unacceptable but relatively petty? Quietly, calmly and in a distinctively, superbly personal manner. Be not afraid. And don't let mammon motivate you. If you are a mystic: see and pass on.

When will the Church regain spiritual audacity? Will it ever again speak with authority? When will it embody Christ and enflesh the mystical life? Will it always let the Empire rule the Kingdom? Does it really believe that distributing billions of dollars solves a problem or merely saves face? Why does it tolerate a Christianity subverted for centuries? And, finally, why does it remain unequipped and disinclined to convey what the people most urgently want and need and what Christ came to give: the mystical life? Let the Church teach one thing: What did the Son of God come to save us from? Un-love. If only we could grasp that and live with the freedom of enlightened lovers! Why do we need a vigorous spiritual life? For moral rectitude? No. For pious satisfaction? No. For psychological poise? No. For soulful repentance? No. For a religious experience? No.

Good grief! What then? Why does a hermit herm? To meet—that's why. All living is meeting. If we could only get this straight and then do it. Not perfectly but moving with awe more and more deeply and mindfully into the profound and mystery of the other. How open, receptive, and vulnerable we need to be! We must reach heroic degrees at being deliberate, attentive, passionate, prayerful, and yielding. I did not choose those dispositions randomly. Each one is required for really meeting. Want to remember them? Think of the first letter of each word: DAPPY.

D = Deliberate
A = Attentive
P = Passionate
P = Prayerful
Y = Yielding

It's a nifty little word. Who would not want to be dappy? Dapper is trite, dappy bright.

Jesus was super-luminously dappy. So were the apostles, in a lower key. So were the early Christians and the lustrous theologians such as Irenaeus, Gregory, Origen, and Maximus. They met and became human by being unself-consciously divinized. We balk at being deified. Too bad. There is no other way to become human. As Oscar Wilde writes in *The Soul of Man Under Socialism*:

> *And so he who would lead a Christ-like life is he who is perfectly and absolutely himself. He may be a great poet, or a great man of science; or a young student at a University, or one who watched sheep upon a moor; or a maker of dramas, like Shakespeare, or a thinker about God, like Spinoza; or a child who plays in a garden, or a fisherman who throws his nets into the sea. It does not matter what he is, as long as he realizes the perfection of the soul that is within him. All imitation in morals and in life is wrong. Through the streets of Jerusalem at the present day crawls one who is mad and carries a wooden cross on His shoulders. He is a symbol of the lives that are marred by imitation. Fr Damien was Christ-like when he went out to live with the lepers, because in such service he realized fully what was best in him. But he was not more Christ-like than Wagner, when he realized his soul in music; or than Shelley, when he realized his soul in song. There is no one type for man. There are as many perfections as there are imperfect men. And while to the claims of charity a man may yield and yet be free, to the claims of conformity no man may yield and remain free at all.*

THE DEPTHS

Meetings that remain shallow and selfish are sterile. Whenever they move unabashedly into deep encounters, they become fecund, and the fruits of the Spirit abound. This is eros, the making of love, which can be richer than any other kind of sexual experience. This is where celibates should excel and where their ministry engages in its most effective apostolate. "Should," I say; but what if they are shallow? Or merely useful?

We must remember that we cannot be drawn by "others," and especially "The Other," except through what the mystics—and now the psychologists—call "the Dark Night." Because most of us fearfully shun the dark nights, the ultimate translucent experience— the kiss of the Spouse—eludes us. We need wisdom and courage. Otherwise we will never enjoy union and we will be deprived forever of the compassion we need to be consumed by the fire of love of God and of one another. Compassion, our passion linked with God's, is the linchpin for the transfiguration of matter by spirit. Love grows or withers depending on whether or not we accept or reject purification in the dark night.

I've noticed how the remarkable love of our community of hermits is tested through intimacy and intensity. Reality reveals itself and gradually demolishes the inner idol of the loved one, the idol that was none other than an idealized projection of the self, the image of what the lover himself lacked. Genuine discovery of the other prevents idolatry, ignorance, and insouciance. Above all, when we are captivated by infinitely attractive Reality, infidelity—strictly speaking, the only sin—becomes unthinkable.

A second conversion occurs when we discover that our Gods have been too small, when we discover that God is not nice. God is not an uncle or a mascot; He is a tornado. We do not tinker with supernatural storms.

We approach with holy fear—not psychological anxiety, but ontological humility. Entering into this presence is like entering the cave of a lion. Who knows if we will come out alive, if at all? Maybe what happened to Enoch will happen to you. Awesome? Indeed! "Enoch walked with God; then he was no more, because God took him" (Gen. 5:24).

Giles, the Swiss hermit, said that prayer was like going off to war or to a dance. In either case, prayer is momentous and precarious and requires heroism—a brave willingness to be divested of slogans, clichës, illusions, and fantasies. Thus stripped and poor and naked, we are disposed to know God as God is. Job's heroic attitude becomes most appropriate for us: "Even though He slay me, yet will I trust Him."

The Roman breviary expands on a phrase of St. Paul's in Philippians: "The Kingdom of this world and all the beauty of life I have esteemed as nothing, compared with the high privilege of knowing Christ Jesus, my Lord." It concludes brilliantly: *quem vidi, quem amavi, in quem credidi, quem dilexi.* "For I caught sight of Him and fell in love with Him, and though darkness came, I nonetheless trusted Him, and so in the end came to love Him with that deep, deliberate, enduring love which nothing can destroy." That perfect comment on St. Paul by Gerald Vann is so accurate it's almost a translation, a lovely literary one. The illusions and baser elements of *amo,* purified in the crucible of *credidi,* spring forth pure and true in *diligo.* The one who endures faithfully to the end succeeds in loving the object for itself. The truly mysteriously "other" prevails in the night while the grasping, craving ego dies and the authentic, liberated self, the pure "I," is given in love to a concrete situation, an existential summons that turns everything into fire—into incarnate God. This is what I mean by meeting *in depth.* In this sense all meeting is living, loving, going out from oneself.

INHUMAN ACT

Meeting in depth is the essential human act. (*Communion* is a superb word, gravid with meaning, but to those with a religious bent it may seem hackneyed). To live is to meet in the deeps. Our formations as distinctively human beings take place there, but always in connection with solitude and silence, without which we lose our capacity for meeting and our taste for the deeps.

It is also crucial to reflect on the *inhuman* act. Obviously, this is the opposite of communion, the failure to meet; in other words, *alienation*. We live in an increasingly alienated culture as technology develops and we deal with reality less directly with more and more screens and implements between us and the other. Fantasies prevail while reality recedes. Excessive communication kills communion, banderlogs despise dialogue. Crowds nurture thugs and mobs, dispelling vitality. The cell phone demolishes both our solitary and our social lives. Despite the possibility of occasionally helping humanity, I am convinced that in the whole wide world it is the most de-humanizing thing. On that phone, used mindlessly and carelessly, we almost always disarticulate, disincarnate, and dismiss the fundamental embarrassment and radical amazement mutually evoked in an authentic meeting.

Isn't it interesting? The dumbing down of Western society seems to match technological advancement. Another match, staggering in its implications, is the present economic catastrophe and the religious crisis. And finally, it would help to have at hand a diagnostic study of the present relationships between a sybaritic practice of religion and a hunger for war. Are we in dire need of a moral equivalent? Should the U.S. president consider joining an Amish community or spending a year in a contemplative monastery? The important thing is that His prayers be true. We all struggle with spurious prayer.

We must first of all distinguish between solitude and isolation. One cultivates adoration, the other alienation. Solitude is personal and full of social concern. Isolation is individualistic and self-absorbed. Alienation is the lifestyle of an isolated individual who grooves on solipsistic existence. To be alienated is to be separated; to be solitary is to be united: alone in the eye of the storm, alone on the surface level in order to be together in the swirling vortex of being. Alienated individuals tend to live, work, and play in crowds. They are often the loneliest people in the world and therefore the most miserable. Not to be able to share is to be shackled. Alienation is thus the essential inhuman act.

There is a simpler way of putting all this but I had to introduce it slowly to a society notoriously soft, boozy, and jejune. Here's the simple fact: We engage in an inhuman act every time we sin. People hate to think about sin even though it is a central (not *the* central) concept in the Christian experience. Sin is the first element Jesus addresses on Earth: "Repent, for the Kingdom of heaven is at hand." We must confront sin. Understanding it conveys a knowledge of God-manhood that is not otherwise available.

We experience the transcendent God as other and distinct but not as separate and over against. When we talk about God, we talk most deeply about ourselves. By His presence, God calls us into more humanization. The denial of God leads to inhumanity. That is why that towering theologian of the twentieth century, Paul Tillich, said that culture must be theonomous because God is the ground of every human existence. Once we realize what it means to be really human, we experience an inevitable horror of sin.

No one likes to self-destruct or hurt the beloved. Sin is never trivial nor merely indiscreet nor something socially unacceptable. It is the very shadow of death. There is nothing noble or heroic about defying God or hurting those who love you or breaking a vow. Either you are faithful or you defect; there is no other option. The sinner's model is not Prometheus who challenges the gods; it is Narcissus who falls in love with his own reflection in the pool and, as he hugs it, drowns.

Sin is an intellectual mistake. We are so oriented to the good that we cannot do something bad without a hallucination. We must make something bad look good in order to do it. Sinners, myself included, are absurd. A human being is the one whom God addresses. Sinners will not listen. They behave as if they were deaf. The original Latin word *ob surdus* means *deaf.* When we ignore God, we lose our vocation.

Ripe as we are for continued conversion. Christ is always calling: Follow me, follow me, more intimately, more intensely. But we balk, clutch, hesitate, compromise, and postpone. We remain unfinished; God remains in pursuit. The tension between us is the groundwork for understanding sin.

Nikos Kazantzakis portrays this phenomenon with panache in his novel *The Last Temptation of Christ.* Will Jesus respond to the call of God the Father or betray it? Jesus is tempted to escape God's clutches, forsake the call of the Spirit, hand His freedom over to custom and convention, become an ordinary man, marry, and settle down.

What tragedy, what disgrace if Jesus had wavered in His vocation, ignored His Father's personal call, sniffed with selfish indifference at this commitment, chucking it! The voice He listened to (obedience) would have spoken no longer, and His own possibilities for becoming representatively human, the most manly man, would have been forfeited forever.

Now one of the chief activities of the risen Christ is convicting the world of sin. As John says in his Gospel's third chapter, Jesus does not judge the unbeliever, the unbeliever judges himself. Likewise, Jesus does not convict the world of sin by infecting it with guilt but by infusing it with grace. In other words, He is gracious to the sinner, and this implacable grace, no matter what, is an embarrassment. Such radical embarrassment jolts the sinner. Being constantly presented with opportunities to convert is both maddening and touching. God is calling and enabling us to live in a brand new way. If we refuse, God's grace seems like wrath. Followers of Christ, by their alternative love stories concretely lived, also convict the world of sin. We all seem to drift and float. We need repentance, life-changing repentance. This is the first step to wholeness.

Sin is not an infraction of a legal proposition; it is not primarily a slip or failure in keeping the law. Frightfully, dreadfully, sin is the breaking of a bond— between creature and Creator, between fellow creatures, between friends, business partners, and above all, lovers. Break the bond, the vow, the oath, commit treason, and without repenting we are doomed. We must call a spade a spade. Betrayal is betrayal. Contradict this, and the passion and death of Jesus make no sense. He was betrayed. Sin crucified Him. It was pretty poison all right, but it was sin.

Every time I hurt another unnecessarily, I sin. I betray a trust. God entrusts me with His kingdom, and all I want is control, esteem, and power. I want to follow my whim and caprice, not that terrible surprise, that Ineffable Good, that Holy One we call God.

THE CALL

To meet or not to meet: that is the humanizing criterion and the goal: intimate union between the human bride and the divine Bridegroom. To begin we need titanic courage; to reach the end we need a fierce, unflagging loyalty. Infidelity is, ultimately, the only failure; perfidy the only sin. And yet think of all the nifty, upright people who play capriciously along the side of the road and never make it to the end. They multiply impressive means to take the place of the end. In this they find success but no glory. A labyrinth of solipsisms replaces authentic human hunger for wisdom: a taste for the right things. As long as we remain unwise we are plagued by unconscious refusal, a series of half-measures, a failure to come to some great *meeting* place. Fear, more than anything else, prevents the final transforming encounter, a ravening experience of life undreamt of on the safe, familiar plateaus of human existence. We are overwhelmed by, and therefore refuse, the fullness of life, the apotheosis of eros, and the refulgence of unleashed personhood, all of which are characterized by an unbearable freedom. We refuse our real self in favor of the manageable ego.

How spectacularly blessed we are—and commonly so! We seem like such upright bags of tripe—at least I do. But I know more certainly than I know anything that the Holy One has chosen us to be His partners in the human experience. We are suffused with divine energy in order to meet the deep, darling otherness, so sacred and sublime and yet searingly secular, that fills our universe. Creation is relational. We are all—animal, mineral, vegetable—interrelated, interdependent. Our quality of humanness depends upon how mindful and reverent our ways of relating are: "The Kingdom of God is between us." As we encounter the immeasurable mystery of otherness, eschewing false judgments, glib attitudes, and arrogant opinions, we are being Goddened, deified. The human Son of God does not want honeyed fans but robust followers, not treacly sycophants but, instead, dynamic men and women who, drawn and captivated by the infinitely attractive personality of Christ, become themselves raw and riveting witnesses of the One, the living God, sharing with Him His divine longing to create, redeem, and glorify. We grow in this capacity to the extent that we become liberated by an upbeat and joyous asceticism from moralism, envy, cowardice, cheap talk, pious piffle, small desires, petty behavior, and, in summary, from the banality of evil and the evil of banality.

Every authentic lover is an outlaw—not a rogue or a renegade but an enlightened person. A delicious but painful process! *Pati Divina*: Who can bear the beams of love? *Pati Humana*: Who can bear the doom of treason? By the law we are trained for bearing—mindfully and merrily. Once we have suffered the plenitude of divine disclosure and the amplitude of human potential, once the Bridegroom is met and espoused, the law becomes superfluous. If you cannot assimilate bridal language, then try this: Once you have penetrated the ground of your being and live in the "ungrund" (the underground), where everything that was an object—measurable and calculable—becomes a subject, when all is one and one is all, at that point, though you are not finished, the law is fulfilled, love is the law. "I live now, not I, but Christ lives within me."

Christ is the beginning and the end, not in isolation but in the flesh, in history, in the mystical body, and in the body politic. Those who don't understand the religious freedom guaranteed by our government try to edge the divine and representative man out of politics and away from the public square (it's a private thing, they say). They have tunnel vision and a vapid fear of God. Their ontological orientation is an endless detour into absurdity. Religiousness is the most unprivate thing in the world, the most blatantly and plangently public. It has been regarded forever by the wisdom of ages as "the work of the people." That's the literal meaning of liturgy, the dramaturgy of the Church. Religion is so universal and irrepressible that it cannot be confined in or by the narrow and nugatory structures of the state. But the flames of this eternal fire ignited by God must by all means permeate the mind as it strives to reach the pinnacle of all human achievement: Christophany, or the ability of graced humankind to live on the same wavelength as God.

I am critical of casual, careless meetings. I recognize, for instance, my weakness as a leader, an abbot. I was too casual, too easy-going. I disempowered myself. I should have resorted to the tough, imperious modes of treatment that seem so rife in army sergeants and football coaches. I am no pussycat. I don't lack courage. In fact, another weakness may pop up here, my daredevil attempts to be wild. Not sexually; I'm too shy and awed by others to ever be so inclined; but intellectually and physically (that's why I've suffered poor health). I know, prudence does not mean taking the safest means to the end but the best means to the end. Often the best is not the safest. But humility often requires us to settle for the second or ninth best.

So, although perfunctory meetings, cozy get-togethers, can impede racing urgently to the end, leaping impetuously into corybantic and terpsichorean modes of encounter could be, if done feverishly or fatuously, counter-productive. I stopped telling young people to live life exuberantly and spontaneously when I found all over the place balloons, kites, and a million paper hearts (years later I still find those dreadful little hearts stuck in the cracks of my floor!). Let me share with you some of my own fumbling efforts to meet in meaningful depths.

The first time I met Jacques Maritain, that towering philosopher, I listened to him with my whole heart
and was drawn by him into such depths that I could
not find my way home. I had to call for help.

One day, walking down a busy New York street, I
noticed vividly, with shocking amazement, a very distinctive, even awesome sort of man. I longed to meet
him. I nudged him gently and asked him carefully:
"Who are you?"

"Abraham Heschel," he said. I was smitten. This
Jewish rabbi and eminent scholar had by his books
influenced me more than anyone.

"Can I come with you?"

"Yes," he said, "Come along but excuse my bad
mood." He did seem down.

"Why are you sad?"

"Morning prayer," he answered.

"Why did that make you sad?"

"Well," he groaned, "I was praying about the Viet-
nam Council going on in Rome."

"Why did that make you sad?" We stopped walking. He stood with me in silence.

He gazed piercingly into my eyes and finally spoke:
"Can you tell me, my friend, how many of your bishops are contemplative?" We walked again in wonder,
which, on his death, he had said is all he ever asked
for.

Other philosophers and theologians, once met, affected me profoundly. E. I. Watkin came to visit me and
fifty years later I am still overwhelmed. There is no one
greater. (His daughter, Magdalen Goffin, a splendid
and insightful writer herself, has recently published
a biography of her father. I am passionately eager to
read it.) Father Gerald Vann came too. What an astonishing, beautiful Dominican! What an exquisite man!
We went to movies and lectures together. We laughed
and wept and prayed wherever we went. I was just a

young monk when I read his first book, *The Heart of Man,* a forbidden gem of wisdom. His lovely book and J. D. Salinger's *Catcher in the Rye* were stunning and popular at that time and both banned in seminaries. Neither before nor since has anyone been so eloquent and so right about love and sexuality. In this area he was my incomparable mentor. I tried to share this flaming insight with my community but failed. A last regression into rigidity and frigidity by frightened and fearful ecclesiastical apparatchiks has knocked the stuffing—they're flutzy, too—out of monks. Christianity has been subverted, monasticism debilitated, and democracy demonized. When splendid, saintly men such as Father Vann vanish (R.I.P.), a vacuum arises and anesthetizes the mindless masses who are happy enough to live a derivative existence in the suburbs of reality. Complacently gormless puerilities lure them into stupefaction. We do not need highbrow meetings for living in the depths. Every meeting—at work, or on the street, in stores and on campus, or at the movies—sets the stage for mutual discovery of the sacred secret writ large in the cavernous recesses of an otherwise bland and fenced-in human puppet.

There are certain social arrangements that are particularly conducive to delightful mental intercourse—for instance, going out to dinner. A key player in this ideal human drama is the waiter or waitress. How heedless and haughty it is to ignore them or to treat them with a cavalier kind of *sangfroid.* Yet a funny, infuriating thing happens to me every single time I go to a restaurant. When I have my mouth full and can't talk at all—that's when the waiter will suddenly arrive and ask, "How is it going?" So, a few years ago I decided to take measures to avoid this embarrassing predicament. I became extremely watchful and furtive. I now look all around to see if I'm safe. No server in this whole section of the building.

Here goes! A good heaping forkful. And here he is at my side. Where the devil did he come from? Always, everywhere the server is asking: "How is the food?" I've resorted to one thumb up; the other one is busy with the fork.

In hotels I enjoy innocent, happy intimacy with the housecleaners. How uplifting and playful they can be and sincerely devoted. They don't have sex on the brain, as so many self-righteous religious professionals do. So they hug and kiss and move on.

Exhilarating moments or hours of intimacy can erupt spontaneously when we are not stuffy, fussy, and self-absorbed. I met the actress Brigitte Bardot at a Corpus Christi parade in St. Tropez. Prayerfully, gleefully we watched and clapped and sang. What a feast! Then she took me by the hand and ran with me down the hilly street and into a crowded, jubilant café where the love was more palpable than the smoke and passion more potent than wine. I was supposed to stay overnight with the Carmelites in Monaco but the querulous friar who answered the doorbell sent me away, reasoning, "because you are an American." So I walked a bit farther and met—and stayed with—Grace Kelly and Prince Rainier and the American chaplain. And consequently, in the middle of that night, I met God. Everything came together: the mountains, the sea, the sunny beaches, and bodacious bathers; the palace, the parade, Brigitte—that lively, lovely friend of whales and of God—the café people throbbing with love—touching, kissing, and philosophizing, the wild ones on the narrow streets, praising Eros, Love Himself in the monstrance. We can't prove the existence of God rationally; but we can monstrate him. And amidst the hurly-burly of St. Tropez and Monaco what seized me and secured my seduction was this super-personal luminosity in the night, this most manly man, this divine union with the original and ultimate Eros. God-intoxication, and that alone, can satisfy human hunger. All this trivial, tiresome talk about sex—what spectacular nonsense it all is! Of course, we could turn it around: simply take God seriously—not solemnly but seriously, not self-righteously but self-obliviously—and forget about sex. Let it empower us but not direct us, let it enliven and enrich our whole being, without fustian or preoccupation. Let it develop fully, freshly, broadly, bursting boundaries, not fortifying them. Let it envelop us. We can't master it anymore than we can master the wind and the waves. It's a drive. Our holiness prevents sexual damage, not our bully-boy techniques, not our arrogant self-possession. People don't seem to mind if a spouse kills someone, but to kiss someone is doomsday. Monks prefer rectitude to amplitude and so their love is shriveled and shallow. We'll slap you on the back and make jokes but refuse to make love. Making love is a monk's life. Celibacy helps us to do that. It is not focused on the genitals but on the beatitudes. That's why monks deserve respect from lay people. They live for the people. Relentless discipline enables them to make love bountifully and so raise levels of life significantly. The punctilious rectitude of auspicious religious life eliminates lovers. No edges, no risk, no heroism, no holiness. My vocation as a monastic founder was to teach this effectively—more by rule and spirit than by formal teaching. Somehow I failed. Earlier in this chapter I briefly reflected on this. I was too casual, assuming this art of lovemaking was so natural it should be easy. But the trouble is, *we* are not natural. We are not corrupt, but we are bent and our education has not helped. Our confusion has reached a peak today, and no wonder, given our attachment to Puritanism while, at the same time, trying to become exceedingly permissive. At any rate, only in a rich erosphere will we trust enough to meet with wild and wise abandon, and thus become God's delight: a disciplined wild one.

The form itself can never be imagined. Recently, while driving in Northern California, I was stopped by a policeman. "Can I help you, officer?"

"Yeah. I've been following you for some time."

"Thank you, officer."

"You broke three laws in the last few minutes."

"What a shame! What particular laws did I break?"

"One, you didn't stop at the stop sign."

"Well, sir, I can put your mind to rest about that. I did indeed stop. In fact, I read a map. When you caught sight of me I was moving out of my long stop."

"I see; you may be right about that. Two, at the next stop you pulled out in front of that red car. You came so close to him I was worried."

"I don't blame you, officer, but that man looked distressed to me and I wanted, first of all, to make sure he was all right and then to bless him."

"And then you don't seem to know where you are going; maybe you are a drunk driver, I thought, now I see you are just different. Back to number two, what a weird excuse! Are you a preacher?"

"No, sir, but I am a Catholic priest."

"What does a priest do?"

"He does anything he can to restore an exquisite humanness to humanity, and the key to that is divine infusion of God's infinite love. So I try to get folks to shake their shanks and look lively, to live more intensely. So I celebrate Mass and hear confessions. Maybe it's providential that you stopped me—I'd be glad to hear your confession."

"Now for three. Are you lost?"

"Yes, sir, maybe you'll help me."

"I will on the condition that you promise to keep all the laws between here and there."

"I promise."

"Now this is not a ticket. It's my card with my phone number on it. If you need help, and I strongly suspect you will, call me."

"Loved *meeting* you, Charles, thank you."

Finally, I try, though not always successfully, to induce a meeting, a real I-Thou encounter between doctors and myself whenever I need medical attention. God is love. That is the gospel message. So is this: A human being is by nature, above all, a lover. What a fierce and fecund thing to be! The Gospels spell it out lucidly and wondrously. So do some rare thinkers, great writers such as Kierkegaard, Soloviev, Tolstoy, Dostoyevsky, Unamuno, and, more recently, D'Arcy and Percy. Walker Percy was a doctor. In some of his love stories doctors play a big role. So do patients. We learn from them in a novel way what tradition has always and everywhere taught us: Love is not enough.

When you get really ill, you come to know this— maybe for the first time. In fact, lovers of a sick person often do the wrong thing. What a sick person wants from most people is not love, but a spacious, flaming grasp of His situation, a quiet objective need of empathetic witnessing. Illness—acute suffering of any kind—is full of revelation. The person so afflicted by harsh necessity or severe illness needs someone to recognize it when it comes.

The doctor, especially, doesn't need to love the patient or to suffer with him but to enjoy him. The doctor and the patient should be mutually interesting. A physician, like anyone else, is repelled by greediness for care. Just as there is, up to a point, an art of dying, an art of healing, so is there an etiquette to being sick.

To get at my illness the physician must probe my character as well as my flesh. Proust dismissed a physician because he never read Shakespeare. There should be something beautiful about all relationships—

most of all between a person who professes to be a healer, such as a priest or a physician, and one who seeks that kind of personal attention.

It is important for me to know that my poor old body hasn't failed me. My illnesses are a natural consummation of it. My quandary is not why am I so sick, but why I've lived so long. I have no trouble with suffering—physically or spiritually. I know I get what I deserve. How do I know? Intuition—mindfully feeling my way *into it,* into the swirling sheerness of being.

I adore old folks who look upon their ramshackle shape as an inevitable diminishment after a peak of vitality. The ruins of a body deserve the same respect as the ruins of antiquity.

It is the small, quotidian meetings, sometimes pleasant and sometimes tedious, that make up our days. All these need to be transfigured.

One of our monks (or nunks, as well call the female members) was in a prolonged funk. (Imagine a nunk in a funk—high dudgeon, to say the least!) Issue followed issue and she wept profusely week after week. I found this annoying and very unmonastic. I was about to chide her but instead I took a long, loving look, which is how I define contemplation. I discovered that she was no sad sack at all but a lovely, vibrant person full of monastic potential and human holiness. That objective, open, contemplative gaze enabled me to intuit the rough, sharp, cleansing tang of her otherness. And she knew I loved her. And her ongoing response was brilliant, radiant, peaceful, and joyous. I never saw her cry again. Her walk, her talk, and her presence exuded hilarity, mirth, and something gloriously sacred.

In George Eliot's novel *Silas Marner* you find this— the meeting and reaping the reward:

> *He turned towards her, and their eyes met, dwell-*
> *ing in that meeting without any movement on either*
> *side. That quiet mutual gaze of a trusting husband*
> *and wife is like the first moment of rest or refuge from*
> *a great weariness or a great danger, not to be inter-*
> *fered with by speech or action which would distract*
> *the sensations from the best enjoyment of repose.*

Pray and read all you want and learn the Bible by heart, but if you refuse to meet the lover, the stranger, the ruler, the one in distress, you miss God.

There is an old Jewish story that makes the point trenchantly. A young fugitive, trying to escape the enemy, had convinced the people of a small Jewish village to hide and protect him. But when the soldiers came and threatened to burn down the village and kill every man if the fugitive was not handed over, the people got frightened and asked the rabbi what to do. The rabbi was caught in this awful dilemma. So he went to this room, took the Bible, and started to read, hoping to find an answer. After a while his eyes fell on the words, "It is better that one dies than that the whole people be lost." So the rabbi closed the Bible, called the soldiers, and handed the boy over to his enemies. The village celebrated with a big feast. But the rabbi returned to his room with mixed feelings.

At that moment the prophet entered and asked, "Rabbi, what have you done?"

The rabbi said, "I handed over the fugitive to the enemy."

Then the prophet said, "But don't you know that you have handed over the Messiah?" "How could I know?" the rabbi replied anxiously.

Then the prophet said, "If, instead of reading your Bible, you had visited this young man just once and looked into His eyes, you would have known."

His vision must expand to the dimensions of the

universe, His heart swell to the size of Secretariat's and the scope of Christ's.

The Rabbi seemed holy precisely because he was so biblical. But therein lay his failure, his escape from responsibility, from the urgent need to attend to how and why he is addressed now by the living God and thus to respond to what is and is not happening historically, demanding that he be fully immersed in the present while effecting creatively the future. Without meeting he cannot act judiciously or lovingly. Biblicism is laziness plus cowardice. So is legalism. Both are smoke screens for moral weaklings.

Think of the massive carnage in the world today due to the failure to meet. The heads of nations, of political parties, of churches, of religions, of families, of business rivals, of lovers, and of friends. Think of the economic chain of heinous events, the painful experiences, and the ruined lives consequent upon one arrogant, egotistic leader who refuses to consult and to listen, or one careless rabbi, one complacent minister, one effete bishop, one religious superior, or an elected committee of twits, for that matter—who, hiding behind the wall, will not meet and will not dialogue. The results are always disastrous.

The whole wonderful adventure begins and ends with Christ. Jesus became man so that we could see the invisible God. "He who sees me sees the Father." And, in another way, a contemporary author says the same thing: "See Christ and you are a Christian; all else is talk." And I'm sure we've all heard the modern lament: "Poor little talkative Christianity."

St. Francis de Sales calls this most manly man "God in His most attractive form." He's intoxicating. So the brilliant French author of *The Stumbling Block*, Francois Mauriac, asserts, experientially, that "once you get to know him you cannot be cured of him." And again: "how eagerly we would listen to you if he would speak to us no longer as philosophers, psychologists and theologians but as men and women who have seen and touched the resurrected Christ."

The ancient Church Fathers went further and claimed that "God became man so we could become God (by participation)." St. Teresa of Avila groans over our failure to experience the living God in Christ. She says: "all of our trouble comes from not keeping our eyes on Christ."

Everything we do must play a part in our transformation into Christ. God already Christened Jesus. Now he wants to Christen us. In this endeavor we don't exactly imitate Jesus. But we meet, understand, love, and follow him. Meeting is key. And the principal way to meet is to pray. That involves much more than saying prayers. Our whole being is unceasingly at prayer. An indispensable way to learn prayer is daily meditation. Here we learn to do one thing. That's all: one thing. Being there undividedly. So efficiency is an effect of meditation. That's why so much of the corporate business world is becoming more and more interested in meditation, as are therapists.

Though that is indeed an effect, it is not the reason we meditate. Why then? To do the one thing necessary: to meet Christ and in Him to attend to God and share in a deified human mode: the divine power to create, redeem, and glorify.

TRUE PRAYER

When prayer is a genuine cry of the heart, who could possibly be trying to edify or impress or want to feel correctly religious? Prayer wrenched from the heart in the exigencies of life is always true. It is significant that the early Christians did not think of a theologian as an expert in exegesis and hermeneutics but, rather, as one whose prayer is true.

We pray truly not when we ask to be catered to but when we long for a larger capacity to engage willingly and skillfully in the task at hand, applying the undivided energy of the whole, focused self on meeting the existential demands of the moment.

One of the Hasidim heard himself being addressed by the Holy Other: "You have lost your share in the world to come."

"Good," he responded, "now I can begin to serve in good earnest."

We do not strive for perfection, not even for "purity of heart," but for whatever it takes to get the job done. The Hasidic image of man is the right one: "Only if we bring ourselves to the Lord as an offering may we be called human." This is no once-for-all commitment but an orientation renewed and intensified over and over again. What do they think is the most important thing to do? Whatever they happen to be doing at the moment.

Pain, joy, success, failure, good times and bad—all must be met with calm deliberation and active participation; otherwise we sink into a detached, derivative existence. So if you want to raise a man from mud and filth you must go down into the mud and filth yourself and lift him into the light.

Can you love someone without knowing her needs and bearing the burden of her sorrow? No, it's not enough to love another in her universal humanity or divinity. We must love her in her uniqueness, including what she lacks.

EROTIC QUEST FOR INTIMACY

I became a celibate monk seeking human and divine intimacy, wanting to become as quickly and surely as possible a great lover of God and His whole creation. I wanted the fullness of life on Earth. I wanted, as God's partner, to participate as thoroughly as possible in the saving act of Christ—creating, redeeming, and glorifying the world. I was and, even more so now, am willing to be divinized, knowing all along how much purification this would entail. I did not want human approval. I wanted to please God and hallow the Earth. Nourished by the church and prompted by the Spirit I wanted to follow Christ, no matter what. Maybe not consciously but certainly subconsciously. This is what everyone wants ultimately: to be alone—all in one, one in all—with God. Sheer intimacy.

Richness and complexity, not sameness, always characterize intimacy. All deep relationships are intimate. Intimacy means inward. So shallowness, crude publicness, and stentorian bravado and garish demonstrations of affection are out of place. This is not secrecy but decency. In fact, all communication is communication *in sacris*. Sacred times and places, but an awesome ambience—whatever induces us to act out of our true inner selves. Reverence is key. Celibates who are trained to dwell at the center, suffused by the source of life and drawn by love itself into ultimate communion, should be most at home with intimacy, however intense. Whoever is deeply rooted can be relaxed and reliable when confronted by love and asked to meet the mysterious other. Meeting others shapes our lives; unmet, we continue to live a derivative existence and our lives remain sterile, vapid, and futile.

Authentic humanness—divinization—hinges on the quality of our relatedness. How deep, how attentive, receptive, insightful, and loving? Mutual presence kills the bloated ego, reduces the separate, simulated self, and establishes concretely, incarnationally the Kingdom of God. We are the Body of Christ; each member enlivens the other. It is through such reciprocity that a fullness of life is reached. Jesus' prayer is answered. We become refulgent with His own glory. Sparks from a thousand mindful meetings set the soul on fire. The body radiates divine glory. As Anaïs Nin put it in her diary: "Each friend represents a world in us, a world possibly not born until they arrive, and it is only by this meeting that a new world is born."

That is how we stay in touch with the real world— not by hanging out in the crowds, not by stuffing our heads with information, not by cell phone garrulity, not by keeping in touch compulsively and indiscriminately, but by letting God touch us with transforming power at the core of our being. That happens when with erotic fervor we daringly, generously meet.

Can we depend on such courage and generosity? Only if we are steadily intimate with God. This requires, whoever you are, a contemplative life, which means that being deeply and directly in touch with Eros, the cosmic theandric person or Superperson himself, you can move with liberty and alacrity into a richer, broader union with other people—with all creatures, actually. During every aspect of the encounter prayer persists at the center, the presence of God is felt, permeating the whole exchange. But the only source of this togetherness is solitude, when we are alone with God at a level of our being to which no creature can be admitted.

Aloneness with God does not foster loneliness, but homeliness, and by that I mean the placiest place of all, our truest home where we are real and most alive; where we are overwhelmed by the onslaught of eros, the Holy One's high proposals of love and His divine, effusive pressure to hallow the Earth and ignite the fire in every creature. We are solitary. If we deny it we self-destruct. Love peaks when two solitaries meet in this silent, uncluttered ambiance, cultivate it, and with stilled minds and skilled bodies worship each other.

God is Eros and all "others" are nourished at this source. For both married and celibate lovers the goal is the same: universal love. To attain this end both need discipline. Each state is unique and the transforming principles and practices will vary accordingly. All lovers need to be intensively but not exclusively committed to each other, faithfully, to the end. Celibates are celibate precisely to excel in universal love. Whenever you have a life dedicated to the development of deep, personal friendships and also to the universal extension of love you have an important, sanctifying kind of creative tension; embraced with hope all of life is enriched. How dare we even hesitate to embark on this challenging adventure?

> *I will make a covenant on your behalf with the wild beasts, the birds of the air and the things that creep on the Earth, and I will break bow and sword and weapon of war and sweep them off the Earth, so that all living creatures may lie down without fear. I will betroth you to myself forever, betroth you in lawful wedlock with unfailing devotion and love; I will betroth you to myself to have and to hold, and you will know I am the Lord. (Hosea 2:18-20)*

Christopher Fry, an amazing poet, read that fulgent passage from the prophet Hosea and was inspired to articulate his own brilliant response to the Lord's wild gesture of ineffable love, quoted in chapter one. Is there anything comparable in all of English literature? Only *Mr. Blue* by Myles Cannolly strikes me as being nearly as luminous as that quote I found in Fry's play *A Sleep of Prisoners*. *Mr. Blue* is an answer to Christopher Fry's prayer. Cannolly does not crawl into Christianity. He bypasses the subverted version we've inherited and approved of, and suffused with pure Christianness he comes leaping and vaulting into the eye of the storm. Keenly aware that Christ is no safe harbor, he dons his crash helmet and moves with outrageous speed into the blessed, bloody heart of reality, where the fire is, a fire lit and kept blazing by the Living Flame of Love.

Most of us never take that leap. We are incapacitated by a very peculiar disease called moderate happiness. Pretty good people do pretty good things, read pretty good books, and have pretty good times. What reduces us to a half-life is pretty poison. Christ came to wake us up, to enliven us and inflame us. If we don't take this manliest man seriously and let His fire, His eros, consume us, we will prolong our mediocrity and a subverted Christianity. We will lollygag in the suburbs of reality, we will choke on the long suck of self, and we will languish in lugubrious levels of psychobabble and schizoid alienation.

What is the alternative? To kneel and pray first thing in the morning or make coffee or tea and meditate in a favorite corner of the house or yard. Celebrate Mass two or three times a week. One-half hour of prayer every evening plus a walk (leisurely—no jogging! Jog later if you must.) Better yet: play with others—anything, anywhere, but play. Pray the Angelus every noon. Keep a vigil every Saturday night. Do something wild every day. Enliven the neighborhood. Glorify the parish. Go to or start a discussion group, reflecting on the best books, reviewing the best movies and videos and DVDs. Go on a retreat every few years. Find a soul-friend. Enjoy and amuse the pastor.

In conclusion: Let us pray to meet God, to know and touch Christ. We will thus continue the Incarnation. Who knows? We may even do greater things than Jesus did. That's what He wants, that's why He came and why He infused us with the Spirit.

O God, who lives in storms and stillness, in suburbs and slums, in much and majesty, in little girls and old men, in prisoners and priests, in nannies and nuns, in cars and planes, buses and trains, in luscious lakes and mountain tops, in deserts and oceans, in schools and hospitals, in Narnia and Arabia—you are in fact the whirling sheerness of Being, the Trinity;

you are, indeed, the Father, Son and Holy Spirit—so you—so you are the whole world.

You dwell in the firmament and in the brightness of our minds and in the ravishment of our hearts. We are smitten by your presence in our pain—a bit of your pain; universal, all-embracing and yet screamingly concrete. You are cold in wintry slums, lonely and sorry in prison camps—rats gnawing at you, and rats guarding and starving you. More often you are being privily pilloried by nice ladies and gentlemen who know about you but ignore you. Help us to touch you.

The Human Adventure

MYSTICAL LIFE

The mystic is not a special kind of person, but everyone is, or ought to be, a special kind of mystic. Mysticism is nothing esoteric. It is not the privilege of a few but an experience every one of us should know firsthand.

Mysticism is infinitely too subjective to teach. It is more readily caught than taught. The supreme objective of the Spiritual Life Institute, with centers in Crestone, Colorado, and Skreen, County Sligo, Ireland, is to foster the spirit of mystical contemplation in contemporary culture so that our social, political, economic, and domestic existence is inspired by it. And yet we wouldn't dare try to teach mysticism. All we can do is set the stage as humanly as possible for the mystical experience.

In my earliest writings I used the term *contemplation* rather than *mysticism*. Now I prefer to use *mysticism*, although contemplation and mysticism are essentially the same. It is crucial, however, to eliminate many of the misunderstandings that surround the meaning of both these words. Though we cannot teach mysticism, explain it adequately, or superficially decide to achieve it, we must know as much about it as we can theoretically and do as much as we can practically in order to become mystical. We especially need to know what mysticism is *not*.

WHAT MYSTICISM IS NOT

Mysticism is not a painkiller. It provides no escape *from* the world but puts us in touch *with* the world. Mystics are not rigid, unbending, or unworldly. Because they are in love with God and with life, they are supple, tolerant, and flexible. Mysticism is not a way out of anguish, conflict, and doubt. On the contrary, the deep, inexpressible certitude of the mystical experience awakens a tragic anguish and opens many questions in the depths of the heart, like wounds that cannot stop bleeding.

Mystics often suffer more than anyone else because they are so sympathetic and compassionate. They may harbor the gravest doubts because their childish, puerile, and spurious faith explodes before them. A veritable bonfire burns to ashes their old, worn-out words, clichés, and slogans. Even their most holy concepts and sacred ideas of God are consumed in the fire of this great holocaust.

Mystics discover through contemplation, a personal encounter with the living God, that they know nothing about God. They know not *what* but only *that* God is. They learn that God is no thing (nothing, *nada*), no what, but pure Who. God is the "Thou" before whom the mystics' inmost "I" springs into awareness. God is the "I am" before whom the mystics echo their own "I am." They stand defenselessly, helplessly, and humbled before God's holy scrutiny.

Mysticism is not what drug enthusiasts call "tripping out" but more like "standing in," alert and alive, with the highest possible focus of human attention on the present moment. It is standing willfully and deliberately in awe and wonder before the unveiled mystery of reality. Mysticism is not a trance, an ecstasy, or an enthusiasm.

It is neither the wild frenzy of religious exultation nor the imagination of lights nor the hearing of unutterable words. These emanate not from the deep self but from the somatic unconscious, and although they may happen in conjunction with religious experience, they do not constitute mysticism.

Mysticism is not the affair of a quiet and passive temperament that naturally loves to sit and do nothing. Mystics are not spooky introverts or isolated thinkers who simply love to ruminate, prowling around in the sanctuary of their own psyches. Most of the mystics I know are strong, robust, and vibrant, obsessed with a Zorba-like or, better, Christ-like madness.

True mystics do not merely explore their own consciousness but savor the Real. They are not aloof from flesh and blood, the turmoil, chaos, and pleasures of the world. Some of the most mystical people are deeply and profoundly immersed in the world, thoroughly engaged in political and social life, rearing dozens of children. They are mystical simply because they are basically and essentially great lovers of God and His whole creation. My favorite mystic is the prophet, Elijah, who is not indifferent but deeply in love with the world. His love of the world does not diminish but enhances his dynamic, irresistible, and burning love of God. It is possible to become totally detached in everything and unattached to God. But then we become stuffed shirts, not mystics. We are not all aglow with the Spirit, consumed with the fire of God's love, but simply "into" spirituality.

Mysticism is not inward torpor but a magnetic, mobilizing peace characterized by the wise passiveness of St. John of the Cross: "I abandoned and forgot myself...leaving my cares forgotten among the lilies." Mysticism is the highest form of action. But the mystics don't always need to take a pole when they go fishing because they have no need to justify doing nothing. Being may compel them to do nothing. When God speaks, the mystics simply listen; when God appears, they simply behold; when God gives, they simply receive. Responding to God's initiative this way distinguishes genuinely positive and gracious quiet from the error of quietism, the limp passivity of the sluggard often confused with the alert stillness of the spiritual athlete. English mystic and theologian Walter Hilton describes the paradoxical activity of such peace: "This restful travail is far from fleshly idleness and from blind security. It is full of ghostly work, but it is called rest...a holy idleness and a rest most busy."

WHAT IS MYSTICISM?

Having cleared away some of the outstanding debris, we are in a better position to say something more positive about mysticism. Mystical contemplation is the experiential grasp of reality as subjective. Not "my" reality, as it pertains to one's external, superficial self, but reality as myself in existential mystery. Mysticism does not meet reality through a process of deduction but through an intuitive awakening in which our free and personal reality becomes fully alive in its own existential depths that open out into the mystery of God. If we can discover ourselves in depth, we discover God and simultaneously discover Christ. We can almost say there is an identity between one's most real, profound, and transcendent self and the real Christ.

If I am a mystic, I have come into ownership of myself. I achieve through asceticism, discipline, and the controlled wildness of love mastery of my own human instrument. Only when I achieve ownership of myself may I give myself to the world and share the contemplation I enjoy, which is the only valid definition of apostolic outreach. If my apostolate is not simply a sharing of my mystical contemplation, my own experiential awareness of God, then it is phony, noisy, and absurd.

We cannot proclaim the contemplation of Christ in an effective and lasting way unless we ourselves participate in it. How can we proclaim or act, however zealously, what we do not know ourselves personally and experientially?

Apostles are not self-appointed but sent by God, after He has touched and transformed them. Such people are rare. When they show up, they always seem to be men and women of prayer; silent and solitary, God-filled and God-intoxicated, not saying or doing much, but keeping God's love alive and God's presence felt in a half-hearted, talkative busy society where people live frightened, fragmented "lives of quiet desperation."

To engage in the natural art of contemplation is to look long and steadily, leisurely and lovingly, at any thing—a tree, a child, a pear, a kitten, a hippopotamus—and really "see" the whole of it; not to steal an idea of it, but to know it by experience, a pure intuition born of love. This is a gratuitous, not an aggressive, act. Being discloses its hidden secrets as we look, wait, wonder, and stand in awe, not inquisitively but receptively. Mystics and contemplatives are never utilitarian, greedily trying to get something out of everything. They simply stand before being, a plant, an animal. They enjoy it and leave themselves wide open to its revelation, to its disclosures of mystery, truth, and love.

Mystical contemplation is more than a consideration of abstract truths about God, more than meditation on what we believe. Mysticism is an awakening enlightenment, an intuition born of love that leaves us sure of God's creative and dynamic intervention in our concrete, daily life. The mystics do not simply find a clear idea of God and hold Him prisoner within the limits of that idea. The mystics are carried away by God into the divine realm of mystery and freedom. Mysticism is pure and virginal knowledge, poor in concepts, poorer still in reasoning, but able by its very poverty and purity to follow the Word wherever it may lead.

Mysticism is a long, loving look at the Real to which we are united by love. It is the highest expression of our intellectual and spiritual life. Its activity is its own end. Mysticism has no utilitarian purpose but is simply looking, loving, being utterly, magnificently, wildly useless. It is life itself fully awake and active and aware that it is alive. Mysticism is awe and wonder at the sacredness of life and being and of the invisible, transcendent, and infinite abundant Source of being. It knows the Source obscurely, but with a certitude beyond reason. It is a veritable vision of the Godhead in the human, earthy context. This act by which we see who we are, not in isolation but against the background of eternity, and so simultaneously and experientially see who God is—this is genuine mysticism.

Mystical life is both the most normal and the highest expression of the spiritual life. It involves the highest levels of participation in the intimate, trinitarian love life of the Godhead. This loving involvement with Ultimate Being issues in our divinization. God is the primary source and active agent of this divine transformation. We are the recipients of divine disclosures and become mystics by grace drawing us into Ineffable Mystery.

TRANSPARENT AND OPAQUE

Whether mystical union is experienced depends partly on our environment, particularly our beliefs, but preeminently on our psychophysical constitution. This accounts for the fact, otherwise inexplicable, that mystical experience, like artistic creation or scientific intelligence, is often shared by members of the same family: for example, St. John of the Cross and his brother.

Not everyone is mystical to the same degree. Some individuals are more easily recognizable as mystics. A psychological factor identifies and distinguishes them from other spiritual individuals who are not usually considered mystical. The felicity and frequency with which mystics consciously experience divine union depend upon their particular temperaments.

E. I. Watkin, my favorite religious philosopher, explains this in terms of the transparent or opaque personality. The opaque personality sees the same comedy as the transparent but never laughs; hears the same music but never moves a muscle; suffers the same embarrassment but never turns red. The inner experiences of the transparent personality, however, always register on His countenance or external behavior. What happens in the spiritual depths, at the center of the soul, rises easily to the conscious surface. What occurs in the deep recesses of the opaque personality will seldom, if ever, become apparent. Transparent personalities are much more likely to translate inner experience into a painting, a song, or a poem.

Both the transparent and the opaque person are in union with God, but only the transparent one becomes conscious of it. Both are drawn by God into the deepest dimensions of the human adventure, the mystical depths of the spiritual life, but only the transparent personality exhibits mystical experiences. Opaque personalities, though raised by God into mystical existence, do not show it or even know it. Despite this, they may be as holy as their transparent counterparts. Theologically speaking, both types are mystics; but phenomenally speaking, only the transparent are, because they experience God's active presence within them and are obviously and recognizably mystical.

Unfortunately, because of our "monkey business," phony mysticism abounds. Like monkeys, people copy the outer behavior of genuine mystics without understanding their inner Godward dispositions. It's what's inside that counts. I remember philosopher Alan Watts comparing a mystic to a musical genius. Strictly speaking a composer like Mozart is inspired when melody emerges from the depths of his mind. To convey that melody to others he writes it down on paper, employing a technical knowledge that enables him to name the notes he heard in his mind.

This fact is important: his technical knowledge does not create the tune in his mind; it simply provides him with a complicated alphabet and is no more the source of music than the literary alphabet and the rules of grammar are the source of our ideas. What music teachers call "rules" of harmony are simply observations on the harmonies most usually used by such people as Mozart. Mozart did not use them because they were the rules but because he liked their sound. A composer needs to study harmony in order to identify the chords that he hears in his mind, but he does not use his knowledge to construct chords unless he is a mere imitator of other people. In the same way, language is used not to create thoughts but to express them, and mastery of prose does not make a great thinker.

The mystics are spiritual geniuses who work the same way as musical geniuses. They have a wider scope because their technique of expression, their alphabet, is every possible human activity. In all mystics, some more than others, *the presence of God is felt.* The mystic expresses this feeling two ways: first, by living a certain kind of life; and second, by translating this feeling into thoughts and words.

People who have not had this feeling observe the actions and words and from them formulate the "rules" of religious morality and theology. There are bound to be distortions. It is strange how foreign any unique religious feeling is to the average human being, even to the professional religious personality. The essential quality in the mystics is their feeling, not their ideas and actions, for these are only reflections of the feeling, and a reflection existing without light is a sham. Therefore, just as great technical proficiency will not make a creative genius in music, so morality, theology, and discipline will not make a genius in religion, for these are the result of religious experience, not the cause, and by themselves can not more produce it than the tail can be made to wag the dog.

When we speak of feeling, we imply an element of rational appreciation of what we feel. Affectivity and rationality are not opposed. Genuine affective responses are rational. Genuine feeling is partly cognitive, but it is also much more than that. According to the Irish poet William Butler Yeats, "We only believe those thoughts which have been conceived not in the brain but in the whole body." A merely intellectual response to reality is not enough because it is restricted and doesn't engage the total self. Genuine feeling refers to a total response, actuating what we are as persons.

THE CODE-CULT CONNECTION

Mystical *life* is the same as mystical *experience* (singular) but not the same as mystical *experiences* (plural). Whereas mystical *life* is indispensable for eminent holiness and consists in an intimate and sacrificial union with God, the union of charity, mystical *experiences* are not. Although secondary mystical phenomena such as visions, locutions, and bilocation may be helpful, they are nonessential, transitory, and fraught with danger.

Christian mysticism is inseparable from the Bible. The doctrines of St. John the Evangelist and St. Paul not only furnish the basis of Christian mysticism, but constitute its most authentic realization. St. John's theology of God as Love, Light, and Spirit, and salvation as new birth in water and the Spirit, carrying with it an unshakable certitude, is deeply mystical. John's Gospel has always been known as the "spiritual" Gospel and contains all the great words of mysticism.

St. Paul, to whom God revealed himself directly, and who preached a mystery into which we are initiated by knowledge and love, the work of an interior God, is no less mystical. Though Paul tries to write soberly of the profound psychic changes that came to him and of the heavenly manifestations he enjoyed, he cannot restrain his pen and communicates something of his own rapture as he attempts to relate what can never be told. His writings are a treasure-house of mystical doctrine. Later mysticism will deviate at times by forgetting the characteristics of New Testament mysticism. But there in sacred Scripture the historic character of revelation and the incarnation, the importance of objective mysticism (the symbolic role of visible reality), and the necessity of liturgy are not forgotten.

It is perilous to dissociate Christian mystics from the doctrine that nourishes them and from the Church that sustains them. Obviously, doctrine plays more than a secondary role in the experience of St. Augustine, St. Bonaventure, St. Bernard, St. Catherine of Siena, St. Teresa, Blessed Henry Suso, Juliana of Norwich, and Blesses John Ruysbroeck. They are typical of all the Christian mystics who also loved the liturgy, especially the Mass, and participated in it fully unto the end. St. John of the Cross was so completely and delicately in tune with the liturgical year that one of his confreres claimed they could tell what liturgical feast or season they were celebrating by simply looking at the saint's face.

No one preserves the unity of mysticism, dogma, and the ecclesiastical institution better than Baron Friedrich von Hugel, a twentieth-century Englishman. In his classic contribution, *The Mystical Element of Religion*, Von Hugel says religion is built only with the aid of a mystical ëlan, doctrinal penetration, and a communitarian institution that subsist in it as varied elements in a state of tension, but also in vital unity. To suppress one of the elements is tantamount to abolishing religion in its richest meaning.

The mystical element of religion is an active infusion of Infinite Spirit into finite spirit. We fragile creatures become acutely aware of our contingence and finitude, and although our first inclination is to withdraw from the divine pressure at the core of our being, we finally capitulate and hurl ourselves into the infinite abyss, into the pure, naked being of the All. But mysticism is never "pure" in the sense that it drives out and replaces the institutional and intellectual dimensions of religion. And genuine mystics, however solitary and exalted, have profound impact on the world around them.

CRISIS, NOT DECLINE

The mystic must not be confused with the psychic who is in touch with another world, the world of extrasensory perception, psychokinesis or mind over matter, and similar phenomena. Psychics are not necessarily spiritual. They may have unusual faculties of perception and be familiar with the ways of a world that is not usually our own, but this is a matter of faculty and knowledge, not of spirituality. If you want to enter into the psychic world you simply have to enlarge your experience. But if you want to become spiritual, you will have to learn from your experience. The mystic is most surely in touch with this world of flesh *and* blood, of hard facts and concrete realities. The spiritual world, if we must use the term, is this world, and a spiritual experience is what we are experiencing at this moment if we look at it the right way.

We have witnesses a psychic revolution that has, in many respects, won the approval of science (biofeedback, body consciousness, neuroscience, and so forth), and one that could, if properly guided, improve our human condition and expand our human consciousness immeasurably. And there is some evidence that a spiritual renewal has begun, though it is neither strong nor deep enough.

It would be appropriate to speak as German philosopher Oswald Spengler did less than a century ago of *The Decline of the West*, except that it now appears to be an irreversible stampede toward destruction. What is at stake is not the means to survive, not even the will to survive, but the *faith* to survive. Our Western civilization was born of the great drama enacted in Palestine two thousand years ago, the drama of Christ's incarnation, passion, and resurrection. This divine drama inspired the great art, music, literature, and architecture that have been the glory of our civilization.

The remarkable voice of journalist Malcolm Muggeridge cried out in dire warning before he died in 1990: If we should now reject the Judeo-Christian origins of Western civilization, persuading ourselves that we can be masters of our own destiny and chart our own future, then assuredly our way of life and all that we stand for must perish. In his article "Albion Agonistes," Muggeridge wrote:

> *The real crisis which confronts us is about faith rather than power, about the question "Why" rather than the question "How"—about man's relationship with His Creator rather than about His energy supplies, His currency, His balance of trade and Gross National Product, His sexual fantasies, and His other passing preoccupations with which the media interminably concern themselves. These are essentially trivial matters easily adjusted when the need to do so is apparent, as in time of war; whereas the God we serve, the salvation we hope for, the light we live by in this world, and, when we come to leave it, the vista reaching before us into eternity—these concern the very fundamentals of our moral existence.*

It may be more constructive to speak of our present human predicament in terms of a crisis rather than of decline. A crisis environment ought to be energizing, a time of idealism, sacrifice, and heroic effort. In this crisis we must face militant and malevolent forces opposed to human growth. Evil is a fungus that worms its way into every fission and all the features of society. Countless abnormalities and an endless malaise are the result. All of us are badly, though often indiscernibly, infected to some degree. This is due precisely to the fact that we are all interrelated and interdependent. The form evil takes most of the time is ignorance, especially ignorance in holy places such as churches, episcopal offices, and monasteries that produce everything except saints.

And in high places as well. Examples abound,

filling daily newspapers and adding spoof and spice to talk shows. I am embarrassed and infuriated by pinhead politicians and gormless critics who create a brouhaha over the deep breathing of society, since such breathing is a sign of health, however tentative and tortured. As long as we are still capable of these deep, fresh breaths, such vital signs can give us hope. The body politic can revive, the common man can become vibrantly uncommon, humanness can be restored; we are ready to become daringly, dazzlingly divinized. This revitalizing kind of breathing of the sociopolitical world is call religiousness. This, above all, was what our Founding Fathers wanted through the separation of church and state, through the restriction of "religion"—not religiousness, which is the basic, fundamental human orientation toward ultimate communion and what we all want, whether we are Catholic, Protestant, Jewish, Hindu, Buddhist, or Islamic. It's our nature.

Where there is no insight, no depth of understanding, no contemplation, there is always a stampede into silliness. And this silliness enthralls us. Look at the salaries of athletes and celebrities! Lebron James earned 100 million dollars before even playing his first NBA basketball game! The economic world is venal and incompetent. I not long ago worked with five business companies, all of them woefully inefficient. No wonder: Efficiency is a fruit of meditation—a highly developed capacity to do one thing.

Entertainment: Besides the occasional singer who can explore the depths of a song, or the rare theatrical production or movie that explores the human experience with insight and understanding, what have we other than mindless diversion? Politics is meretricious. A world full of wars, how smart is that? Social life? With sex on the brain or squeezed into bodily fissures and fleshy protuberances, what hope is there? Eros has been banished from marriage and from monastic life. Without sexual love no one can become holy—no bishop, no priest, no nun, no monk, no businesswoman, no married man, no single person. Only sexual love can sanctify. How did we reject sexy saints in favor of rectitude?

CRISIS IN CONTEMPLATION

Our contemporary global predicament may be described as a spiritual crisis, a crisis in contemplation. Our frenzied tempo, the waist-high culture of our schizoid societies, the disintegration of education, the loss of our roots in nature and the home, the loss of symbols, of community life, integrated personalities, and uproariously happy people, the degradation of sex and matter (air and water pollution and the rape of the land), our preoccupation with violence and war—these characteristics of our modern way of life are far from being unrelated. They are all manifestations of one central fact: an impoverishment of the mystical life.

We are naturally contemplative. But our mystical powers, left unexercised for so long, are seriously atrophied. They can and must be reactivated if we are to become integrated personalities, and if our world is to become humanized and God-centered. The mystical way is the only proven way for changing human behavior radically and permanently. And yet the one central treasure of the Christian Church, which less than one tenth of its membership knows anything about, is its profound and incomparable contemplative tradition.

According to Aldous Huxley's *Grey Eminence*: "The mystics are channels through which a little knowledge of reality filters down into our human universe of ignorance and illusion. A totally unmystical world would be a world totally blind and insane. From the beginnings of the eighteenth century onward, the sources of all mystical knowledge have been steadily diminishing in number, all over the planet. We are dangerously far advanced into the darkness." A civilization that denies the place of mysticism or shuts out the possibility of it sets us inevitably on the road toward a philosophy that is not so much a "love of wisdom" as a hatred of wisdom. Everywhere there is activity. Everywhere there is busy-ness. Everywhere there are organizations, projects, and programs. But they emerge from an inner self that is not quite at home or at ease with itself, but rather acts and thinks and judges from its superficial spheres, from the achievements of mere intellect or mere calculation, or from the impulses of power, possession, or pleasure. Action without contemplation is blind. Action of any kind—political, economic, social, religious—is not wise except for proficients in the art of meditation and prayer. Louis Lallemant, S.J., a reliable spiritual guide from the seventeenth century, says: "If we have gone far in prayer, we shall give much to action; if we are but middlingly advanced in the inward life, we shall give ourselves only moderately to outward life; if we have only a very little inwardness, we shall give nothing at all to what is external. A man of prayer will accomplish more in one year than another in all his life." A generation before Lallemant, the greatest of all Christian spiritual guides, the sixteenth-century Carmelite reformer St. John of the Cross, said that those who rush headlong into good works without first having acquired through contemplation the power to act will accomplish little more than nothing, and sometimes nothing at all, and sometimes even harm.

We must revive our depths again; we must rediscover our souls. We must all have, as a permanent and constituent part of our lives, prolonged periods as well as moments every day when we become still and contemplate, among other things, ourselves, and with living heart and soul ask ourselves one of the innumerable questions we have suppressed during the busy day. An atmosphere of prayer, the literature of the world's great religious traditions, manual labor, and tranquil creative activities should serve as a moving center in which we recompose the personality disintegrated into a thousand threads and reweave that personality into proper unity.

We have to pull out of the human anthill, the asphalt jungle, the daily chase; we have to become present to ourselves. We cannot give what we do not have. Self-possession is not the end, but it must happen en route or we will never get to the end, at least not a distinctively human end. Only a deeply contemplative attitude can permit us to take a strong stand against the powers of time and of the world around us.

Our central religious thrust today is dominated by a transcendental hunger and thirst for God, a hunger not very often or very well fed by our churches. Countless Christians have left the Church because they were not being nourished on the contemplative bread of the Mystical Body of Christ, on the Spirit, but were being regulated by the rules and roles of religion.

Theologians, bright with flaming talents, taking the world seriously, developing their science in contemporary style, creating fashionable theological trends, have become celebrities. It is a heady experience. Theologians are now wordmongers instead of Word-listeners, that is, mystics. They are shockers, straining to tell the world something novel or contrary. But we need shock absorbers who receive, assimilate, and digest the eternal, single Word of God.

We are fed and sustained by mystical theology; amused and confused by any other. Yet we are being led thoughtlessly from one vogue to another. It's so tempting to be faddish and accommodating; to leave

our solitary, silent stance before the source of wisdom
and become washed but in the "sauce" of endless dialogue. It's so easy to blame the old myths, the old symbols, the old structures. But where does the trouble
really lie? In our own routine, barren experience of the
Truth. "See Christ and you are a Christian; all else is
talk," said J.D. Salinger, quoting the Vedanta swami
Vivekananda.

We will never see God as long as we refuse to stop,
take time, enter into holy leisure, and contemplate.
We will miss God in the busy hustle and bustle of our
loquacious liturgies. We will miss God in our hurried,
routinized, self-centered prayer. We will miss God in
our frenzied activities. We will miss God above all in
our education, whose goal is supposed to be contemplation, according to Plato, Socrates, Aristotle, the Fathers of the Church, Thomas Aquinas, and any ancient
or modern educator worthy of our attention. Without
mystical vision, our education is a farce, our civilization a sham, religion an opium, liturgy a corpse, theology a fad, and apostolic outreach the most popular
and pietistic escape from the God who said, "Be still
and see that I am God" (Ps. 46:11).

PURE CHRISTUS

On the feast of St. Augustine, "prince of Mystics,"
I was released from the hospital after an episode of
congestive heart failure. I went for a walk on Carlsbad
Beach, gratefully aware of the beauty, power, and permanence of the ocean. I was still, absorbed introspec-
tively, ruminating on my own human diminishment
and on the intensified struggle of my own brave little
band of Carmelite contemplatives.

Rising out of the water is primordial. History, science, religion, combat, literature, the arts, and, of
course, evolution and sheer human and animal enjoyment depend on this aquatic experience. It has a

lot to do with our sexuality—our own vast sea and its tidal waves of energy. It is all so wondrous. It is massive and magical, the largest source of our dread and delight. The surface of the Earth is mostly water, and it dominates us. The mystery of the sea, whether in Galilee or Hawaii, threatens us and fascinates us. We can never master this terrible force but must cope with it creatively, cooperatively, and awesomely. Our own erotic sea is the same—all this beauty and power require from us a degree of individual ingenuity that will enable us to be so personally and uniquely sexual that the oceanic megalasaurus will not incapacitate us.

Aphrodite the Goddess of sexual love, has limitations. All she can do is make introductions, establish connections. Then we must traverse our way through the delirious and dolorous phases of human intimacy and, ultimately, of divine union. This is called sexual intelligence.

It has taken me nearly a full page to say that. But on the beach one day in Carlsbad, California, I realized it in only a moment, in a religious experience. Externally, hardly anything happened—a boy, exuding health and happiness, radiating youthful ardor and hope, rising out of the sea with his surfboard, yelled across the beach to me with a vibrant, cheerful "hi" and passed on into whatever, leaving his mark on me for all eternity. My whole being resonated with the heartbeat of all reality, namely *Puer Christus*, Boy Christ.

Surfing has always been my favorite analogy of the ascetical-mystical life, of balanced human existence. Surfing is a series of disciplined acts, or asceticism, followed by ecstasy, or mysticism. Here you have a perfect combination of two basic human impulses: dread and delight. Note the discipline as the surfer gets up early in the morning, polishes his board, and carries it expectantly toward the sea. There he faces an empty beach and aqueous immensity and confronts the cold, raging waves. Arduously he paddles out into the deeps. Capping this whole assiduous glissando, with the patience of a cat, looking, sniffing, and spanning the horizon, he waits, not lackadaisically for any old wave, but contemplatively for the perfect one.

Waiting is his secret and his genius, and the results are lusciously rewarding. Eventually the surfer spots the longed-for wave, rumbling toward him with exquisite power and majesty. He moves deftly and adroitly into position and takes the wave at its rampant momentum, then relaxes, resonates and rides, rides, and rides: sheer ecstasy, the delicious fruit of contemplative, disciplined mindfulness, God suffusing and animating this pinnacle of action.

Mystical life is a carefully crafted balance between two polarities: Don't just stand there, do something; and don't just do something, stand there. One without the other is inhuman. Unless God alone knocks us off balance, it is our indispensable obligation to develop a deliberate harmonious self, interrelating reverently with others, God, and the universe. Our own growth will be authentic only if we learn to unite asceticism and mysticism, discipline and delight, suffering and celebration. Only this smooth and undulating rhythm of life engenders human wholeness, holiness, and uproarious happiness.

The Human Problem

SECULARISM AND PRAISE

Christianity was once an integrating motivation for every dimension of social, political, and cultural life in the western world. But now the Christian presence is no longer a force to be reckoned with. It has become so innocuous it hardly evokes hostility. Secularists willingly admit that civilization owes a debt to Christianity as a historical factor and, even now, a cultural artifact. Without any creative power, however, Christianity becomes subservient to a secular culture. We owe this cool attitude of benign atheism to the three most prominent secularizers of our time: Karl Marx, Sigmund Freud, and Frederick Nietzsche. According to Marx, God and religion, the "opiate of the people," are simply forgotten by the socially active mind. Freud dismissed religion as a cop-out. For Nietzsche, God was dead; the old religion needed to be replaced by a new religion with autonomous humanity at its center.

Secularism is Godlessness. Secularity, however, properly understood, liberates the wild unstemmable

Spirit of God from rigidly enclosed spaces, allowing the fire to permeate an entire culture, uniting sacred and profane.

Our contemporary culture of alienation is characterized by a distinctive form of secularism. According to Irish Jesuit Michael Paul Gallagher, God is not only missing but not missed. We suffer from vapid faith, religious indifference, and flattened, horizontal theology. Until recently the Numinous was always a mystery. Now we try to measure it. Vertical theology has always taught otherwise: True religion does not present problems to be solved but a mystery to be lived. We heard God's death knell tolling centuries ago when moralism replaced mysticism. The net result: How unlike the Bride of Christ the lumbering Church has become! How mousy our lives; how mincing our convictions! We have secular minds with religious patches.

Our present respectable secularism is more socially and politically decimating than any of our previous forms of antitheism. As St. Thomas Aquinas taught: We do not believe in a creed; we believe through a creed in a Person. This personal, subjective, supremely involved relatedness to the Beyond-in-our-midst is much more than belief in revelational propositions. It is faith, an ultimate trust that cannot remain only one discrete part of life. Faith must integrate every element of life. Otherwise it ceases to be the underlying trust that enables us to endure and enjoy all the agonies and ecstasies of life.

Religion is infinitely more than one dimension of life. It is the lightning source of life's direction, the matrix of every humanizing and deifying connection, and the motivating force in us by which meaning unfolds. Religion is not merely a comforting, useful, and sporadic element in our civilized portfolio. All life—industrial, social, and political—is fatal without it. If religion isn't everything, it's nothing.

THE DECLINE OF PLEASURE

Western civilization is in peril. Culture is not only in decline but in revolt against life, beauty, goodness, and truth, against holiness and against God. The brilliant social critic Malcolm Muggeridge called this our "modern liberal death wish." By that he meant that we keep letting too many things happen to us. We get used up as means to some economic, political, or military end. Without noticing it, we lose our dignity and our glory as joyful, God-centered human beings. As Walker Percy wrote in *Lost in the Cosmos*, anyone who is not depressed today by the state of our culture is really sick. With eyes to see and ears to hear, how can anyone today not be a cultural pessimist? But the spirit of humanity is irrepressible. Even today (and, in fact, forever), there are inescapable experiences of corybantic hilarity, Dionysian delight, and Zorbatic madness. These rare moments of insight and communion resonate with harmony, clarity, exuberance, and, above all, with something more: a pure, erotic, unitive experience of the All in one, the One in all, an artistic virtuosity hard to define. Plato called it "divine madness."

Now and then I have been deeply moved by an inspired media event, stormdingled away into impetuous, scrumptious glee. Particular experiences come to mind: a production of T.S. Eliot's *Murder in the Cathedral* in St. Patrick's Cathedral, Dublin; Handel's *Messiah* at Christmas in St. Mary's Cathedral, Sligo; hearing Sister Sharon recite Francis Thompson's *Hound of Heaven* by heart in our own hermitage chapel; hearing our community of monks sing "Day of the Lion" and Sister Susan sing " His Eye Is on the Sparrow" in our Holy Hill Chapel in Skreen, Ireland; watching old videos such as *Becket, A Man for All Seasons, The Honeymooners, What's Up doc?, West Side Story, Shane,* and *High Noon*; listening to LeAnn Rimes sing the U.S. national anthem, Frank Sinatra sing "My Way," and Madonna sing "Don't Cry For Me, Argentina"; listening to Seamus Heaney's new translation of *Beowulf*, Charles Laughton's recitation of *Bible Stories*, and Anthony Zerbe's reading of T. S. Eliot's *Love Song of J. Alfred Prufrock*; watching *Les Miserables, The Dialogue of the Carmelites*, and, on the Charles River, the Boston Pops celebrating the Fourth of July and, in the theater, *Riverdance*.

There are still artistic glories: Salvador Dali's *Christ of St. John of the Cross*; the breathtaking works by Andrew Wyeth and Diego Rivera; the paintings of my friends Leslie McNamara, Sean Jennings, Anne Marie Dowdican, and Karen Gilg. There are instances of architectural splendor as well, such as Frank Lloyd Wright's Taliesen West in Scottsdale, Arizona, the Lincoln Center in New York, Le Corbusier's unique church, Notre Dame de Haut at Ronchamp, France, and the St. Louis airport by Japanese architect Minoru Yamasaki. Although athletic performances have become increasingly money-driven and lackluster, Michelle Kwan's figure skating thrills nearly everyone. And who will ever forget Doug Flutie's "Hail Mary" pass in the last desperate seconds of a Boston College football game and, more recently, the New England Patriots' dazzling display of teamwork in their Super Bowl victory?

There is also some good literature to raise our hearts and minds. An ecstatic experience recently engulfed me as I read Edith Pargeter's *The Heaven Tree Trilogy*. And I not long ago finished, once again, F. Scott Fitzgerald's *Tender is the Night*. Has anyone ever managed with such adroitness and cogency to reveal the dark brutality lying just below the surface of this civilized glittering society? My own community has been inspired for decades by J.R.R Tolkien's *The Lord of the Rings* as a metaphor for our monastic life, as well as by C. S. Lewis's *The Chronicles of Narnia*, and, more recently, despite the Christian fundamentalists' protests, by J. K. Rowling's Harry Potter books, for both lighthearted reading and insight into the human condition.

It is even more rejuvenating to discover the bright hilarity of the heart of human existence. Nowhere is this discovery more felicitous and fulgent than in the life and writings of St. Teresa of Avila. There we find humanness in bas-relief, caught and conveyed so simply and saliently in *Teresa of Avila: Ecstasy and Common Sense* by Tessa Bielecki.

SIGNS OF OUR DYING CULTURE

Now, with that positive propaedeutic, I am ready to be properly critical of our culture. The bright moments I've listed are rare and sporadic. Since this is not a book on culture but on humanness, holiness, and personal vocation, I will simply mention in passing some unmistakable signs of our dying culture.

Decline of Pleasure

The first sign is the *decline of pleasure.* As Thomas Aquinas says, "No one can live without pleasure." He means deep, soul-satisfying communion. Too much communication kills communion. None of us is ever really pleasured by mere excitement, titillation, media glut, noise, or feverish activity. When our human actions conjoin the infinite Act—pure love or Eros—then we experience divine union and freedom in the resurrected order of being. Apart from that, all is distraction and illusion, a stampede into silliness.

Loss of the Sacred

The second unmistakable sign of our dying culture is our *loss of the sacred.* Without a sacred center, there is no sanity. Then we become obsessed with trivialities and mindless routine. Ultimate concern withers

and we regress into vapid preoccupation with unful-
filled infantile longings for esteem, power, and control,
which the Gospel calls a "Gadarene rush into the sea"
(Matt. 8:28-34). This becomes a frantic hunt for the
key to happiness, a prodigious waste of time doomed
to failure because there is no key within a thousand
miles of the entire secular arena.

The Sufis tell a story about this kind of absurdity.
A Sufi master lost the key to his house and was looking for it on his hands and knees in the grass outside.
Along came a group of his disciples who asked, "Master, what is wrong?"

He said, "I have lost the key to my house."

They said, "Can we help you find it?"

"I'd be delighted," he said. So they all got down
on their hands and knees and anxiously tussled the
grass.

As the sun grew hotter, one of the brighter disciples asked, "Master, do you have any idea where you
might have lost the key?"

The Master replied, "Why, yes. I lost it in the
house," to which they all exclaimed, "Then why are
we looking for it out here?" He said, "Isn't it obvious?
There is more light here."

The house represents happiness, intimate communion with God. The key is the contemplative life where
all of our days are shaped by experiential awareness
of God's presence. We've lost that key: a recollected
mindfulness, a capacity to make free decisions based
on ultimate commitment. Now we find ourselves in
an effete scramble for ersatz happiness outside in the
suburbs of reality where the action is, where the lights
are on, where the crowd ekes out a pseudo-existence.

Though we are miserable trying to compensate for
that esteem, power, and control we were robbed of in
childhood, we find a bit of solace in the solidarity of
the crowd. Everybody seems to be there, looking for

happiness and meaning in the wrong place, where there is more light and distraction, and therefore more opportunity to be deceived, deluded, and anesthetized. We have become like the people who ate the poisoned grain in the following telling story worth telling over and over.

Once upon a time in a kingdom long ago and far away, the cherished crop of grain, so lovingly harvested and preciously stored away, was found poisoned. Anyone who ate it went insane. The distraught king and his advisors anguished over what to do. There was clearly very little other food available to sustain the people. They had no choice but to eat the grain. "Very well," decided the king, "Let us eat it; but at the same time we must feed a few people on a different diet so that there will be among us some who remember that we are insane." Who of us today is feeding on a sane, unpoisoned diet?

Language Pollution

The third sign of our dying culture is the *humiliation of our language*. Superb verbal expression is key to knowledge, wisdom, insight, and communities of love. We are destroying life on Earth by pollution. The worst kind of pollution is verbal pollution. Verbal pollution has driven wisdom out of work and play, out of public discourse and private conversation, out of homes, schools, commerce, the political arena, and the industrial-military complex.

Wisdom is "a taste for the right things." Bad language cannot convey good taste. Noisy language cannot convey wisdom. Without the matrix of silence, words become empty, flat, and shopworn. Worst of all, they become brutal, vulgar, and hateful. Our words are so rotten it's hard to find a beautiful novel anymore, engage in good conversation, produce a bright, fulgent movie or play. We can not watch television without being savaged by linguistic atrocities. Language no longer reveals coruscating truth, iridescent beauty, and sheer goodness. One of our best and most sacred love words, the "f-word," is now ugly and hateful, used as noun, verb, or adjective, a curse in every other sentence with every other breath. Our mindless use of the word has killed our culture in a singular dramatic way. One of our most pernicious pathologies today is our addiction to ugliness, an extremely peculiar phenomenon being transmitted aggressively in and through the media. Beauty is out, especially out of our language. Much more needs to be said about language. I'll do that in the next chapter.

Dumbing Down

Linguistic atrocity leads to a fourth sign of cultural decay: the "dumbing down" of Western society. Here's a "dumb" list that highlights our moral chaos:

1. The bland barbarism of our social conventions, mirrored in so much of the media. Only a culture as moribund as ours could produce TV shows like Elimidate, Sex and the City, and most of our talk shows ("show" is the right term).
2. The mendacity of politics.
3. The manipulative behavior of government.
4. The mediocrity of democracy, where everyone and everything are reduced to the lowest common denominator.
5. The trumpery of ecclesiastical apparatchiks.
6. The credulity of crowds who listen avidly to famous nitwits and notorious tyrants and pay them handsomely for their shallow opinions—some receive $50,000 or more per speech!
7. The morbidity of crowds who gather to watch boxing and wrestling matches between killer men and now killer women (I never thought I'd live to

see it). And the lunacy of crowds willing to support new stadiums that cost over 500 million dollars, looking on cheerfully when sports stars sign contracts for millions of dollars while teachers are underrated and underpaid.

8. The pathology of crowds who gather to watch strip-tease performances. Recently a record 100,000 people came together in Mexico to watch a stage full of men strip. This is not just a Mexican phenomenon, nor does it merely appeal to low-class audiences. I recently gave a retreat to Episcopalian bishops, priests, and their wives. At the end I agreed to have dinner with them. Astonished at the absence of the women, I asked, "Where are your lovely wives?" Their response was alarming: "They are at a four-star male strip-tease show." Unabashed, the priests puttered punctiliously with their gourmet preparations. The women arrived oohing and aahing about male muscularity, testicularity, and ah! The allure and glory of flesh without spirit.

9. Cruelty to animals for humanly selfish reasons. Hunting for fun is the only unequivocal evil I know. But even worse is the perverted pleasure men find in such hideous games as dog and cock fights. Walter de la Mare's poem "Hi!" comes to mind:

> *Hi! Handsome hunting man,*
> *Fire your little gun.*
> *Bang! Now the animal*
> *Is dead and dumb and done.*
> *Never to peep again, creep again, leap again,*
> *Eat or sleep or drink again. Oh, what fun!*

10. The inability of our highly developed civilizations to prevent war and reduce the destitution and starvation from which half the world suffers so abominably.

11. The fatuous and cowardly leadership that let the Judeo-Christian inspiration of the Western world peter out. Without that prophetic vision we perish. Shore up the fragments all you want, once we lose biblical altruism, trinitarian relatedness, and the covenant of love, we become rootless and ruthless, incapable of ravishment, revision, and renewal. Without biblical transcendence, an ascent into truth, awareness of the Ineffable, we grovel in downward transcendence. Looking for an infinitely satisfying creaturely attachment, we are hurtled into an endless succession of addictions and idolatries.

I myself know this parlous territory by heart. I have occasionally been so enchanted by the profound mystery and exquisite beauty of a woman in the cinema, a novel, a biography (Dorothy Dandridge and Josephine Baker, for instance), and in real life as well, I have felt, however briefly, that such a shockingly gorgeous embodiment of God must convey infinity—an intellectual mistake! A lifetime of purity and reverence, given to me gratuitously, not acquired, has inured me to lust, but left me vertiginously open to illusion and romantic fantasies. How pathetic!

12. The ravages of technology, a condition of human enslavement resulting from our unwise use of technology. We have become servants of the machine rather than vice versa. What was meant to free us from overwork and brighten our leisurely mindful life has done the opposite. We are ensorcelled. We have become functionaries, robots, and automatons, as lifeless and abstract as the mechanistic masters we envy and adore. Systems have replaced wonder and worship.

We are trapped on an information highway where there is a boundless supply of facts and derivative knowledge about things, but very little intimate and immediate knowledge of things, very little contemplation or mystical life, very little I-Thou experience of communion, very little exercise of our basic, fundamental human rights to intimacy, ecstasy, and fecundity.

Another deathblow to our culture is the ubiquitous cellular phone. Last week I stood next to an oafish bloke who bought an airline ticket without interrupting his private phone conversation. The ticket agent was stunned, her patience severely tested. A thousand versions of such idiocy occur daily on planes, in restaurants and libraries. Even the sacredness of churches and remote wildernesses are ruined by the cell phone's intrusion. So is meditative walking.

The most costly deprivation of all is the tragic loss of presence. So many serendipitous marvels, the unique and unrepeatable theophanies that unfold with glorious particularity on the street, are precluded by the phone that estranges callers from their surroundings. Loquacious encounters on the phone repudiate presence in the here and now, meeting the stranger, opening up to the mysterious other along the way.

13. The wayward aspects of the feminist movement. By wayward (as opposed to genuine) aspects of the feminist movement I refer to those aspects that abrogate tenderness, chivalry, good manners, contemplative home life, flirting and courting, shyness, and the intuitive life.

14. The typical unhealthy and inhuman diet of the average American. We do not eat good food as men and women of leisure, deliberately, with pleasure and gratitude. We eat fast food in a frenzy as workers and functionaries with the cell phone at hand. We have business breakfasts, power lunches, and

TV dinners. Contemplating food and the special friends with whom we share it is more nourishing than consuming the food. When deep attentiveness accompanies our meals, they become so sensuously cognitive that peak human experience is inevitable. Good food and good talk set the stage for a deep satisfaction of mind and heart as well as body.

15. The global ecological disaster. The apotheosis of dumbing down is ingloriously achieved by our deplorable state of pollution. We've poisoned our air and water, littered our city streets, cut down our forests, raped the Earth, filled the world with noise, and threatened the very life of humankind.

ENCULTURATION AND CALL

These are fifteen blatant signs of deculturation caused by the galloping secularism of contemporary society. I largely blame our churches and their failure to enculturate; that is, the churches' accommodation of our waist-high culture rather than enculturating it—transfiguring matter with spirit, hallowing the Earth, and integrating the profane with the sacred. Since Christianity has lost its creative, formative power and no longer plays an integrating role in the life of modern societies, transfiguration must occur differently today. Each one of us, existentially and subjectively, must do what we once relied on tradition to do. We must personally incorporate and unify all aspects of our existence. This requires a vital, critical faith, an immense trust in God, in life, in one another, and in the communion of saints, and, most importantly, a vibrant spiritual life.

The spiritual life is our personal response to the intimate call of the divine. This call or vocation is not inherited from family or infused by social pressure. It unfolds to the degree that each of us is trenchantly aware of an inner voice. No other force can call us to attention and rivet us in irrevocable conviction and commitment. When we lose this sense of personal call, we no longer feel significant. We become more mechanical and materialistic, progressively more herded and dehumanized. All life can be summed up in four words: *God calls, we respond.*

The sense of unique personal vocation, being divinely called, seared, and sealed, began to erode late in the twentieth century. Today, even in Catholic Ireland, there's increasingly little trace of it. Commitment, "riding for the brand," has become a quaint, old-fashioned notion replaced by rampant, disconnected individualism and selfishness.

The opposite of this shallow and fruitless lifestyle is a vital mystical life. This means moving out of a dead space into new and rejuvenating freshness. "I will make all things new," Jesus said (Rev. 21:5). Has there ever been a revolution as radical as this? No wonder the blessed Virgin Mary, the rebel-woman whom God chose for His revolution, sang with such serene gusto the most socially challenging lyric ever sung in human history, the *Magnificat.* In the whole body of Jewish-Christian Scripture, few texts are more widely known and more vainly repeated than Mary's song. Its language is not that of sweet maidens, but Maccabee warriors: it speaks of dethroning the mighty and exalting the lowly, of filling the hungry and sending the rich away empty. Mary's praise to God is a revolutionary battle cry.

Mystical life is the pure intuition of God born of love. It is a direct and immediate knowledge of the Numinous. It is not anti-rational but the highest level of cognition. Mystical cognition is practical knowledge in and of the world, seeing things as they really are, interrelatedly and interdependently. Caring for the Earth we cherish and loving the world we know comprise the only authentic exploration into God. That is why one of our brightest German theologians, Karl Rahner, contends that Christianity in the future will be mystical or it will be nothing at all. Either we are immersed in mystery or enmeshed in misery.

IN PRAISE OF PRAISE

What can we do to attack secularism at its root? We can praise God, which is the essential aspect of worship. Praise of God, pure and simple, emancipates us from the secularism that inhabits us. Praise must not be occasional or sporadic, a flight from what we take to be reality; it must be a positive duty, a formative factor in the shape of our lives and a sustained challenge to pseudo-reality, to the vanity, clamor, and disguised idolatries of the world. When we praise God, we acknowledge our contingence and God's transcendence. There's no distance between Creator and creature but an ontic difference, a difference that evokes holy fear—that is, holy awe—and ontological humility.

Praise acknowledges what is true about God whether I am grateful or not. This means that praise and gratitude are not identical. We must distinguish between them. Because God is God, we praise Him. Benefits or not, we adore God. Ineffable Being, Sheer Love, God is inherently praiseworthy. The root cause of our human dilemma is the refusal to honor God as God in silent awe, verbal praise, or rapt adoration. Once we have forgotten God, we praise everything except God. We adore Marilyn Monroe, Elvis Presley, or, heaven help us, Britney Spears. (A few years from now the reader will likely ask, "Who was Britney Spears?") Oh dear! I myself love her.

"All things work for good for those who love God," wrote St. Paul (Rom. 8:28). Therefore, we praise God for everything, whether in agony or ecstasy. This does not preclude our painful desperate cries of terror and dread. Jesus' whole life was praise of God. He was on the same wavelength as the Father; still He bellowed from the cross: "My God, my God, why have you forsaken me?" (Matt. 27:46). The apex of His praise was expressed not in seraphic jubilation but in terrible ululation, an agonized, almost atheistic, howl. With what exquisite pain Jesus missed the tangible, visceral care of His Father; and that plangent missing was itself appropriate praise. If only this age of selfism would begin to miss God!

When our focus at prayer shifts from the character of God to the enhancement of self, we lose our center, which is an unflinching orientation to the other, the Numinous. We lose our sense of the sacred and our capacity to admire and affirm, with no designs on God. In praise we do not bargain or entreat. We are too overwhelmed by an intimate sense of the All.

In perverted, secularized worship, we banalize praise by seeking help to bolster our false self-image, fabricated by shallow, vapid conventions, pseudo-events, and cheap fantasies. We all want to get something good, some kind of self-improvement out of the service. This is a crime against leisure. We have had some success in minimizing the male-centeredness of worship. But we have done something even worse by accentuating the self-centeredness of worship and enhancing our own parochial and usually political agendas. The perversion of public prayer will prevail as long as our motivation is self-centered rather than God-centered.

Society today is suffering shipwreck in an oceanic upheaval of values. We have reached near-despair in the wake of worldwide disillusionment. Multitudes are drowning or merely floating along in a stupor, accepting passively the tenets of a world gone mad. Call that madness what you will: the Empire, the modern or postmodern world, pretty poison, the techno-barbaric juggernaut, or even the impressive Celtic Tiger, as we say in Ireland. We are willing to perish in madness if only we all go down in euphoric togetherness. The masses are often offended by the few unwilling to perish with them.

There's only one solution: We must all swim for our lives, for "leisurely mind," for "Zen Mind, Beginner's Mind," as Suzuki-Roshi put it, and in this contemplative lifestance, choose life, wed the Spirit, and worship. Jesuit paleontologist Pierre Teilhard de Chardin once defined humanity as *homo adorans*. For *homo adorans,* worship is the one thing necessary. We recognize the infinite *worth* of God and so we *worship.* As protestant theologian Paul Tillich says, when we take God with ultimate seriousness, that's religion. And if we are religious at the center, what do we do? We praise God with such grateful awakeness that we know, perhaps for the first time, what it really feels like to be alive, alive to the Numinous as well as the numerous in the One.

SEVEN SIGNS OF PRAISE

Seven ways to praise God out of grateful awakeness come to mind, each beginning felicitously with a sibilant sound.

The Psalms. These dancing songs of David are full of deep human feelings but gather them into an aliveness to God with praise as the apotheosis of their meaning. No privatization here; no isolated comfort for the pitiful individual; no preoccupation with the "I," "me," or "mine"; no narcissistic reveries and longings. Instead, the psalms focus on the Holy One and on the way this infinitely divine and merciful force govern the world at the heart of things with personal passionate presence, sheer Eros. Our response is gratitude for all the gifts that make life so livable. Praise is that thin thread that unites us all, gladly and gaily to the Godhead.

Silence. Our own noxiously noisy world, outside and inside of us, makes intimate contact with the Word impossible. The Word is our source of truth and reality. "The Word became flesh" (John 1:14). To be smitten by that embodied Word is happiness. To respond to every challenge and invitation of the Word is education, or what religious teachers call revelation. To be directed by the Word is wisdom. To be uninspired by the Word is deliberate deafness or "absurdity." "Be still and see that God is God" (Ps. 46:10).

Solitude. To be alone with God is everyone's deepest desire. When we are alone in deep reality, we are steeped in communion not only with our Creator but with all of creation. In crowds everyone is there, but no one is in communion. The Holy One longs to be in communion with each one of us in solitude. "I will espouse you, lead you into the desert, and there speak to your heart" (Hos. 2:16). Our crowded lives remain untouched by the divine. Periods of solitude dispose us for contemplation. We become aware of the Ineffable who touches us at the core of our being. When we are personally touched by the living God, we are transformed. We become vital witnesses of Divine Eros. *"Oh, beata solitudo, solo beatitudo!"* the ancient monks used to say.

Sickness and Suffering. We are so active, restless, and securely in control that the more passive and receptive aspects of our beings become atrophied, leaving us dehumanized. We lack wisdom, compassion, and tenderness. Empathy becomes foreign to us. This can be catastrophic. The chief psychiatrist at the Nuremberg trials said that the most devastating Nazi evil was the absence of empathy. One possible definition of human ugliness is "To be hearty without a heart." To respond positively and creatively to human diminishment, whether it is mental fatigue or bodily indisposition, is to follow Christ. To follow Christ is to

be so faithful to our calling, our commitment, our vo-
cational destiny that suffering and sickness along the
way are hardly noticed because love is all-consuming.

Sacrifice. To live is to love and to love is to die. That
is the gospel's evangelical message. Love is "to die for."
This is so true that even fraudulent lovers can't skip
the intransigence and ubiquity of a nature that needs
to die to express a love-life. There we have the unfortunate history of scapegoating. "Lovers we are, Lord
God, but not unto death; so accept our offerings." And
we sacrificed thousands of magnificent beasts. This
false worship went on until one of the scapegoats was
so startlingly, stunningly beautiful, true, and good
that the worshipers were unbearably embarrassed—
and forever. Now, freely and mindfully, we present
and offer ourselves at the altar with Christ, the final
scapegoat, to be sacrificed and simultaneously made
whole, not vicariously but virtuously, that is, in a distinctly human way. We enjoy more life and more love
while we are stripped of all our egotistic trappings.
The false self, the egomaniac, dies. The authentic self
with a pure heart rises with Christ into the resurrected order of being.

Sabbath. One day a week all of us should spend
our time making love—the sexually organic way does
not exhaust the possibilities—but in a prayerful, playful, and festive way, creating a public erosphere in
which a community of love grows out of a celebration of love. We must break our ordinary workaday
routine—the grim pursuit of business, the unrelated-
ness of our functional, busy, independent selves, the
utilitarian fuss over money—and simply enjoy God by
enjoying one another in such depth that we are called
out of our used-up, narrow, niggardly selves into an
openness and a freshness that hurtle us into divine
union.

Sabbatical. As life becomes more and more intense and we become increasingly stressed, the sabbatical becomes indispensable—weeks, months, or a year off to retreat, retrench, review, and renew. One word, unpacked, says it all: *recollection.* We need to collect our spent forces, our dispersed energy, our flagging spirits, our original intuition and, above all, our authentic calling, our divine summons. Our lives are so crowded and harried, we settle for habitual mindlessness. We need time to read, rest, think, and love. We need time to be alone with the All-One. We need sabbatical time.

During His famous Harvard address in 1982, Alexander Solzhenitsyn, Russian dissident and Nobel Prize-winning author, pinpointed a major error in the Western world: "You have forgotten God." We never forgave Solzhenitsyn, and he fell from favor. Yet Solzhenitsyn was right; and it is our fault. We have long ceased to be living witnesses of the living God. Are we drawn and captivated by this infinitely attractive, super-personal God? In the absence of such dynamic witness, secularism fills the vacuum: If God is not supremely important, He is not important at all. There is only one way to respond to the Absolute and that is absolutely.

Verbal Pollution

here can be no healing of the Earth, no reform of state or Church, no restoration of the unity and felicity of family, no beauty in the arts or entertainment industry, no reality in the media, no truly liberal education, no city civility, no mindful work, no renewal of humanity unless there is a radical renewal of language. The most corrupting influence in the world today—and the most tolerated—is verbal pollution, a pollution begun in childhood and fostered at home, on the streets, in school, in the marketplace, in Congress, in the White House, in churches, sports, and even between lovers. The most gruesomely grotesque feature of our cultural decline is the ugly shambles of our language.

The most blatant form of this cultural malaise is strident street language, by no means confined to the streets. It is no surprise to hear it, as if it were an acceptable style of communication, among the pious and the politically correct. By street talk I mean hollow words devoid of meaning or words that are vain, violent, and vulgar. I am not referring to simple, straightforward exchanges or earthy comments among street people but to the quotidian twaddle that repudiates the scared Word, the Logos.

Nothing creates a climate of culture so cogently and plangently as words. Build a beautiful new home, school, or office, fill it with bad language, and the place is ruined. Send a young person to the most expensive and prestigious university in the country, and no education will be possible if the student is inundated there by bad language. I have not met a student in years, anywhere, who has not been lacerated by linguistic atrocities, shackled passively and respectably by the bland barbarism of academic verbosity and college crudity. The university climate, Catholic or not, is universally smarmy. But such garrulous humbug is by no means limited to the halls of academe. It's just that one would expect word vendors to be eloquent and the educative atmosphere they create to be crackling with fulgurous truth.

The spontaneous and convincing words poet Maya Angelou spoke to TV talk-show host Oprah Winfrey on the subject of language vastly encouraged me while watching television one evening. Angelou is accustomed to giving huge, festive parties in her home. She mentioned that if and when anyone invited to the party uses really foul language or tells dirty jokes, she herself graciously but firmly escorts this unfortunate person to the door. She then added something not many of us consider but is nevertheless true: The language used so mindlessly and unconscious of its dehumanizing effect lingers venomously in the curtains, the furniture, and, in fact, the whole ambience of her lovely home long after the guests have departed.

In *The Humiliation of the Word*, French lay theologian Jacques Ellul goes so far as to distinguish between the truth and reality. This "everyday reality" for which we stand he calls a lie. It is the Big Lie of

Technological Society. The technique of schools, politics, social compulsions, the military-industrial complex, and even religion is to fashion and foster the Lie: the pseudo-events, the images, the fantasies, the deception people want rather than facing the terrible beauty, the naked truth. With our deranged language, we have turned the world upside down. There are no absolutes, no permanent values, no public philosophy, no reliable, traditional stepping-stones into Ultimate Reality. We suffer this essential deprivation because we have no primordial words and have profaned our scared words. They are now trivial and trite, used to blemish and blaspheme. Most talk is small talk, that is, chirpy chitchat and specious prattle. The rest is acrimonious invective or unctuous flattery: the tool of propaganda.

What we regard as reality is in fact a subtle sham, the super-sham: what we might aptly call the Empire as opposed to the real world, a modern Tower of Babel that we have constructed by gigantic heaps of words, words that enslave us by their mendacity, manipulation, and mediocrity. Our boredom mounts. We do and say so much, but just below the superficial flourish, the windbag chatter, is a terrible tedium. Loose words, uprooted, unconnected with the original Word ("In the beginning was the Word," John 1:1) cause confusion. We choose the wrong revolution. We give ourselves over to the wrong prayer. We idolize the city—or is it the suburbs? We adulate gurus and therapists while we criticize and crucify priests. We prize our own individual experiences while we ignore or even deny the one mystical experience at the heart of things—the prayer of Christ, the prayer of the Church. We substitute facile beliefs for a vital faith. We join the wrong movements. Most movements today, some flourishing in the Catholic Church, are spurious. They come and go, their banality inevitably short-lived. Their words, clichés, slogans, and disguised idolatries sputter and split, generating hot air and ashes instead of salutary action. Such power-fired, self-righteous eruptions are as nugatory as they are trendy and tawdry.

FEMINIST JARGON AND SHODDY POLITICISMS

Though there are clearly genuine feminist concerns, much feminist rhetoric is simply jargon that has had a baneful influence on the English language. On this subject Madeleine L'Engle is particularly helpful. In *Walking on Water*, she expresses a sane view:

> *I am a female, of the species, man. Genesis is very explicit that it takes both male and female to make the image of God, and that the generic word, man, includes both. God created man in His own image male and female.*
>
> *That is Scripture, therefore I refuse to be timid about being part of mankind. We of the female sex are one half of mankind, and it is pusillanimous to resort to he/she, him/her, or even worse, android words.*

A young friend wrote me a letter saying. "We swam in a person-made lake. Then we went to a lesbian bar and were person-handled." It was inevitable. It will get worse. It is a perilous situation. When language is limited, we are thereby limited, too.

When language is weak, prayer is weakened, and so is theology. Some recent translators have done to Scripture and the Divine Office what Bowdler did to Shakespeare—tried to remove anything possibly offensive from the text. We tired of Bowdler and returned to Shakespeare. Schools of theology and houses of prayer may yet grow weary of linguistic fashions and return to expressions of faith that are raw, rich, and robust. Why must language be reduced to the lowest common denominator in order to be meaningful? Why must all prayers be nice? There's nothing nice about the cursing psalms! We need depth and breadth if we are to know and cherish our heritage.

Our present compulsion to avoid the masculine pronoun is a huge distraction. L'Engle states the problem trenchantly. In her chapter entitled "Icons of the True," she writes:

> *We are in a state of intense sexual confusion, both in life and in language, but the social manipulation is not working. Language is a living thing; it does not stay the same; it is hard for me to read the language of Piers Plowman, for instance, so radical have the changes been. But language is its own creature. It evolves on its own. It follows the language of its great artists, such as Chaucer. It does not do well when suffering from arbitrary control. Our attempts to change the words which have long been part of a society dominated by males have not been successful; instead of making language less sexist they have made it more so.*

Indeed, we are in a bind. For thousands of years we have lived in a paternalistic society, where women have allowed men to make God over in their own, masculine image. But that's anthropomorphism. To think of God in terms of gender at all is a dead end.

To substitute the word *person* for *man* has ruined what used to be a good, theological word, calling up the glory of God's image within us. Now, at best, it's a joke. There's something humiliating and embarrassing about being a chairperson, or a chair. A group of earnest women have put together a volume of degendered hymns, and one of my old favorites now begins "O dear Mother-Father of personkind."

Next to radical feminists and trivial academics, politicians seem to have the most pernicious effect on language. We were shocked by President Nixon's dirty tricks and dirty talk. But, sad to say, no one seemed upset when the first President George Bush used spectacularly shabby language to announce to the nation our engagement in the Gulf War. "We're going over there to kick ass," said he. What an embarrassment! Oh, for the finesse of Attila the Hun!

Shoddy language both leads to war and is an effect of war. Quoting L'Engle again:

> *We cannot Name or be Named without language. If our vocabulary dwindles to a few shopworn words, we are setting ourselves up for takeover by a dictator. When language becomes exhausted, our freedom dwindles—we cannot think, we do not recognize danger, injustice strikes us as no more than "the way things are."*

I might even go the extreme of declaring that the deliberate diminution of vocabulary by a dictator, or an advertising copywriter, is anti-Christian. That is why politicians may be as responsible for the decadence of the language as radical feminists. Politicians have invented some of our worst euphemisms to palliate or deceive us: We no longer have prisons, just correctional facilities; no longer poverty, just low-income levels; no longer poor children, just culturally disadvantaged ones; no longer destruction by bombs, just pacification; no longer military invasions, just protective reaction; no longer killing civilians, just collateral damage; no longer old people, just senior citizens; no longer lazy students, just underachievers.

Word pollution makes bureaucratic bungling seem harmless, renders anti-social behavior acceptable, and erases unpleasant images of poverty and social injustice, thus lulling people into apathy, and giving war an innocent look. It has been a long time since a national shudder has been detected in the face of America's techno-barbaric juggernaut.

PSYCHOBABBLE, GOSSIP, AND VICTIM LANGUAGE

We live in an environment whose principal product is garbage. We garble and ruin words, such as actually, virtually, meaningful, awesome, frankly, devil's advocate, at this point in time, there for me (or not), y'know, hopefully, okay, like, man, I know where you're coming from. Pointless conversations and the limitless proliferation of words poison our cities and our minds simultaneously, for the sake of advertising and propaganda. This kind of febrile and venal verbiage constitutes 80 percent of our garbage.

One half of that percentage takes the form of psychobabble. Psychobabble must be distinguished from genuine psychological language—so terse and true that it doesn't hide but unveils reality. In contrast, psychobabble is a language unfit for the quest of holiness or even wholeness, but instead, is a pitiable kind of cant, or high I.Q. whimpering. In Sophie's Choice, William Styron catches in a poignant scene the sophisticated wretchedness and the pious pretensions of this therapeutic age. Sophie and her chums are sitting languidly by the sea. The chums are rapping rhapsodically about their various forms of therapy, a Pecksniffian business referred to by Walker Percy, the latest, greatest Catholic writer, as "the long suck of self." The chums, annoyed by Sophie's silent largesse of contempt for their feckless hauteur, asked her, "What's your problem?" Sophie, who had escaped from a German concentration camp, said she had no time for nebulous drivel over unearned unhappiness. What a deft observation! What a perceptive commentary on our psychological age! What Sophie implies is a clear direction into both sanity and sanctity. It is an echo of the mystical teaching of the Roman Catholic Church, especially the doctor of mysticism, St. John of the Cross, a sixteenth-century Spanish mystic who, with St. Teresa of Avila, reformed the Carmelite Order.

A few years ago, renowned men and women in the worldwide field of psychotherapy gathered in Phoenix, Arizona for a convention. They came to an extraordinary conclusion: There was insufficient evidence to indicate that their professional work was often helpful. Instead, evidence showed that in many cases they did more harm than good. I have before me the names of twenty-five friends who have been in therapy for years. Only one has been helped; the others have been damaged.

My generation tells horror stories about confessors who hurt them by insensitivity to them and the Word they were supposed to listen to and convey. Will the next generation accuse their therapists of fatuous inanities and slick adjustments? Something like that is bound to happen. Just as there are good and bad confessors, so there are good and bad therapists.

Gossip also can be a pernicious form of verbal pollution. Although the abuse scandals that have rocked the Church in recent years have caused unspeakable pain for too many people, at the same time, too much of the priest-bashing that occupies a great deal of the media's space and energy is nothing but gossip. The lives of too many outstanding and innocent priests have been torn to tatters by lies, and the priesthood as a whole has been unfairly and carelessly demeaned by a lunatic media without conscience, respect, or discernment.

These are delicate matters, and we must discern and distinguish between minor lapses in chastity and the pernicious abuse of one's office. There are indeed those whose abuses are so dire, whose behavior is so predatory, they cannot be trusted to return to their priestly functions, and the Church must find other ways they can serve in safety. Unfortunately, the demon of gossip has blurred any such distinctions in the public eye, and many fine leaders who pose no danger to any under their care—child, adolescent, or adult—are forced to resign, even when properly repentant, humbled, and chastened. If they had been forgiven and kept at their posts, they could have been far better leaders and servants than before. Jesus knew that sinners make good leaders.

We live in an age of victims, so our language is becoming a tiresome, weary language of victims. While the truly heartbroken victims remain silent, an endless chain gang of victims has trudged noisily into our consciousness, uttering groans and grunts quite incommensurable with their burdens. *Discrimination*, a key word in education, is now known only in its pejorative sense. Seminal words like this get skewed from misuse or overuse.

Abstraction—the inadequacy of words to life—is one of the worst traps of academe. This is certainly true of our seminaries. In the words of the great contemporary theologian Dorothy Soelle:

> *What is called scientific theology is normally conveyed in a language devoid of a sense of awareness. It is unaware of the emotions, insensitive to what people experience. It has no interest and no appeal. It has a dull flatness because it leaves no room for doubt, that shadow of the faith....Any theology that wants to communicate with real people must however use a language that shows awareness, brings them and their practical experience and leads to a change in being and behavior.*

Soelle highlights a false academic theological language that has three appalling results: the neglect of emotions, feelings, and experience; the absence of doubt; and the loss of dialogue. Only practical experience, closely scrutinized, will change this deplorable situation.

Theologians must speak beyond the academy. The divinity schools of American universities are ghettoes—respectable places, but parochial, insular, full of half-dead people speaking an almost-dead language. Our society needs contemplatives and prophets who will speak the tragic, comic, mystic truth to people dehumanized on a raped Earth, in a ravaged culture. Only with Olympian optimism could we expect a contemplative mind, a prophetic voice, a Christened Zorbatic personality, to emerge from our seminaries—from either the conservatively stuffy ones or the liberally sappy ones.

What is required of us? Escape from our homemade prisons, from our habitual forms of banality. We need to do this immediately, a gigantic task that needs moral grandeur and spiritual audacity. If we don't risk our lives in apocalyptic warfare and go out into the desert and face the Dark Night of the Soul—our own, and the Night of the Church and State—if we do not take the longest stride of soul man ever took, then there is no reconciliation. Unless we are inspired by and stand under the judgment of the Word—the Ultimate Truth—we will end up thinking what memorable social reformer Saul Alinsky said we would: "Reconciliation means I am in power and you get reconciled to it."

To speak somnific, soothing words, to trivialize the pain of despair, is an act of great cruelty and contempt to an oppressed and depressed society, to a culture in ruins. We need humble words, honest words, clothed in splendor—the shining truth—to humanize human beings.

Bad words, sloppy, careless, merely modern words can spoil even the sublime vocation of a spiritual director, a soul-friend, whose one purpose is to help others into Divine Union, into the love of God and His whole creation. There is nothing individualistic about this. Care of the soul and care of the Earth unfold simultaneously and interactively. This unique and dramatic event is hampered when the counseling model takes over. Pampering or normalizing the skin-encapsulated ego is something entirely different. The Word does not prevail. Pat words and answers do. Therapy couples and groups can be the most isolated in the world: "Let's take care of our own psyches and let the world stew in its own juice and hoist itself on its own petard."

SPORTS, TELEVISION, AND VERBAL STRIPTEASE

The very nature of sports events should save them from the honors of talk. Far from it! Late in his career, announcer Hill Stern made a charming confession about his vocal fuss as the original television sportscaster: "I had no idea when to keep my big, fat, flapping mouth shut." If only his heirs had listened! If I go to heaven and hear the voice of John "Boom-Boom" Madden, I will ask out! How lamentable that good athletic games must compete for attention with the compulsive concatenation of blah-blah-blah that pretends to be commentary. Sports columnist Red Smith suggests a cure—"No banalities, no pseudo-expert profundities phrased in coachly patois, no giggles, no inside jokes, no second guessing, no numbing prattle." He said that in the early 1990s. The whole thing is worse now, unbearable and seemingly incurable.

Television is the chief source of verbal corruption. The plethora of talk shows—freak shows, really—has reached the apotheosis of foolishness, fanaticism, and ugliness. The crowd-pleasing trick is verbal striptease that allows one to expose the naked self, as pitiful or resentful victim, and thus for a brief, idiotic moment to become notorious by default.

MTV tries to be equally lubricious, specializing in the degradation of youth. Now the managers of MTV have branched out into publications: words, words, words, in a tumid effort to extend idiocy. Capitalizing on what they saw as the indolence and apathy of young people, they published a magazine called *Like Who Cares*. They featured a section for reader response to the most vulgar question of the age: What sucks? MTV then became even more wantonly irreverent by adding to its program the idiotic "Beavis and Butthead." Even worse shows, such as *Elimidate* and *Sex and the City*, have followed on other networks.

Oh well, we lived through the lunacy of the music gangs from Led Zeppelin to The Red Hot Chili Peppers. Elvis Presley and Andy Warhol stole not only the show but cascades of our glory.

Long ago President Carter applauded Presley as a model for young people. More recently, and unbelievably, we issued a U.S postage stamp in his honor. And then there's Madonna—chatty, cheeky, and so unlovely. Lady Chatterley, come back! Or better yet—(Saint) Josephine Baker!

Television pollution is our own fault. All we've got to do in turn it off, or, preferably, get rid of it. Who needs it, anyway, until the Boston Celtics rebuild their exquisite game of basketball? So pull the plug and snuff out the oceanic surf of gabble.

It is far more difficult to elude the real-life blather. We get trapped in airplanes, barbers' and dentists' chairs, waiting rooms, restaurants where we are always forced to sit in the crowded, noisy section, theaters where talkative nitwits surround us, and churches where loquacity replaces liturgy and soporific sermons cancel priestly prophecy.

THE INCARNATE WORD

God speaks, Jesus is the Word: "The Word was with God, and the Word was God" (John 1:1). From beginning to end, the Bible deals only with the Word. This Word is both act and mystery.

The Word commands with absolute authority. We respond, "I am commanded, therefore I am." The Word spoken by God from the beginning is incarnate in Jesus. We know that Jesus listened so perfectly to what God said that He responded fully and so was indeed the Word. Jesus bears in himself the Word of God, so that He can say, "I am the Truth" (John 14:6). "I am the Life" means "I incarnate the creative word"; "I am the Way" means that the word is the guide.

"God speaks" means that the question of truth—sheer reality—has been raised. The question of falsehood and the pollution of language is raised in that same moment of truth. The "anti-God" is named the Liar. Is this why we cannot bear to face our own modern conspiracy in the cultural lie, why we debunk our heroes and adulate our anti-heroes?

Polluting the language is falsifying the Word. The vocation of the Church is to contemplate the Word, conserve it, penetrate it freshly every day, and then communicate it. "By your words you will be justified, and by your words you will be condemned" (Matt. 12:37). This reminds us of the ultimate seriousness of words. Words involve commitment and reflect authenticity. We will "render account for every careless word" (Matt. 12:36). The Word is the means by which God chooses to express Himself—thus the gravity of words. If we speak the truth in a world of acceptable lies we, as witnesses of pure veracity, become martyrs. Pope John Paul II, a living witness of immutable truth—branded in the nature of things and revealed in tradition and the Bible—was, ironically, the world's favorite martyr—and continues to be so, even in death. The world (more correctly, the Empire, the fallen world, the popular fabrication of pseudo-events, false values, and half-truths) loved him or simply ignored him, the speaker of the Truth, a contemporary hero who tried to restore to the human word its fullness, its refined ferocity. Like all great heroes he was overwhelmed, broken, and crushed by the truth of this word he had to speak. Shades of Augustine, Joan of Arc, and Kierkegaard.

Preaching is the most frightful adventure. If the preacher is not inspirited by the Ineffable, if the words spoken are not born in silence, in eternity, then the words become very subtly and insidiously the Lie that fills the sound and fury of one merely modern aspect of this age that is dying of hunger for the truth.

What is required of the Church? Fidelity to the Word. It must become detached from every sociocultural milieu and remain permanently and robustly attached to the Living Word, to the ongoing command of God who speaks at the heart of things.

We worry when the Church loses or abandons imperial power for the sake of love. We suspect anarchy when the Church refuses to be political except as lover, as Bride of Christ. But it's either poverty or "archy." Poverty is an evangelical imperative. "Archys" are power plays, power plants, and power persons. If the Church is powerless—like Christ—it has no archys to rely on. God is love. Period. Jesus embodied that love. So does the Church—more or less. The glory of that love must not be mistaken for an archy. In a shrunken age it may seem spectacular, but it is no spectacle—just the splendor of the Word exploding amidst the egregious folly of our wooden, wastrel words.

THE "ARCHY" OF INCLUSIVE LANGUAGE

The final linguistic catastrophe is the American Catholic bishops' approval of inclusive language in the ancient, sacred texts of the liturgy. The bishops came to this disastrous decision not out of theological reflection, religious experience, or episcopal wisdom but out of fear of the loudest lobby in today's church. Many of the most deplorable mutations in human history were due to this same fear.

I have spoken with many bishops, and each one deplores this and many other decisions. But their attachment to and resonance of the Word, the Gospel Truth, has been drowned out by the dull drone of "position papers," by conferences and committees. The Church, refusing to enter the Dark Night of the Soul, sets up its own "archys" to match the "archys" of the Empire. Who is brave enough to stand alone, in the dark, in the sheer "unarchyness" of the Church, a voice in the wilderness, contesting the relevant rabble? Will one man, like Bishop John Fisher in sixteenth-century England, say no to the Empire, resist the crowd, numbed and cowed by the Imperial Lie?

The truth is simple: God has spoken. Who is overwhelmed? The Word was made flesh. Who will be faithful to that flesh? Only heroes. *Orthodoxy* literally means "right glory." To enjoy right glory we need the "right words." Only contemplatives to whom the Eternal Word is revealed can speak with humble and unswerving conviction, with personal and unwavering authority. Contemplatives do not represent the crowd or modern man but the Poor Man, Jesus Christ, People like this who penetrate and perpetuate the Word are speakers of the Truth and witnesses of Ultimate Reality in such a remarkable way, their orthodoxy may be mistaken for anarchy. In fact, the more God-centered and obedient they are to the Word—and therefore to the Church, the Mystical Body of Christ—the more "unarchy" they will be, and only as such are they spiritually authentic and politically significant. That is why the priest must make a stupendous effort to preserve and present a pure mind and heart. Bombarded by so much pietistic poison, he needs to be heroic, His language purely eloquent. Dag Hammarskjöld, former Secretary-General of the United Nations, and a good example of a contemplative in action, thought that good language was a moral imperative for priests, politicians, and the proletariat. "To misuse a word," he said, "is to show contempt for Man. It undermines the bridges and poisons the wells. It causes Man to regress down the long path of evolution."

Everyone needs to approach language with reverence. Dylan Thomas said, "I write for the glory of God and I'd be a damned fool if I didn't." Exactly! Can you imagine, for the glory of God, writing gobbledygook?

Let me now be positive about language. According to linguistics scholar Peter Farb, in *Word Play*: "Something happened in evolution to create Man the talker." I'd say God created us to participate in His own Eternal Word. We are talkers. Speech is our most exalting tool, the toy, the comfort, and joy of the human species. The pity is that talkers so often blurt so far beyond the line of what is needed and desired that they have to be listened to with either boredom or contempt.

Whenever language is good, it is luminously gravid with truth. Professors A.M. and Charlene Tibbetts of the University of Illinois say it all in one pithy paragraph that concludes their book, *What's Happening to American English?*:

> As our public rhetoric becomes more churlish and illogical; as our plays, movies, and works of fiction become more slovenly, violent, and dirty; as our scholarship becomes more pretentious and inaccurate so

our American spirit loses its magnanimity and grows weak and mean-spirited....To abuse language is to abuse the very idea of being human. Wit, kindness, intelligence, grace, humor, love, honor—all require the right employment of language for their embodiment. In the decline of American English may also be seen the decline of the American as human being.

THE ART OF CONVERSATION

On every level of society, whatever our way of life, we have lost the art of convention—good talk. On this subject I can make an experimental comment. I have lived with four communities of monks, in Arizona, Colorado, Nova Scotia, and Ireland. We have worked on the art of conversation for forty-five years.

Fantastic! But it will take as many years as we have left, though we are a young community, to enjoy consistent good quality. It's up and down now—sometimes dialogic ecstasy, other times, the pits. One Sunday, for instance, we went from an exalted experience of community prayer into a breakfast conversation that was inflated, uninspired, downright boring, and worst of all, totally unconnected with the peak experience we had just shared and the feast day we were celebrating. Our lives as monks—shepherds of being who savor the Word and therefore speak with gusto, muted by awe, wonder, and wise patience—were momentarily defeated. But the struggle goes on with deep commitment.

At least, I hope it does. I live now in complete solitude in Oregon. I do talk to the cats and they make me laugh uproariously. I must say, though, that I am very careful what and how I speak to the cats. Awe and reverence are key. I owe this gentleness also to the birds and squirrels. So I do not slam doors or bang things around. And if perchance I bump into a chair or table or wastebasket, I apologize. I am horrified in movies when irate people throw dishes, phones, and furniture at the walls. How brazen, barbaric, and downright silly!

Fortunately, the struggle continues in an oasis of verbal purity and delight. In thirty-three years, I have never heard a bad word uttered by one of our monks. We are not only revolutionary because our Crestone center, as far as we know, is the only solar-heated monastery in the world. In a far more crucial ecological revolution, we work toward a cleaner planetary environment by creating a cleaner verbal atmosphere, freed from the pollution of dirty talk.

The ecological question is: How can we clean up the Earth? More specifically, how can we acknowledge and preserve the inherent goodness of animals, vegetation, air, water, soil, and silence? The supreme ecological question is: How can we clean up our language? It can and must be done. The Native American Indians did not curse. The Japanese do not curse. Our monks do not curse. In most decent places, smoking is forbidden. Then why not bad language?

If certain base words have crept into our vocabulary and seem impossible to expel, then why not transform them? Because so much of the population is functionally illiterate, our efforts to clean up must be kept simple. A few ugly words dominate our vocabulary—at least our street talk and movie language: *damn, hell, piss, shit, bitch, bastard,* and most of all, the super word of the modern age, *fuck.*

If these words cannot be eliminated, they can certainly be transformed. The devil is damned—we can say so. Hell is hell. When used verbally and meant as such, it's a good word. If we make a hell of our lives, we will probably end up in hell. That's a meaningful sentence. We can refer to bitch and bastards as such, but reverently, and only when appropriate.

According to the Bible, folks pissed against the

wall. Not bad. No fuss. If a neighbor sees a bull go into your house and you ask him later on: "Guess what I found on the kitchen floor today?" and he says "Bullshit," that makes sense.

We think of the ass as a stupid animal, but our tiresome use of the word, anatomizing our anger, is the truly stupid thing. If you say that the ass played an important role in the life of Jesus, you are making a correct observation. If you say the only attractive thing about your neighbor is her (or his!) ass, you are making an extraordinary observation—or suffering from callipygian cupidity!

As for the super word, fuck, this is a valid word of old Germanic and Middle Dutch or English origin. I'd be a happy man if I heard the word used properly just once before I die. The fourth greatest book I ever read was called *The Love Book*. I lost if half a century ago and have never seen or heard of it again. I forget the name of the female author. It was a book about matrimonial lovemaking—sacred poetry like *The Song of Songs* or *The Spiritual Canticle*. The key word used over and over again with holy fear and tender affection was *fuck*. So it's a perfectly pure word—If restricted to the love chamber and used with reverence.

We suffer from a final problem, the biggest and most terrible problem of all: Our language is obliterated, the conducive climate devastated, the possibility of education made utterly impossible when the Name of God is taken in vain. This is sinful. When we do it, we have no access to the Word. Speech self-destructs. It is probably the most serious sin most of us commit on a daily basis, mucking up the whole atmosphere and tempting the wrath of God. We take God's Name in vain both piously and profanely.

Whenever we casually refer to God or Christ or Jesus, using these names without fear, love, awe, and adoration, we are peril. The Holy Name of God is the sacred center of Judeo-Christian tradition, the heart and soul of Western culture. His Name, Our Father, shatters our autonomy, our original sin—which is also our modern sin: our egotistic attempt to name things, to decide what is right and what is wrong, what is good and what bad. We bow before the Infinite and at the sound of God's Name. And though Wholly Other and transcendent, we know God is not separate. So we bow with wonder and radical astonishment before God's creatures, the things God found so good in the act of creation. This creative act of God keeps things from falling apart. So do we, insofar as we are co-creators, alive to God and therefore responsible stewards of His creation. Everything matters. That doesn't mean anything goes. It means doing what is right and saying what is true so that "all things shall be well, all manner of things shall be well." Fourteenth-century English mystic Julian of Norwich knew this secret when she discovered God in a hazelnut.

As Brian Moore, the author of *Catholics* and many other fine novels, said, "When our words become prayer, God comes."

The Human Vocation

"Who Do You Think You Are?"
DEPRIVED & DISSATISFIED

Our modern society is increasingly stuck in a mind-kicking whirligig. Most of us are hurtled, day after day, into a breathless grind of persistent deadlines, clock dominance, impossible schedules, several jobs, clamoring children, and chores to be done. Agriculture and industrialism have created a glut of material goods and a great poverty of time. We are deprived of space in which to play and enlarge the mind; we are devoid of everything except maintaining and servicing our material existence. That eats up twelve to fourteen hours every day.

It's not that most of us are outrageously unhappy; rather, we are vaguely dissatisfied. The work we chose to do is fairly good work but it does not reward us the way we expected. The family we were so anxious to build is found plausible by friends and neighbors but leaves us restless and tense. We have enough amenities for comfort and convenience, we know possessing more won't make a significant difference, and yet we are not centered or in deep peace. Absolute felicity would be fatal. We need to be provoked, challenged, and disturbed, otherwise we float and let too many things happen to us. Thus, much of our uniqueness and glory leak away. If our unease were creative it would be a plus; but it's enervating and so interrupts the humanizing process the spirit engenders in us.

What then is wrong with us? What can we do? It's worth quoting once again the *New York Times* drama critic Walter Kerr, who expressed the problem this way: "We are vaguely wretched because we are leading half-lives, half-heartedly, and with only one half of our minds actively engaged in making contact with the universe about us." In the face of all our recent accomplishments, Mr. Kerr knows that may sound strange. But it's not, really. Why not? Because the remarkable work we have done is the half-life we have led, brilliantly. Still, we feel distressed, and rightly so, since the work we've accomplished is due to the unfortunate fate of having engaged only half of our faculties, while the other half of our instincts, affections, and energies has been permitted to atrophy.

We are equipped with a human faculty for overcoming this wayward but common dichotomy. It's our basic human instinct; it is, notoriously, the chief monastic impulse, a hunger tearing at our guts to seek wholly and entirely, to do and be engaged by, the "one thing necessary." Understood deeply and profoundly: to be alone with God is what everyone wants. *Monos* is the Greek word for it. The embodiment of that fundamental human disposition whenever and wherever it is found is called "monk," one who attends to God, not over and above everything else but mediated by created being.

The more God-centered I am then the more intellectual, social, sexual, and political I am. This simply means that without being a scholar, a social activist, a

sexual animal, I am—precisely because I am a monk—
a man aware of the Ineffable; I am a touched sinner,
scorched by God's terrifying tenderness. God's irre-
ducible worldly presence makes me love ideas, people,
and multitudinous exchanges of ecstatic, erotic love
more passionately, not less. I look forward to a defying fecundity to the extent that now my disciplined
life, by excluding sensuality and expanding sensuousness, prepares me for personal intimacy so consuming that the inflated and intrusive ego is annihilated
and the self, authentic, pure, and present, is simply
there—there to love, to be wounded, wasted, and wed.

EVERYONE IS CALLED TO THE DESERT

Everyone, therefore, is called to be a monk today,
an archetypal monk at least: one who, in his or her
own way, undergoes the desert experience. Grace in-
undates the cultural chaos of our twenty-first century. As Wes Seeliger suggests, we are not asked to
be settlers in this modern form of barbarism, but to
pioneer our ardent way through this desert into a vision of beauty and a realm of virtue that will draw us
compellingly into a loving awareness of the Ineffable.

What is required of us now is to leave the glitter,
the glut, and the noise and move swiftly and steadfastly into the wilderness. What we desperately need
is a radical shift in terms of lifestyle. We need what
Jesus offered us when He rose from the dead—not
some nice adjustment, some smart improvement, a
better life; no, we need life on a new axis, an absolutely new order of being. We know this in a deep-down
level of our being but not achingly, shockingly enough
to do it, to make the radical shift, to follow Christ, to
live in and for the Kingdom. Everything depends on
this choice and on our realized freedom to make this
choice.

This is a radical shift indeed, but not as unique to Christianity as it may seem. If you read the Jewish theologian Abraham Heschel on the prophets, you will see what I mean. Their God, he says, is not wholly other, a strange, weird, uncanny Being shrouded in the unfathomable darkness, but the God of the covenant, full of pathos, intimately involved, urgently there, always there, pressing for new life. Equally impressive and impassioned were Sufi mystics: Al-Ghazzali, Hafiz, and Rumi, the Persian. The Lover leads us into the desert to speak to our hearts.

All that we knew, believed in, and cherished will collapse in the wilderness. We recognize how barren our faith, how banal our lives, and how effete our spirits were—much too weak to cope with the onslaught of chaos and the demonic force of secularism. Without a vibrant people nourished on a concrete spirituality, transformed by their life in Christ, there's not enough pure Christian energy to dislodge the occupied forces of the Empire and detach ourselves from its enslaving tentacles: mediocrity, mendacity, and manipulation. The two outstanding fruits of the desert experience are freedom and wisdom. Until the desert remakes us we will be manacled by modernism or, even worse, by postmodernism, and forced to continue dumbing down, enticed by nonexistence itself.

I use the "desert" metaphor both negatively and positively. Negatively, the desert refers to the cultural chaos of our megalopolitan monstrosities where there is neither space nor time to think. There's no conducive environment for leisurely work, no mood mystical or mysterious enough to lure even business partners into the sacred depths where authentic meetings take place, and no beauty to seduce the mind and the heart into playing and praying so that consumption does not preclude contemplation. Positively, the desert is the wilderness, an unspoiled, uncluttered environment that provides so much silence and solitude and such an opportunity for a salient simplicity that one can hardly resist the invitation to be still, to be wise, and to cultivate, with wild and wonderful abandon, the life of the spirit.

We need more desert men and women—exquisite, savvy humans who know their way in the desert, who know what is going on there, who can interpret it and manage it. All of us need to be archetypal monks. It's an attitude, a disposition, and a perspective, a *Weltanschauung*—a basic worldview with God at the center, each one of us longing and yearning to be alone with him.

In the West, we have three forms of wisdom: religious, philosophical, and scientific. The Asian "way" is none of these. It is experience. Take, for instance, the experience of sensuousness: You drink water and know for yourself that it's worth trusting yourself to the water. Relax, let it support you—and move. It's a glorious experience. Direct and immediate experience is the only thing that saves us from addiction to social conventions. In this sense the Eastern Tao and Christian experience are the same thing. So, what students of Buddhism and Vedanta call transformation of human consciousness we in the West call "mystical experience." What both Tao and the mystical experience want to highlight is the concrete life of the spirit.

CALL TO MONASTIC LIFE

But that's not enough. Eros, the Infinite Lover, the Hound of Heaven *calls* me—and you—to be His own existential monk (that is, to live monastic life in a monastery with its training, its discipline, its vows, and intense way of following Christ). To be the man of the hour, to be the woman wrapped in silence, but with the irrepressible Word!

No one in the Church is more necessary, more urgently needed, no one more desired by God. The desert is the monk's world, and today the world is a desert. Ideally, our occupation should be our vocation. Work and play should be identical. Hindus think of creation not as work but as play. They call it *Vishnulila*: the play of God. Our word *lilt* means the same sort of thing. Hibernian lilt is playful, beautiful, and full of the possibilities of rich disclosures. As Emily Dickinson says, "The supernatural is simply the natural disclosed."

Also, our idiotic, materially driven way of life is corrected in monastic life whenever those twelve to fourteen hours typically spent in servicing our material existence are spent in cultural activities—praying, singing, dancing, gardening, and careful, mindful craftsmanship. The daily work is play. In other words, understood deeply, the major activity of the day, for the monk, is making love.

"Making love" is no banal reference to sexual happenstance, but to the hard quotidian work it takes, and the wild wonderful deeds one needs to risk, in order to transfigure matter by the power of the spirit. This is an incomparable adventure, full of sangfroid and sweat, magic and meaning.

God *calls* us all to life, to the enjoyed fullness of life. Very few respond. God, then, with supreme prejudice, summons a bunch of us. That is who the Ineffable, Holy One is—the One who summons us into a concrete way of life that draws us into a deep authentic existence, into habits of the mind that enable us to be, under any circumstance, the brand-new image and likeness of God we are created to be. And that is who we are—each one of us, called, summoned, and, if faithful, transformed by the Spirit as we pursue wholeheartedly the Center, outside. The Center, mind you, is outside. Although our intention is activated and dynamized, the Center draws out, out, out into unimaginable otherness. Once we get that straight our lives become simplified.

Though a divine summons always involves a following of Christ, the way for each of us is extremely particular and utterly experiential: Experience—real engagement or union—is contagious. It involves being "oned." It is Trinity-centered, community-centered, never isolated or separated. Unified! The ramifications are personal, public, and political.

A busy day at work, then, far from being unprayerful is, in fact, one genuine expression of the contemplative life. The multiple things attended to in a day's work are not just means to an end. Each moment, every event is an end-means. The rose, the rabbit, and the rain are not merely symbolic. Each one pulsates with reality, with truth. The revelation of the rose itself is repeated nowhere. Watching the rabbit run or the rain pour is truth enough. It is in the grit of earth that we find the glory of heaven. It is in our being robustly human that God enables us to share His own divine life.

MONK AND LAY ALIKE ARE CALLED TO LOVE

Revelation—Scripture and tradition—makes it clear that there is an incomparably close connection between love of God and of neighbor. So, when a human lover says to his spouse, "with my body I thee worship," he's hardly a breath away from saying, "My Lord and my God, I adore you."

Despite billions of Gothic and Romantic novels, regardless of saints such as St. John of the Cross, Francis, and Therîsë, not withstanding the love poets and writers such as Dostoyevsky, Soloviev, and Walker Percy, and ignoring the perfection of love itself in the life of Christ, we have left unexplored the mystery of love, and therefore, the meaning of our lives.

You want a real sexual revolution? Fall in love and then sustain it forever. You want an industrial revolution? Work heroically and make your whole day of labor playful. You want family life enriched and renewed? Don't hang our there lackadaisically or co-dependently. Let its intense energy of love hurtle you into your way (Tao), into your own human adventure. You want an outstanding education? Reduce schooling to a minimum (it's the false god of the twenty-first century). Read with classical discretion, think rigorously and creatively, meditate, and then risk everything for a higher purpose, in response to a summons. You want to pray? Then live dangerously and cry out for help, for forgiveness, in gratitude, and above all, in adoration.

To exist is to love. To exist with authenticity is to love with fidelity. I called this an impossible task. I know this from personal experience and a lifetime of soul-friending and counseling. Still, it is a task each of us must undertake at the cost of everything.

Yet, it is not enough to say God is love. That's like saying, "Drink eight glasses of water a day." What we need to know is, What does God require of us here and now in this existential situation? And, equally pressing, how can we satisfy these requirements? See Jesus and, in love, follow him; the Way will open up before you. For a hundred reasons it will always be a way of the cross. It will also be wild and wonderful, and the joy, found nowhere else, will be boundless. In this unique unfolding of selfhood there is no method and no system. Strictly speaking, there is no "interior life," no "spirituality." There is *tao*, your *karma*, your *kismet*. Though steeped in traditional wisdom and buoyed up by the communion of saints, ultimately, there is only *your way* (Frank Sinatra was right)—a way hewn not from individualistic eccentricities but from personal experience.

THE CALL

I want to clarify that aspect of vocation referred to as "summons," which I see as something much more concrete and compelling than the general, universal "calling" of all human beings. I would estimate that 70 percent of the human race rejects God's call. While this negative response to love dehumanizes each one of us and intercepts the evolutionary process, it does not necessarily compel us to join the road to perdition. Still, ignoring the "call" courts, unfailingly, some kind of disaster. Look at our schizoid society, our collapsing culture, our downward transcendence.

No call means no awakening, no shocking experience of life, neither terror nor delight. Nothing to shake our shanks and enliven us. Without the Numinous, we are nothing but a crowd of nitwits, numbskulls, and nudniks—that's what Jean-Paul Sartre found so nauseating. Who wouldn't? On the other hand, hearing the call is an invitation of wildness—to a destiny reached by the allure of every concrete situation. We are fashioned by the situation if we perform the tasks it requires of us. Deeds comprise the contemplative life.

The call has nothing to do with a specific direction in life. It is a deep, repetitive resonance in the depths of the soul that awakens us and calls us to attention. In response we develop a perceptive appreciation of things as they really are—interrelated, interconnected, and, in some sense, "oned" by Eros. The contemplative life begins to unfold.

SPIRIT

It is not at all helpful to think of either the call or the summons as the voice of God from above, a mega-message from out of the clouds. That's the sort of image cultivated by Dan and Ron Lafferty, two devout Mormons who were serious devotees of Joseph Smith and Brigham Young, the founders of Mormonism. According to the Lafferty brothers, the murders they committed were carried out in the name of faith, as Jon Krakauer notes in his excellent book on this subject, *Under the Banner of Heaven*.

God influences us in a totally different way. While we make courageous and consistent efforts to become, through ascetical-mystical life, enlightened lovers, an inflowing pressure of Spirit has a deifying effect on us, that is, *calling* and summoning us into the fullness of life, the life of the Spirit. The purpose of a true Church is to transmit, cultivate, and bring to fruition that spiritual life.

The desiccation of our theological thinking moves on through our tumultuous decades as if no significant, seminal events have occurred. Paradigmatic shifts are happening so rapidly that society remains stunned and uprooted. The religious reality underlying the startling phenomena of our times hardly recognizes these staggering mutations in the areas of science, art, ecology, economics, politics, education, industry, and ethics.

The ignored reality is change. What is enhancing is not just theological statement or sociological formulae, but the very condition of our spirit as it is molded by the divine.

We are constantly being distracted from the "one thing necessary"—love of God and His whole creation—by an extreme polarization that gives life to the multiple others. It is the essential polarization between the Church of Jesus and the various institutions that claim membership in, or even leadership of, that Church.

Our culture ignores the divine. Drenched as we are in that culture of ignorance, we are enthralled by nescience. We gape at screens. Reality evades us. We stuff ourselves with information and remain bereft of knowledge. We wear ourselves out with successive pseudo-events and are starved for experience. Feverish activity so exhausts us we never reach the pinnacle of human achievement, namely, contemplation or the pure intuition of the Real born of love.

Jesus didn't whip into and fly out of our human realm as a singular, sovereign individual offering us a quick look at a divine kind of being with human identity. No, something more: He left a presence—spiritual, ecclesiastical, visible, and permanent. Whatever power it took to represent Jesus resided in that presence. Spirit was its source, and its energy, and its end. All its accoutrements, institutional and administrative, and its moral powers have one purpose: the generation and communication of Spirit. If it departs from that dynamic thrust it begins to decay. This presence is His Church, the body of holiness, its members. That means all of us, in union with the Founder.

It is indisputable that the Church becomes less and less capable of exercising the moral authority and spiritual power that Jesus irrevocable bestowed on this Church. The bishops are in a panic and the priests are in a slump. Jesus' first command to this Church was "to preach." Only a few are capable of engaging in intelligent discourse about creation, incarnation, and redemption, or about what is in the heart of man. Why such a shameful state of affairs?

Because a few hundred years after Constantine blessed the Church as Empire rather than Kingdom, the embodiment of Jesus' spirit, lured by political and military force, ceased to be solely immersed in its exercise of moral and spiritual power. It became captivated by its cultural accretions and neglected its spiritual roots. It was purity that characterized the original Presence—purity understood as undispersed energy. The Church had one focus—the life of the Spirit—and was unwaveringly committed to it. Despite centuries of spiritual decline and a fractured focus the Church always had luminous figures who both witnessed and defended the life of the Spirit. Until recently. Now a pandemic fear, coupled with laziness, stifles the Spirit. Here and there an intrepid follower of Christ will

break through the massive myopia of the crowd, the
establishment and the self-righteousness of the "good"
people; will become free of institutional bondage and
take a "human" stand *against* the techno-barbaric
juggernaut. We all know that law, clung to inordinately, kills the Spirit. We have not yet acknowledged the
most dangerous threat of all: How an arrogant and
narcissistic piety snuffs out the living flame of love.

Unignited by Jesus' fire, His Church—even the
storm troops, the religious orders—leaves unspirited
the changing situation of the world. Ecclesiastical apparatchiks remain woefully incapable of halting the
mechanization of civilization, but become instead venomously affected by it. The Presence is abraded. The
Sacred is not rediscovered in the marketplace. That
would be wonderful. No, the tragedy of these postmodern times is that with Kingdom and Empire becoming
undistinguishable, each a pawn of secularism, genuine holiness is counterfeited in the Kingdom by a pale
moralism and in the Empire by a paltry correctness.
In both cases the Spirit is being throttled by mechanization, a malaise that may indeed be the most dehumanizing feature of our contemporary culture. Much
of our misery is due to our lackluster revolt against
a system that promises death to Spirit. Why is the
Church such an ineffective witness of the living God?
Of His flaming Spirit? One obvious reason is that
church people try too hard to imitate politicians, en-
tertainers, scientists, and psychologists. Much more
could be accomplished by a few God-intoxicated people. Only to the extent that its members have seen
and touched the resurrected Christ can the Church
contribute what it is uniquely capable of contributing.

THE SUMMONS

The summons, on the other hand, implies a specific
purpose, a definite direction, and a deliberate destiny.
Who am I? I am the person who was called by the

Spirit. An invisible higher force is leading.

I took my own summons with terrifying seriousness. What did I regard as my summons? An impossible task: a radical renewal—a new model, actually—of
monastic life based on (1) the ancient rule and spirit of
the Carmelite Order, (2) the Celtic monastic tradition,
and (3) the wilderness experience. The other powerful
influence is, of course, life as we know it today. The
only way to provide authenticity is to wed ancient and
contemporary modes of existence, seeking all the time
and environment that is beautiful and a community
as exquisitely human as possible.

Now comes the hard part—the impossible task. In
essence, what comprises high-quality happiness? The
answer is deep, reverent meeting that, however bustling, is always erotic—that is, caring—and manifestly
open to the mystery of each otherness.

MY OWN CALL AND SUMMONS

What I want to say now, though, does bring me closer
to that subject. At ten to twelve years of age playing
and reading were the outstanding activities of my life.
How I loved to play—alone or with others: alone on
our front steps on Cass Street in Providence with one
ball that did all the stuff I wanted it to do, or across
the sandy, rocky street on the grass with a jackknife,
utterly absorbed in a half-dozen versions of mum-
blety-peg; or with others, with my classmates playing basketball or my neighbors, brothers and sisters
playing baseball and football, or on lusciously bright,
cold nights skating in Roger Williams Park to the tune
of "The music goes 'round and around and comes out
here."

The playful boy-Christ, loose and lively in Nazareth, was always on my mind. As noted above, in the
Orient *lila* refers to God the Father's leisurely hilarity

in the act of creation. Jesus caught that divine luster in His own lilting life of redemption, a life both hidden and hallowed. Competing in sports was exhilarating, winning was satisfying, losing was sanctifying. Anticipating the game was half the fun. So was savoring the victory and brooding over the loss. But most fruitful and fulfilling was the recollection of resurrected moments when, beyond reason, plan, and natural capacity, an energy burst forth, a rhythm unfolded, and a shot was made that swooshed silently into the hoop but shook the order of the universe.

Then, the *pìîce de rësistance*: Out on the hill, overlooking the railroad tracks and our deep-lived home, I'd find a grassy place to sit and meditate and, when God pleased, to pray. This mulling of mine that verged on prayer was always full of longing and yearning for play itself—pure unadulterated play, the apotheosis of carefree care, of wild abandon, of unmeasured and unimaginable give and take, of lovely tricks and lively pranks—of deep, profound exchange, a swirling soulfulness that human industry and psychotherapy know nothing about, nor does education (that is, schooling). And, astonishingly, neither does a solemn, self-conscious mysticism.

So, between my tenth and twelfth years the following intuition dawned on me during my hillside reveries: The happier I was, the more delightfully playful and wholeheartedly engaged on sea and on land with my enjoyable others, the more lonesome I became. Out of this loneliness sprang the poignant, plangent cry of my heart, my prayerful longing and yearning of God alone or for the way He plays at the heart of the world in His infinite exchange of love, of Eros, the trinitarian love-life of the Godhead, each person relating with reckless—wreckless, indeed—and altruistic abandon to the other.

I worked as well, driven to work by all my elders, in the garden, in the cellar, in the woods by Echo Lake, building, painting, digging, and so forth. But it was the interweaving that happened between playing and praying that shaped my identity. Daily Mass and a keen sense of living the liturgical year were pivotal, Serving mass was awesome, a radical break with what was often shabby behavior before and after—or so they tell me. Somehow I think they were onto something. But how do you cope with family members who seem so sober in the early morning?

One day in my twelfth year, Father Kelly brought us altar boys to Bristol, Rhode Island, where the Columban Fathers have a beautiful house with a huge, sprawling lawn that stretches from the highway to Narragansett Bay. Hovering over the bay on a promontory of lush, green hillside stands a striking crucifix—a gleaming, white, broken body of that most manly man, that perfect representative of the human race, Love itself embodied, enfleshed—absolute beauty crushed for us and nailed on that dark weather-tortured cross.

After a very satisfying ballgame during which even the fight seemed right—a bracing encounter anyway— I slipped away to encounter my living God, focused for me in that powerful crucified image. Wrapped in awe and silence I knelt, I gazed with naked intent (no petitions) on my Lord, my Beloved, my Model. Though I cherished everything else, the beautiful place, the quaint New England convergence of land and sea, the frolicking with my dear friends, the picnic, the Columban Fathers, and the image I always shed last, Libby O'Neil, my, my—my what? I don't know. But Jesus alone mattered. Mattered, that is, ultimately and with extreme urgency. I knew then—from my parents? My siblings? My cat? My teachers (the Sisters of mercy were terrific in every way)? Of course, but all of life seemed to say the same thing: If He is not all-important, He is not important at all. I knew that there was only one authentic way I could respond to the Absolute and that is absolutely.

I, by God's grace, have never strayed from the divinely ravishing onslaught. It's all I ever wanted. This alone explains why, though enraptured by life, its experiences and challenges, I have, since my twenties, longed for death—death, more living than life: the supreme love. This commitment did not leave me sinless but it did keep me sane—and, above all, faithful. I am so implacably foolish that even the Holy One cannot protect me from mistakes, blunders, and balderdash. But he can make lust and violence and even the subtleties of narcissism incongruous and antagonistic. His call may be so perilous that comfort and consolation become foreign to me. I am required to live on the edge, to so mock and tease catastrophe that I never dream of being good. "God alone is good....So why call me good?" asked Jesus with whiplash cogency. My own summons, like many others, obviates a good conscience. A good conscience would embarrass me and inundate me with guilt. A great tide rises within me. All I can experience is anguish. A feature of my summons: to build a mixed community. So, though a hermit, I live with women.

Being drawn by the Spirit into the fullness of life is never a private affair. It is personal and, as such, issues always into a community of love. But the heart of adventure lies in a deep personal, solitary encounter.

That is why, when I was a twelve-year-old lad, I knelt there on the grass with Him, come what may. Deep in my heart I heard Him say, and felt it in my loins, "Follow me." And, this time, with such finality. I could not temper or mitigate or postpone. He meant, "Now." Oh, not in a creepy, copycat sort of imitation. He doesn't need groovy fans or Jesus freaks. He wanted this bloody scamp of a boy to follow him truthfully, therefore in "My Way." Any other way would not be true or real; not God's will, not the way of the cross.

A few months later, at age thirteen, I was gone. My Carmelite training began. And it goes on. I am, now in my eighties, still becoming a Christian, an apostolic hermit, a Priest. Identity comes, though, only by hearing the call, obeying the summons, and being faithful unto the end. The call awakens us; the summons engages us; the fidelity proves us.

Finding myself at the foot of the cross I was being summoned, drawn by the irresistible force invisible but irrepressible, into a particular, earthy way of following Christ. Now I felt bound by duty and dynamized by destiny.

So I did all the things one needs to do (with the help of Sister Trinitas, a Christ-woman if there ever was one!) to be embarked on an adventure that would take me away from Providence to the Carmelite Minor Seminary in Wisconsin. Four years later I'd be a monastic novice in Brookline, Massachusetts, then a professed friar and philosophical student at Holy Hill, Wisconsin. A few years later I would study theology at our Carmelite monastery in Washington, D.C., and at the Catholic University of America, then ordination to priesthood at Josephinum Pontifical Seminary in Columbus, Ohio. Right away, I was sent to our novitiate in Brookline, where I spent some of the happiest and most peaceful years of my life. While there, I studied psychology and education at Boston College. Mostly I shared with the novices a deep, joyful monastic experience. It was idyllic. The most significant thing that happened during those quiet, contemplative years, though, was the discovery (or formation?) of the "Brookline Gang," a wild, holy, vivacious group of children who inspired me, challenged me, and played with me. Today such activity would arouse suspicion; then it was sheer, pure, God-intoxicating celebration. That bond among us endured. To this day, we are close friends.

My summons shaped up this way externally: From the Novitiate in Brookline to the Carmelite parish monastery in Milwaukee, it was a comedic existence there. Was my response to the absolute summons absolute? I doubt it. I would define the years there as "happy turmoil." I did, with God's grace, begin the *Spiritual Life* magazine. Then I went to the desert and began the Spiritual Life Institute, the heart of which is the apostolic hermits of Our Lady of Mount Carmel, a mixed community of men and women—friars no longer but monks who embody the ancient monastic impulse: To be "alone" with God and therefore "all one" and who, without being modern or new-agers, do have an attractive, captivating style that is simply and gloriously contemporary.

A HUMAN RESPONSE TO A DIVINE SUMMONS

I trace this development, however briefly, in order to convey the earthy and worldly exigencies of a human response to the divine summons. Deeds are required. Tasks must be performed. Risks need to be taken and one's own destiny embraced. Jesus' life and death proved the trust-worthiness of His Father. We not only live for Christ but in Him; because we share His trust we live with wild abandon. We are inordinately attached to nothing, not even our good conscience or our reputation, or our impeccable moral image. We are committed to life; to live is to love and to love is to die; to love is to fall, inevitable, but love falls are the least heinous. Love is erotic, is sexual. Love is the greatest of the virtues but the most threatened and endangered—endangered by sin.

We who are summoned to follow Christ and live in Him can answer the question existentially—in this manner: When I, in an act of love, somehow fall, I *fall* with Christ. My following Him does not cease. I do not prefer anyone to Him, any pleasure to the pleasure of

His company. As Christ-man I make mistakes but do not betray my Lord and Friend. In fact, it is because of Christ, with His grace and by His power, that I enter these living situations.

CONCLUSION

There is a difference between the call and the summons. How droll that despite the plethora of psychological studies on piffle almost nothing of significance has been done on such a crucial issue as the effect that a lively consciousness about being "called" has on identity. Quite an impressive case could be made about our schizoid society suffering such identity confusion precisely because of its inexcusable oblivion of the call. Much light could also be shed on the pedophilia crisis among priests and the catastrophic infidelity among priests, religious, and friends.

When we think of our identity—becoming a vital self by responding to the primordial call and erotic summons—we want to belong to something larger than ourselves. In this our contemporary culture of alienation, our deepest hunger is to belong. David Spangler, in his nifty little book *The Call*, provides genuine comfort in this regard by reminding us of the scientific discovery, made in the 1960s, about the background radiation of the universe. This music of the spheres, this magnificent universal order, is a result of an original creation or explosion referred to as the Big Bang. The uniform background radiation proves the Big Bang. Likewise, the incarnation proves the Big Love. As Spangler writes, "There is a background call in all of us, in all creatures. This is the call of love, the original radiation of creation."

We say God so loved the world he gave His only Son. Hindus say God gives itself. The deity dismembers itself and out of this love all the worlds are born. The worldwide revelation is that we are valued and we are loved. We do indeed belong. To belong means intimacy, ecstasy, and fecundity. God's commanding us is His way of flirting; espousing us is what He does intimately with elaborate subtlety, an act that transforms us. Luring us out of dead spots into more life is ecstasy. Fecundity is what happens when spirit weds matter. Look at Mary, mother of God—that's it.

To belong—as we do, and as I've tried to articulate it here—means to participate. If we want to get wet we get into the water; if we want to get warm we get into the sun. If we want, above all, to be lovers we immerse ourselves in Love, into the One who is by nature "for the others." His act of loving surrender and sacrifice lives on in us, so we are divinely empowered to give ourselves to the world, to one another, and to the purposes of God in the world.

The Big Love *calls* us to be transformed by love and to transfigure all of matter by love. When we respond to the call, we become magnificently alive—a contagion in the world, a challenge, even a scandal. We represent and to some extent execute a radical shift in the world. We make God the center of the sociopolitical world. It's an axial, revolutionary change. We have moved beyond Christendom with its ephemeral power, beyond Christianity with its meticulous moralistic and immobile doctrine. The call is to Christianness: We must have one single, passionate reason for everything we do and that reason must be Christ.

The solution is to live whole lives wholeheartedly, with the whole mind actively engaged in making contact with other creatures and ultimately with the Wholly Other who suffuses everything with His being, His presence, His power, His love. This is the essential mystery we live in. If we have a heightened consciousness of this we are mystery spelunkers, that is, mystics. We enjoy what Rabbi Abraham Heschel calls "awareness of the Ineffable."

The Summons, whatever shape and form it takes, will be absolutely urgent, crucial, ultimate. The fuss is over. It's ridiculous. It's embarrassing. It's time for heroic love. Nothing but fire!

At this point it may help to call forth four people who became canonized saints, each in singularly unique and distinct way, but all of them sanctified by love, consumed by fire. That is what we will do in the next chapter, beginning with St. Paul and calling attention to his gentle ferocity.

Love Letters of Wrath and Reverence

S t. Paul of Tarsus was a revolutionary on fire with
the love of God, fascinated by Jesus and imbued
with Spirit. He could not tolerate any ludicrous
attempt to tame God and falsify love. God's presence
is unbearable, His love immeasurable, ever-burning,
breaking, making new.

When I was theological student, we spent most
of our time studying the Pauline privilege, which is a
tricky way out of a problematic marriage situation. We
learned nothing of Pauline passion. And all we ever
heard about the passion of Christ was how it spent
itself at the end in that long, lonely, agonizing walk up
Mount Calvary.

An appreciation of Paul's passion would have rescued me long ago from measly pursuits. I've wasted
so much time, for instance, writing inane, innocuous
letters. Finally, I did resolve to write only love letters.
That doesn't mean mushy, sentimental stuff; it doesn't
even mean pleasant. It means that I address myself
carefully and passionately to whomever I write about
matters that deserve loving attention. Nice people in

a neatly run society often find such letters shocking, insulting, rude, righteous, embarrassing, improper. It isn't even safe to talk that way, they say; so why put it in writing? It's a risk, I know, but perhaps a prudent one, since prudence means taking the best, not the safest, means to the proper end. Sometimes the best means are the least safe.

Religious people are particularly finicky about what they write because they are supposed to be paragons of virtue, which they equate with impeccable propriety. Such a dour outlook may force them to be morally upright, but certainly not great lovers.

I find the epistles of St. Paul so refreshing! They are love letters, vehement, volatile, but never irreverent. Paul is a thoroughly passionate man, so his letters are passionate. He is passionate about God and the things that pertain to God, especially Christ and the members of His Mystical Body.

The passion of God has irrupted in Paul's soul. Divine pathos has laid hold of him. Paul is a marked man. He has seen God suffer. He made him suffer: "Saul, Saul, why do you persecute me?" (Acts 9:4). So love of God, according to Paul, is not all sweetness and light. Paul's God is a God of love, but also a God of wrath. He warns us: "Observe the kindness and severity of God—severity to those who fall away, divine kindness to you, if only you remain within its scope" (Rom. 11:22-23). It is only against this background of wrath and severity that Paul speaks of love and goodness; otherwise His doctrine of divine agape would make no sense.

Paul, who represents God and proclaims His word, is loving and wrathful at the same time because he is passionately concerned and in anxiety that Christ be formed in this to whom he writes. This passion permeates Paul's letters. One astonishing example is the marvelous mixture of valediction and malediction at the end of 1 Corinthians: "If anyone has no love for the Lord let him be anathema. Maranatha (may the Lord come)! The grace of the Lord Jesus be with you. My love be with you all in Christ Jesus" (1 Cor. 16:22-24).

Precisely because he is such a great lover, there are things that Paul hates. So we find him raging with anger against the Galatians. Nothing like the petty barbs of rancor and annoyance that sputter between a president and members of the press, televised across the nation, and nothing like a jejune pap that drips from some parish pulpits every Sunday or the pompous ecclesiastical pronouncements that make it so difficult for the Church to speak, in imitation of Christ, "with authority"! No, nothing like that, but strong invectives, denunciations, and pleadings: "O fools of Galatia, who has bewitched you?...My little children, of whom I am in labor again" (Gal. 3:1; 4:19). This Pauline bombast mounts in fustigating fury until it reaches a paroxysm of vituperation in the fifth chapter: "I wish those who unsettle you would castrate themselves" (Gal. 5:12). A gentle suggestion, after all since he leaves the decision up to them, unlike the suggestion of a famous religious conservative preacher, popular today, that the state castrate convicted rapists.

LOVE AND HATE

In Paul's letters there is a fundamental complementarity of love and hate. Each feeds the other and is intensified by the other. This fact is extremely significant. We foolishly tend to think of God's love as nebulous and otherworldly. The truth is that biblical *agape* is far more earthly, human, and worldly than the Greek idealized *eros*. You will find a good explanation of this in Gerhard Kittel's New Testament *Theologisches Wörterbuch:*

> *The essential characteristic of love in Israel is actually its tendency toward exclusiveness. The Greek eros is fundamentally universal, undiscriminating, undisciplined, broad-minded. The love which is commended in the Old Testament is a jealous love which chooses on object among thousands and holds it fast with all the strength of its passion and its will, brooking no relaxation of the bond of loyalty. It is just this jealousy which reveals the divine strength of such love. It is no accident by which, in the Song of Songs (8:6) love strong as death is inseparably connected, in the poetic parallelism, with jealousy hard as hell. Jacob has two wives, but his love is given to only one of them (Gen 29); he has twelve sons, but loves one of them more than all the others (Gen 37:3). God has set many peoples in the world, but gives His love to the elect nation. With this He makes a covenant which He loyally keeps and jealously guards as if it were a love of marriage (Hos. 1ff). To break the law is a break of faith, to worship strange gods is adultery, calling forth the passionate jealousy of Yahweh.*

This channeling of love into a passionate and definite relationship with jealously guarded boundaries was not abrogated when Paul, knocked off his high horse on the way to Damascus, turned totally and irrevocably to Christ and joined His small community of believers. This Christ whom he loved did not embody the God of universal amiability but the God of Israel, with all His personal and possessive characteristics.

Once Paul embraced the Christian faith, that central theme of the Bible, *personal, passionate presence*, dominated his personality and intensified his love life in every possible way. Having grasped significantly the ineluctable centrality of *Emmanuel,* God with us, he understood with similar clarity the egregious absurdity of seeming to live without Him. Paul came to regard sin, the rejection of God's love, the denial of His presence, as the most insane and inhuman act we could possibly commit.

Every sin we inhumanly commit widens the gulf between us and the real world: the Kingdom of God established by Jesus Christ. This hideous gulf represents being at loggerheads with God: disharmony with ourselves, with others, with our natural environment, and with the One who suffuses all and sustains it by His creative presence. Such conflict is a universal experience and remains uncertified until each one of us is remade, reborn, transfigured, Christened—call it what you will. This alone is dynamic revolution, the only effectively enduring and positively beneficial reformation in the history of the world.

That is why renowned psychiatrist Karl Menninger wrote a book entitled *Whatever Became of Sin?* It isn't the peccadilloes Dr. Menninger is worried about. No one can completely avoid making mistakes and sometimes getting carried away. What is seriously damaging is the overall misdirection and disorientation of a lifetime. In this sense our omissions are very often worse than our commissions. So is our dalliance and our diffidence, and the accumulation of human diminishments.

Think of sin as the parallel of old people saying to the young, "You'll get over it, you won't mind it when you're my age." Think of sin as the drabness of life, the deadening of the spirit by routine, the killing of the spirit by the letter, the failure to live, to love, to adventure, as a kind of oldness, deadness, numbness, a fear of stepping out of line. Yet all this comes dramatically to an end on the cross. See death, and all is old and sad; God in death, and all is suddenly new.

St. Paul said that the law made sin worse. For when we sinned, the law said, "Now you have had it. Now you have God against you," and this shut us up inside our own sinfulness. But we don't worry about the law when we have the wrath of God to contend with; and we know the gentle fury of God's wrath if we've had any experience of His love.

Without faith and hope in God's love, we tend to hate God; and God hates what we have made of ourselves. But God loves Christ, and Christ loves God; Christ in God loves us, and we in Christ love God. This love is manifestly present in us if our relationships are animated by Christ's spirit, by the reverent, in-depth way we attend to one another.

God's persistent love, experienced as love by those who accept it in faith and hope, must be experienced as wrath by those who reject or ignore it. That is the teaching if St. John of the Cross, who says that it is the same "Living Flame of Love" which purges, wounds, and cauterizes. Yet also warms, soothes, and comforts. So Paul urges us to immerse ourselves in that divine love which casts out fear, but warns us of the divine wrath that summons us to accept that love. And the wrath of God is the inevitable consequence of God's passionate pursuit of every human person, every person foolishly foiled by insouciance or insubordination. Reciprocally, the ardor, fervent constancy, and stunning fidelity of God's love is confirmed in Christ and revealed as unspeakably, immeasurably wonderful. The awful mystery of God disclosed in Christ is all the more ineffable. What a pathetic plight we would founder in forever without Christ! So Paul cannot afford to be pedantic, academic, disinterested. He is embroiled! And he is responsible. By the grace of God, divine pathos, he will overcome. And indeed he does, attested to by the extraordinary evangelizing consequences of his prodigious energy.

So much of the love talk today is often nothing more than sentimental posturing. Even our anger is often little more than a bit of petulance over a peripheral private wound suffered in a childish skirmish and therefore not of paramount importance. Unfortunately, there is a widespread compulsion today to "feel comfortable" with every one and everything and to identify that feeling with love or goodness.

But Paul speaks as frequently and potently of the wrath of God as of the love and both in terms of a steadfast and militant realism. This doughty defender of the rights of God does not permit us to wallow in sentimental illusions about God's love, nor delusions of our own lovable-ness, nor about our harmony with the Creator, creation, or ourselves. We must face the formidable abyss between ourselves and the Wholly Other. We must allow the radical rupture in our relationship with God to be healed. We are by birth, as members of the human race, children of wrath (Eph. 2:11-13); and this wrath sets the stage for the drama of divine love, and is indeed itself a vehicle of that love. Paul never forgets this human predicament. He strongly resists those who do and roars with indignation!

But he is not depressed by the human condition. He knows nothing of Jansenistic rigorism or Calvinistic grimness. Nor does he vainly luxuriate in "high IQ whimpering" *à la* Sartre. He faces the problems of a recalcitrant human nature, copes victoriously, and becomes free. He then unwaveringly proclaims the way to freedom, the way out of the "flesh," the world of endless means, naïvely referred to as "civilization as we know it." Like a thunderclap, Paul expresses the way out of the maelstrom and across the abyss into freedom by pointing to Christ and announcing with wild joy and wonder: "We have a pontiff"; we have a bridge over the gulf between human and divine.

Paul rampaged all over the eastern Mediterranean from Antioch, Syria to Rome, Italy, pouring out written and spoken words, worrying the philosophical bones of Greeks and Romans with biblical metaphors, flailing Jewish minds with biblical scorpions. He was an unrelenting gnat on the rump of the world. To be rid of him they finally cut off his head. But not before he had transformed an awful lot of matter in the fire of his spirit, the spirit of Christ in him.

A MARRIED MYSTIC

Elizabeth of Hungary was born in 1207 in Pressburg. She was "perfect in body, handsome, of dark complexion." At fourteen she married a childhood friend, Louis (Ludwig) of the Thuringian court, at the castle of Wartburg. They were deeply in love. She died in 1231 at the age of twenty-four.

Elizabeth was thoroughly human and completely natural. She was a saint because all her good human stuff was raised to the limit, the utmost possibility of her being. She was—and this is the essence of sanctity—a great lover. She had a generous heart with an incomparable capacity for self-giving. The life of the spirit in her raised all her naturally good and lively vibrations to a higher dimension, giving them a quality of glory and finality, as it lifted her loving soul into the sphere of Infinite Being. The risk involved was enormous, the love was perilous, the courage demanded was heroic. The sanctification of Elizabeth was as dangerous as an avalanche, sweeping away all the boundaries and landmarks of a well-ordered life and renewing the face of the Earth. The base of her whole sanctifying process was her passion—pure eros—the fire of her unbridled, exuberant nature. Her zestful, Zorbatic involvement in life has a lucent quality that even the most casual observer cannot overlook.

Elizabeth was a great lover of God and creation. Her passionate devotion to the living God subdued inordinate desires and addictive human behavior. The fire of God's grace drove out sloth and indolence. Her soul was on fire with the white heat of the mystical life. White heat cannot be contained. Why shouldn't the blood catch fire from a white-hot soul? It does. That is why, in Elizabeth's case, her spiritual life was, among other things, a vibrantly rich emotional life. Elizabeth did not find the love of God incompatible with a real, natural, burning love of a human being. When Louis "took the cross" and went off crusading, she knew the pain of parting, of anguished and unappeasable loneliness. In her unbounded and vehement love, her grief over the absence of her husband was unreasonable, despairing: screaming and weeping she rushed through the castle like a person demented. She sank into a sea of sorrow, submerged beyond rescue in the dark waves of depression. No pious prattle or friendly stroking could assuage her. Neither could brilliant rationalizations. There was no need, for she was glorifying God by her passionate human feelings, by her erotic flesh and her boiling blood.

In her husband's absence she hungered for his caress; when they dwelt together she expressed her affection for him with a boundless measure of blissful joy. She even demonstrated her emotion publicly with unself-conscious abandon, kissing him "right heartily with more than thousand kisses on the mouth!" This bouncy, sexy Hungarian princess made her husband happy in the ways that fiercely devoted, playfully saucy wives usually do. And Ludwig reciprocated with equally fierce devotion.

Elizabeth was not wedded to things. Who, in love, ever is? Ultimately she was married to God alone. Paradoxically, her prince, her spouse, was part of that "alone." After all, God is not one more thing, not even the highest or the best, that replaces another thing. He is the All. As Thomas Merton explains in his classic *Contemplation in a World of Action*: "The one thing necessary is not that which is left when everything is crossed off, but it is perhaps that which includes and embraces everything else, that which is arrived at when you've added up everything and gone far beyond."

This holy woman was driven by the mightiest power in the world, the love of God: not the love of God in a vacuum, not even the love of God in her head, but God's supra-personal love, intimately in touch with and enflaming her own untamed nature with terrific force. She was ingenuously oblivious of her radiance from the divine fire within, but she suffered from the scorching heat of its purifying flames.

What stands out in the spiritual life of this remarkable woman is her full-bodied, creative participation in life, her own brand of personal, passionate presence. Look at her care of the sick and poor: a far cry from our sensible and practical welfare work and organized charity. Elizabeth is passionately personal and intimate, inspired by her love of persons and by her own willful determination—however hard and unpleasant—to be her best self. A "best" self is always one that overflows. And so the princess sought out even the most scurfy lepers. Publicly and secretly she regarded her royal position with arch scorn, as she took the lowest places and engaged in the meanest and most disgusting services to make others happy.

The words of Mother Teresa, doing "something beautiful for God" in India, might have been spoken by Elizabeth herself in thirteenth-century Hungary: "Without our suffering, our work would just be social work, very good and helpful, but...not part of the Redemption...all the desolation of the poor people, not only their material poverty, but their spiritual destitution, must be redeemed, and we must share it, for only by being one with them can we redeem them."

Like Christ, who multiplied enough loaves to feed the multitudes, so moved was He by a hillside of hungry people, Elizabeth cleaned out her palace pantry to feed the hungry townspeople. As did Mother Teresa after her, she gave the poor not only her care but also her heart. She did not merely feed them from her opulent and privileged position but dressed like them and dwelt with them and shared their poverty as well as their freedom from the pomposities and absurdities of the shackled rich. Shortly after her marriage, she rescued a deserted leper and put him in her bridal chamber. Her mother-in-law was horrified; but her husband understood. Her perfection was so relational and right that God's hold on her did not deprive her of charming imperfections and colorful eccentricities!

RICH EMOTIONS

What a boon it is to find such strong emotions in a saint! If you strip a saint of her feelings, you dehumanize the best image and likeness of God available to us. Sweet and vapid froth may characterize dainty men and women, but certainly not a saint. A holy human being is an unparalleled example of wholeness, a well-ordered version of wildness. Such a live person cannot be deprived of the vital force of emotion, a reality that must invest the mind if it is to catch fire and move from mere notions into vital motions of love. When the Lord God of Israel becomes my Lord, my friend, my beloved, then an emotion of high quality, profound depth, and creative energy takes hold of me, and I begin to live life fully. The pettiness, coldness, and mediocrity of my former existence now seem bizarre and grotesque.

Only persons of powerful passion commit themselves unconditionally to supreme values and thus realize union with God. Earthly love takes possession of unclaimed territory. That is why a vacuous life is a precarious one. An uncommitted person is bound to fall prey to worldly allurements. Paltry passions give way to the latest fads and fashions, the most popular opinions and the lightest opposition. But if we love God passionately and intensely, then we do not need to draw narrow boundaries around our love of His creatures. There is no bad love, only bad relationships. We cannot love too much. Bad relationships are due to insufficient love, a love that is either diverted or distorted by an inflated or insecure ego.

Capacity for love is perhaps the only indispensable natural foundation for holiness. I must possess the power and impetus, the wings of the soul, to forget myself for another's sake, to prize another more than myself, to face fear and pain for another, and to risk my life. Friendship with God depends on this.

All human friendships depend upon a central Godward dimension. A hundred really good friends cannot take the place of God; nor can they quench the divine thirst that impels us into silent and solitary prayer. Elizabeth was a prodigiously active woman, but her action was the fruit of her contemplation. Every weak age in the history of the Church is an excessively social and horizontal epoch. Why is this? Because people who are without God are bound to panic and, in their hysteria, to become excessively important to one another.

The saints had all sorts of defects. But not one of them was ever apathetic. Have you ever witnessed suffering enclose a friend and exclude you? It's almost unbearable. The real lover will go to any extreme to overcome such exclusion. I read about a mother who sat on the street for hours every day with her blind son. She stayed with him in the bright light of a summer day with her eyes shut so that she might not be better off than he. We all have done something like that somehow or other in the course of our lives. When our Saluki dogs were lost in the woods of Nova Scotia for many wintry days and nights, I used to walk for miles without a flashlight into the wet thickness of the pitch-dark woods, not only in search of them but, even more, to share their plight.

Elizabeth's whole life was ruled by compassion far higher than this: the dynamic effect of an extraordinary convergence between God's passion and hers. The God she loved was not a separate God but a God *pro nobis*, for us, a God in love and incarnate in history. Elizabeth found God in the crowned king and the village clown. She perceived Him most of all and was supremely enraptured by Him in her princely husband. One day at Mass her gaze fell upon her spouse in his festive array. She was so deeply moved by the beauty of the sight that she forgot she was at Mass until aroused by the bell! There was nothing merely "soulful" about her brand of Christianity. Too bad D.H. Lawrence and Nietzsche didn't know about her! They would have been less appalled by the sickly, soulful style of Christian living they so roundly and rightly deplored in their writings.

Though there was something noticeably luminous, even ecstatic, about Elizabeth, she was more earthy than ethereal; and not esoteric at all. Creatures attracted and delighted her but did not imprison her. The more she loved God, the more she seemed to prize creatures. She never gave in to the pilgrim's temptation, which takes two forms. One is to weary of the road and build a premature refuge in the creature for warmth and protection against the troubling immensity of the invisible, the call of eternity. The other is to evade the responsible suffering that loving participation in the contingent and continually changing human situation demands of us, by turning in childish, petulant spite against all lovely or worldly creatures and all sociopolitical events as base or contemptible, declaring flight our only salvation.

It was not aloofness or affluence that made Elizabeth noble. She rescued palace life from the officious boredom, tedious trumpery, and extravagant pageantry to which bored and fettered people are prone. Nobility in human beings intensifies their personal response to created goods. Desire and hunger for created happiness increase because they mirror eternal values. Everything becomes far more valuable to one who has been touched and seized by God. The greedy and lustful are out of touch and do not know how to adore.

Elizabeth's life was a passion precisely because it was a challenge: a choice between an abundance of consumer goods and the absolutely consuming God. Through her primal intuitions and humble, attentive attitudes, Elizabeth perceived penetratingly and perseveringly the difference between the light of a thousand candles and the brightness of the sun. Her struggle was between her ego and her higher self, between her petty role as princess and her regnant role as bride of Christ and, therefore, as suffering servant. Our human struggle is always with God, His unconditional demands of love, His relentless pursuit, and haunting, heartbreaking summons. If we back away from this central human contest, we who are gamblers and contesters by nature are bound to fabricate another contest, dramatizing and dressing it up with panache and panoply characteristic of daredevil Evel Knievel. We see this same phenomenon in all the fanciful forms of demonology prevalent in human history. The macabre image of an externalized, circumscribed entity of evil called the devil must certainly be one of our most famous defenses against a duel-to-death with God, as well as one of our most blatant projections of personal rapacity and capacity for evil.

Our goods demoralize and debilitate us when we get hooked on them. We become so enthralled by the goods of this narrowly limited world that we do not even recognize how merciful and wise God is when He takes away some good before it destroys us. Everything we have, from the commonest to the rarest, is a gift: to be prized, indeed nurtured and multiplied like the Gospel talents, but never hoarded, and never valued more than Giver. Creatures are supportive. Without them we would cast about convulsively in a hallowing wilderness. But they cannot sustain and satisfy us forever. That fact need not discourage us anymore than it did Elizabeth of Hungary. All we need to know, as she knew with such carefree certainty, is this: When the support of creature breaks under us, the only abyss we can fall into is the hand of God.

Elizabeth did not allow creatures, not even human beings, to become the all-absorbing end of her life. But neither did she treat them as mere means, functional adjuncts of her own self-realization or sanctification. Elizabeth did not love God instead of or in place of humanity, which happens when our neighbors become casual mediums, no longer persons. Love "practices" on them, sees them no longer, goes straight through them like a glass—to God. This is a sinister exploitation of the human person who is treated thus as mere thing and degraded to the status of a chance concomitant of God's service. No, as with Elizabeth, the stranger must become a friend for my Friend's sake; not just an instrument or occasion but a person whom I love. But I never lose sight of my missing Friend. I hear the name by which God calls him. As Mother Teresa again demonstrates: "The difference between them [social workers] and us is that they were doing it for something and we are doing it for somebody....We give it and we do it to God, to Christ, and that's why we try to do it as beautifully as possible."

The glory of God's creation outshines all ugliness. The merely natural, the ego, is dead: the narrow self who saves his love, chooses its recipient, and gives it only to a few. The liberated man raised up by the risen Christ has come alive; the same human love, and no other, streams from the new God-born self, extravagant, burning, now awake to keenest sensibility; unfettered for the first time, boundlessly free from every barrier of selfish caution, from every parsimonious withholding, bold enough to dare an overflowing tenderness, sowing now with both hands, conscious of inexhaustible risks. No condescension, but *agape*. Disposed to all, a slave to none. Giving to all, but belonging to none but God.

We are so thwarted by small, narrow, and oblique paths. We were secretly pledged long ago by God to hidden laws whose mysterious inexorability our teachers of methods of perfection cannot fathom. Elizabeth of Hungary knew how limited and lackluster all spiritual practices and religious programs are, and how ineffective even highly developed techniques can be. She knew she could not sanctify herself. Her attitude is caught in the striking words of Rainer Maria Rilke's *Stundenbuch (The Book of Hours)*: "I weigh and count myself, my God, but Thou has the right to squander me."

THE PASSIONATE MAIDEN

Joan of Arc was born in 1412 at Domremy, a little village of Champagne on the bank of Meuse, and was burnt at the stake when she was only nineteen. Her original trial and verdict were officially made void in 1451 but she was not canonized until 464 years later in 1915. Joan of Arc had enough passion to evoke the hero locked up in the unconscious soul of France. Through the voices of her "saints" she heard the cries of the living and dead of that great nation. She took those voices seriously, responded to the challenge and made history. The ramifications of this history reached far beyond French borders. England and then America were also profoundly affected. There are historical reasons for saying that we owe our faith to Joan of Arc.

Joan took the world seriously, loved it, and sacrificed herself for it. Through her life of prayer and contemplation she learned her missions, a purely earthly and worldly one: to expel an enemy, free a people from unendurable political misery, and set a rightful king on his throne. There was no spiritual overtone. Like Elizabeth, Joan was faithful to two kings, the King of Heaven and the king of France. She feared only that in betraying one she would betray the other.

Joan understood that the misery of her world was rooted in sin. Such distress was not simply "willed by God." Revealed in it lighting flashes of terror and human anguish was the offended will of God, the transgressed law of the Most High. For God had promised that His laws would secure honor, peace, and order only so long as they were obeyed. Men mocked at this instruction, destroyed the dikes that God's wisdom had created; and the floods of wickedness flowed in, raging and ruthless. Joan must come to the rescue. The angel tells her nothing but that she, the "daughter of God," must lead the fight for the Father's will against the evil of the world. A little girl from a Lorraine village is the chosen one of God, for she herself feels responsible for the sin and fate of her people. Joan lays the blame nowhere but on her own shoulders and takes her stand before God, asking His command.

Where worldly reality is so dense that seemingly no glimmer of divine light can break through, where opposing forces of evil rise up in all their violent ugliness, there lurks the temptation to despair: to doubt the victory of God's will. There lurks the temptation to assume that certain areas of human life: the political, the social, the economic arena are hopeless, inherently lost, beyond redemption. We feel we must flee this arena to remain untainted; renunciation of the world becomes the sole means of protection from it. If we are "dragged into" it, we will as part and parcel of it, be delivered to its evil powers, refusing obedience to God in order to survive. The disorder of the world is incurable, we say; the world cannot be reborn or remodeled. We can only create and fortify special enclaves within the world, governed by particular regulations, which enable us to follow the will of God alone. The world is doomed to destruction and is hardly worth anybody's bother. Why be concerned? Why sweat it or shed blood in battle for it? Better to confine ourselves to the eternal sphere, the realm of the imperishable or "purely spiritual."

TAKING THE WORLD SERIOUSLY

The passionate maid overcame all such temptation. She was in the world, in the midst of its awful vanity, in order to be tested by it. The will of God would indeed fulfill itself in the world; hence, the world must be taken with utter seriousness. God is an incarnated God. In the vanity of the world sin is committed and confusion wrought, but there, too, we find fidelity, steadfastness, and redemption. Joan's mission was to subject the mighty vanity of the world to the will of the Most High God. This was no empty test, no artificial contrivance, no exercise in pure obedience. Laid upon her was a task capable of fulfillment, a genuine opportunity for her to save her people and secure their liberty. But she was charged to try, not to succeed. Ah! There's the crux of it!

Joan's mission was supernaturally received, to be fulfilled by natural means: troops, strategy, gold. No legions of angels were promised her. St. Michael was to advise her, not fight for her. She was not invulnerable to cut or thrust, nor immune from mishap or illness. She was a sober saint, a truly peasant woman. There was no romantic air about her behavior. People asked in vain for signs and wonders; she asked for soldiers.

She conquered as she fell, preferring death to adjuration. She conquered, and her funeral pyre, which could not consumer her heart, remains a symbol of the utter powerlessness of violence over the soul. She fell, of course, forsaken, conscious of defeat and shame. Else her sacrifice could not be complete; victory must be won at such a price.

In the intensity of Joan's human struggle to stamp the lost and refractory world with the seal of God's will, the question of personal holiness or personal salvation sinks into insignificance. Joan "sought" these only in unconditional surrender to her mission; for her, questions of manner and method did not arise.

It is remarkable that in Joan's life, as in Elizabeth's, a systematic asceticism plays no part, or at least we are not aware of it. Prayer is certainly primary. No Christian life, ordinary or extraordinary, is conceivable without prayer. Joan prayed a great deal as a shepherdess with her sheep. Mass was celebrated daily in her camp and daily she received the Body of Christ in the Eucharist. The withdrawal of the sacrament was the worst and most malicious torture of her long martyrdom. Joan was so totally immersed in existence, so unequivocally caught up in a worldly God-centeredness, she did not need to prod and push herself into life with a stiff upper lip. Life itself was her asceticism precisely because she was so passionately alive, so willing to suffer whatever the glory of her nation and her God required of her.

But the question of asceticism as a spiritual practice, as a turning away from the world, as bodily mortification, did not seem to occur in her life at all. She
knew nothing of the great controversy about the holy
poverty that had occupied ecclesiastical circles for decades. She knew no fear of the things of the world.
She loved magnificence and even luxury—fine weap-
ons, clothes, and horses—as naturally as she loved
her village simplicity and the rigor of camp. She did
not shrink from accepting joyfully silver armor and
splendid saddle and harness; she chose costly material for her banner, and bright colors, loving it "forty
times more than her sword." During her examination
before her persecutors she replied with simple pride to
a question about her horse. "Which?" she asked, "For
I had four." With unruffled tranquility of spirit she accepted title and coat of arms, presents and privileges.
She did not shy away from the excessive enthusiasm
and adulation of the people who swarmed about her
as she rode into the provincial capital. She had no fear
of the splendor of the court with its feasting and mas-
tered its ceremony with untroubled grace. She hated
only the noise and roughness of the drinking bouts.
She reveled with the rest in knightly play with steed
and lance.

Joan is the maiden with pure and undivided heart,
absorbed by a singular passion. But her maidenhood
is in no way hidden from men with veil or enclosure.

Her attitude is so unmistakable in its sheer ap-
proachability, in its consecrated inviolability, that
men never appear in the guise of enemy or danger,
but as comrade, brother, friend. The cordiality, the
ingenuousness, the graceful freedom of her fraternal
attitude toward her soldiers and knights are extraordinary; her faithfulness to the king unexceptionable,
utter, passionate. There is never a thought that any
of these male relationships might constitute spiritual
danger.

Joan of Arc dreams of returning to the arms of her parents, to her forsaken flock of sheep, to her spindle by the fireside, and this charms her in the midst of camp life more than all her triumphs. She is a brave and obedient child, lost for the sake of a great love: love of God and of her people, but worked out in the nitty-gritty of her worldly situation. For this reason she is assuredly an inspiration and a saint for our age.

True passion create the mighty dynamic strength of a Paul, an Elizabeth, or a Joan of Arc, whose energies were all controlled and directed by a lofty ideal. These three inflamed individuals represent the ardent, vibrant tradition of the Church. How did we ever become so uninspired?

THE LITTLE WAY

The lives of Joan and Elizabeth give us concrete instances of Christian passion in person and in action. Since they may seem too heroic to be typical, it seems good to describe the passionate nature of St. Thérîse's "Little Way." This is a not a lifestyle Thérîse Martin discovered in France at the end of the nineteenth century. It is the Gospel way discerned by the "Little Flower" in her Carmel of Lisieux as she struggled with every fiber of her being to surrender unconditionally to the overtures of God's Love.

Thérîse of Lisieux, an ordinary French girl brought up in a representative family in a bourgeois society, grasped with unusual perspicacity the general paradox of Christian discipleship: maturity and childhood are somehow identical. Christ himself made the recovery of childhood the condition of discipleship and human maturity. In her *Autobiography*, Thérîse emphasizes this paradoxical identification and shows in a very unshow-offy manner how this little way is the key to understanding prayer and the mystical life.

My own experience as spiritual director of so many people who have come to join our community but could not make it has led me to the following conclusion. In almost every single case the candidate who left could not survive in the stark simplicity of the contemplative life because in that person the integration of childhood and maturity never took place. I have found this to be equally true in most instances of religious or ecclesiastical defection (excuse the word, but it's a good one). Many divorces are due to the same problem.

Without the dialogue between Jesus and His Father that runs like blood through the life of Christ, we would be forced to interpret His time on Earth as catastrophic. It is the dialogue that gives positive value and meaning to His life and death. So, when His disciples asked Him to teach them to pray, he simply introduced them into the realm of this child-father dialogue. In order to experience the passionate fatherhood of God, the disciple must become passionate child: "Unless you become as little children you cannot enter into the kingdom of God" (Luke 18:17).

In order to become wholly attached to God as Father, belonging to Him with unconditional childlike trust, we must become wholesomely independent of our human parents or any earthly equivalent. Though enormously difficult for Thërîse, spoiled as she was by her father and an older sister, she did it. This was the crucial act that paved the way for her freedom and sanctification. As Freud made so painfully clear, this liberating step is difficult to take. Even today, many parents exert excessive control and a deadening influence on their children, especially grown-up children, and turn "the family" into a false Kingdom of God. Many young people are still inordinately attached to their parents and their parents' world. It is discouraging to reflect on how often the religious life and even marriage are spoiled by parental interference and family attachments. It would be salubrious for all of us to meditate more frequently on the vehemence with which Christ addressed Himself to this subject. His call is so total that once His voice is heard, we cannot even "look back" (Luke 9:62).

We cannot turn toward God without turning away from what is not God. We will discover and savor everything all at once in God, but later. First we must make the leap. Every true vocation is Zorbatic: "Every one needs a little bit of madness, otherwise we will never cut the rope and be free." We find this madness, this mature childhood, in the doctrine and experience of the great Christian mystics. We find it also at the creative center of any good spiritual writer.

Trying to describe prayer, many of the mystics found that the best image was a child speaking to the father; and the father is God. The best possible prayer is the great filial prayer of Christ, the Lord's Prayer, a prayer for all of us, at all times, on any spiritual level. As St. Teresa of Avila points out in her writings and demonstrates in her own life, the highest degrees of contemplation can be reached in one Our Father well said. Our prayer, even the Lord's Prayer, is no good unless it expresses our own inner truth or, at least, what we most desire to be true. Our lives must be as childlike, ardent, and truthful as our prayer.

I found an insight into this subject that is so stunning I am going to quote a whole page from an article by the distinguished Irish philosopher Fr. Noel Dermot O'Donoghue, O.C.D., a professor at Edinburgh University:

> *Essentially the Christian way of childhood is a way of entry into the Trinitarian mystery of fatherhood, filiation and that eternal breathing of love which is the Holy Spirit. The life and death of Jesus of Nazareth is the revelation of eternal childhood in*

*history. The Eucharist is the most complete reca-
pitulation in practical surroundings but now open
to all that is, to God and men and all creation. It is
a creative involvement in the dynamism of creation.
It identifies with creation at the point where all creation is prayer, a response to the God who creates
because He loves. It is not easy to achieve, because
it demands detachment from the possessive self and
from all that is finite and particular, and it is never
finally achieved. But it must be emphasized that the
detachment is only the negative side; positively what
is in question is a deep warmth and tenderness, an
all-fathering, all-mothering love, for the child of God
shares His father's attitude towards creation. It is
in the child as beauty is in the flower; it is only in
maturity that a human being can make His own of it,
can detach the ideal of it and make it a loving ideal.*

*As I see it, the basic dynamism of prayer, espe-
cially mystical prayers, is the affectivity of childhood,
enlarged, refined and purified through experience.
Experience presents us with much that is easy to accept, but it also presents us with the cross, and this
is not easy to accept, certainly it is not easy to accept
with open arms. Yet it is only insofar as we open our
arms to the world and that we can open our arms to
God in filial love. It is the cross that extends our affection beyond the particular; in fact the very process
of detachment from particular love is no small part of
the experience of the cross. Mystical prayer is essentially the expression of a love that has grown beyond
the particular, especially of the particular persons.
This love is full of pathos and loneliness, for it is an
exile in the world; it is always being misunderstood
in its most innocent and spontaneous expressions
and manifestations, for the world can only understand love grossly, having lost childhood. It is deeply*

marked with the sign of the cross; otherwise it is not genuine. Yet if there is any state that may be termed blessed and heavenly it is here it is found, here and in the most perfect days of childhood.

I think it must be admitted that the mystic will always be at odds with the world. There is nothing worldly man, especially if he be a successful and respected clergyman, judges so quickly and so harshly as the mystical and the mystic, since he has by the very nature of this gift the simplicity of a child and leaves himself wide open to the judgment. Yet I do not despair that the world may change in this matter. Rather, it seems to me, the world will have to change in this, or else one has to despair of the world. For today, for the first time in history man can destroy himself, and there is nothing more certain than that man will destroy himself utterly unless there is a change in the forces within him from which his decisions spring. The balance must shift from the performance principle and all its attendant ambitions and hatreds in favor of the creative principle which has its final basis in the simple, spontaneous, as yet undifferentiated affectivity of the child. This is the way of mystical prayer. It is not a way of our own doing. It is the work of the Spirit of God. Our work is to prepare for His coming. Our prayer is that He may transform our prayer into the eternal love of the Son for the Father.

The spirituality of childhood that dominates the Christian tradition requires no strongman acts, no glittering achievements, no spectacular successes. It requires total love that lasts forever. Such a commitment to perfect love may not involve anything big or dramatic at all, but demand instead a passionate fidelity to a hundred little things.

THE CHILD, THE SAGE, AND THE CLOWN

I share the secret of the child, of saints and sages as well as of clowns and fools, when I realize how wondrous it is to carry fuel and draw water. Once the spiritual significance of such ordinary earthy acts dawns on me, I can skip the yoga and koans, the mantras and novenas.

We find pain and pleasure, ecstasy and enstasy, human and divine, in the common place. All these good, natural experiences usher us, if we let them, into the presence of God. It's better to stay home and smell a flower, bake an apple pie, or sweep the floor than have a spooky, spurious religious experience at a prayer meeting. It's better simply to enjoy the sunshine or a good movie than meddle curiously with occult. It's better to romp with the dogs in the backyard than rap with the intellectuals on campus or at church, if the dogs in the yard help us to be less egotistic and more God-centered.

Ordinarily the best contemplative activities are those where contemplation is least emphasized. Self-conscious, highly structured retreats can be less conducive to contemplation than the average city dump. The higher experiences of the spiritual life are most desirable. But they are most likely to occur if we are at home with and enjoying the daily things that fill our lives. They provide the only foundation we've got for sky-high peak experiences. If there's no foundation, there's nothing. How can we relish the higher things of God if we cannot enjoy some simple little things like a glass of beer, a boat ride, a hot tub, a good kiss, a belly laugh, walking in the rain, lying in the sun, anything that comes along as a gift from God? The inner truth of these good things is always accessible. If we stay in touch and remain faithful to them, we will be ready when God comes. But in this age of immense sophistication, vast achievement, and jaded sensibilities, the rediscovery of the secret surprise of customary objects are very rare and precious, enjoyed almost exclusively by unspoiled children, uncanonized saints, undistinguished sages, and unemployed clowns.

There is among us today a great dissatisfaction. Just below the swinging surface we suffer a dreadful tedium. But the ways we have chosen out of our torpor are extremely limited precisely because they are extreme. In our panic we want drastic, frenzied alternatives such as getting out of the Church, religious life, marriage, or getting off the Earth. We want ecstasy, which means, quite literally, standing outside, going beyond, being beside oneself. What we want is a way up or a way out, beyond the regular, repetitive commonplaces of life like cleaning house or weeding the garden.

It really doesn't matter what type of work we do or what our vocation is, the big illusion is the same: that self-realization and fulfillment lie on same fare perimeter of existence to be reached by escaping from and transcending the ordinariness of life. And for those of us who take this desperate route up and out, the prosaic dimensions of life are rendered even more boring. It is a sort of Peeping Tom mysticism; after a few lusty moments of glee, we are left thwarted and frustrated.

SACRED AND PROFANE

Our penchant for the ecstatic has distorted our concept of the sacred. We think of the sacred exclusively as time off or time away and set it up in official opposition to the profane. There are important aspects of the sacred that do indeed distinguish holy places and hallowed times from the profane. But such meaningful nuances and proper distinctions do not exhaust the meaning of the sacred. Any rigid demarcation of the sacred extends monstrously the boundaries of the profane and highlights its sphere.

The distinction between sacred and profane must be made; but it must also be overcome. This happens when, becoming like little children, we return to the world of simple things and common place events with renewed wonder and refined fascination.

We certainly do need corybantic moments, mountaintop views, serendipities, and periodic forays into unaccustomed space. But even more important is coming back, moving deeply within centering down, and dwelling there. From this ontological point of our being we can enjoy a Christic, incarnational view of the universe. The realm of everyday experience will be reaffirmed and reappreciated with our everyday minds. Once God reveals Himself in the breaking of bread, there is no need for miracles. If God has spoken and the Word was made flesh, "tongues" are superfluous. Since God has touched humanity at the core of our being, why care about healing our extremities?

If we follow the lead of the child, the sage, and the clown we may learn to discover and celebrate the sacred within the profane and respond to divine disclosures in both the squalor and splendor of the world. The child, the sage, and the clown are at home with things, seeing the shining insides and detecting all the mysterious connections among creatures. They overcome polarities and reconcile opposites. With their keen insight and cosmic inscape they can feel the vibrations of the whole Earth.

Their kinship with all that is makes them superbly compassionate. They know what it feels like to be a betrayed man, a lonely woman, a porcupine, a loon, a broken chair, a ripe mushroom, or a steaming mug of coffee.

If children, sages, and clowns sometimes profane holy things, it is in order to reveal the holiness of the profane. The king's crown is handled like an old straw hat while an old matchbox is guarded like a treasure chest. By means of their naïveté, eccentricity, or buffoonery, they humble the exalted and exalt the humble. They puncture and lampoon inflated nobility, uncover and mock vulgarity. They restore thrilling significance to the simplest of things: a penny, a cane, a shy smile, a rakish wink, a pat on the head, or a hop, skip, and a jump. Their lives glow with extraordinary luminosity amidst the most ordinary circumstances. In a million undreamed of but perfectly natural ways they show how the fat lady, rocking away on her porch, or squeezing onto the subway, is Christ. "Come, let us have a cup of tea" is hardly distinguishable from "Come, follow me." The beauty and majesty of so much driftwood teach us the same lesson; so do exquisitely artistic creations made of old matchsticks and pieces of soap; so did those frames of glory that one hung on the walls of our main lodge at our Nova Nada Hermitage: dribs and drabs of nature's debris that Tessa found on the forest floor and brought to life again by her imagination, dexterity, and recreative love.

Unfortunately, we have not been inspired enough by children, sages, or clowns. And so we have lost our only possible way into the Kingdom of God: the passionate way of childhood, wisdom, and humor. We have behaved more like a chain gang than children of God, as we moved desperately from methodological meditation to pharmacological mysticism into charismatic intoxication. Instead of breaking out of our prison the way Paul Newman did in *Cool Hand Luke,* we have smuggled into our enslaved way of life hopeless forms of diversion, secular techniques, and religious devices, from demonology and witchcraft to magic, occultism, and astrology. Progress, bigness, happiness, and novelties of all kinds have been promised us as long as we remain in our prisons.

British spiritual writer Caryll Houselander once

said that the divine architect made the doorway into heaven so small that only children can manage to get through. I would say the same thing about our prison doorways. Only children can get out. So Christ adamantly insisted that we grow up, be reborn, and become as little children. Everything else is prison talk and prison behavior, no matter how eloquent. Once we are out in the clear we can forget about the high-flying gods and the subterranean demons. We can stop flexing our muscles and revving our engines and abandon all other ego trips that made prison life bearable. Now we can relax. We are close to Earth again. No need for heady Apollonian flights into space or Dionysian descents into fuliginous darkness. We are already close to God. As mature children a new path has opened up for us, the Little Way, a Way of utter simplicity, of ordinary pleasures and common place delights.

Baal Shem Tov, founder of the Hasidic movement, particularly cherished the following story, found in the Talmud:

> Rabbi Beroka used to visit the marketplace where the prophet Elijah often appeared to him. It was believed that he appeared to some saintly men to offer them spiritual guidance.
> Once Beroka asked the prophet, "Is there anyone here who has a share in the world to come?" He replied, "No."
> While they were conversing two men passed by, and Elijah remarked, "These two men have a share in the world to come." Rabbi Beroka then approached and asked them, "What is your occupation?" They replied, "We are jesters. When we see men depressed, we cheer them up."

These two men knew the way of the child, the sage, and the clown!

AUTHOR'S NOTE

The reflections on Elizabeth of Hungary are based on notes I took years ago on various "lives" of Elizabeth and on old notes of "emotions in the sanctifying process" based on a dialogue with Ida Gorres, who, I am sure, is the one most responsible for my own love of St. Elizabeth and who formed many of Elizabethan sentiments expressed in this chapter. The reflections on Joan of Arc are based on notes after a lecture by and visit with Cardinal John Wright, and originally published in *Desert Call* (Winter, 1973).

The Human Spirit

The Human response to God's initiative, the exquisite act we call prayer, must, if true, possess three qualities and be personal, passionate, and present. These impressive characteristics make prayer the human act *par excellence.* The person who does not pray is not fully human.

Prayer is not a need that psychology and sociology can explain. It is an ontological necessity. Only ontology can explain it. To live without prayer is to live without God. One goes through the motion of life but is, in fact, a dead soul. We pray because God is present. Once we sense the Divine Presence and become aware of the ineffable, we are bound to pray. The whole liturgical life of the Church is due to key insights called the "deposit of faith." When I realize that God has more life and is more real than I, then I inevitably pray.

Prayer is not for the sake of something else. We pray in order to pray. It is so good in itself that it needs no reason or action outside itself to justify it. If God addresses us there is nothing to do but respond. This attentive presence to God is not a duty but a pleasure

and privilege. Whenever our culture is in serious decline, there is a regrettable decrease in the pleasure of
God's company.

The essence of Christian life is worship. Our worship reveals whether we serve God or an idea of God.
As Abraham Heschel was fond of saying, "Prayer is of
no importance unless it is of supreme importance."

Is a certain high quality of piety required for prayer?
No. But a high quality of life is required. Prayer should
be full of life, but living itself is not enough because
we can let too many things happen to us and miss the
prize, the full life of Spirit. We need to be selective and
mindfully discriminating. We need to make deliberate
choices. Being is a blessing and living is holy. And yet,
to be or not to be is not the question. Seeds of suicide
and destruction exist within life itself. The question
is, therefore, *how* do we live or not live? Are we reverently related and faithfully committed or not? Are we
centered in the sacred and rooted in the holy or not?
Can we not feel the excitement, the chase, the Hound
of Heaven closing in or, unbearable dread, the Hound
(the Love) closed out? In a definite sense quality living means "style." The saints had style. If you are a
"touched sinner," a contemporary saint, a disciplined
wild man or woman, you are bound to have style; not
fustian but pure and simple style.

Living prayer will also be true. Truth is maintained
only when the words remain sacred, pure, and, as
much as possible, primordial. Without these holy, reverent words, prayer becomes vulgar. Evagrius of Pon-
tus, one of the original Christian thinkers, said: "The
theologian is one whose prayer is true." He means all
of us, of course, when our hearts are open to God's
revelation.

The Jews stake everything on this ability to direct
the human heart attentively to the Father. Their word
for this is *havanah:* an act of *appreciation* for being

able to stand in the presence of God. The basic attitudes of worship are evoked: awe, wonder, and radical amazement. *Havanah* also means witnessing to God, being zealous for extending His rights. How often Christians behave cowardly in the face of evil. Not only do we not protest; we even support the evildoer with such inanities as "She's following her path" or "He's changed his vehicle." Inanities like that make infallible truth more attractive to me than ever!

We find a good example of *havanah* in Matthew 26:41: "Stay awake, and pray not to be put to the test. The spirit is willing enough, but human nature is weak."

So, one reason we pray is that God commands us to pray, and not out of fear of judgment or punishment but with a liberating obedience we offer gladly. This involves no passivity. We pray for strength to combat the urge (so typical of modern man) to declare that all is nothingness; for stamina and the will to fight evil in ourselves and our milieu. Fighting is an important part of prayer: fighting for our freedom, our stillness, and our life; fighting for victory over selfism. The struggle with God Himself is paramount. We must insist that God reveal and declare Himself and enter into our salvation. It seems to me that God is more likely to respond to our universal emergencies than our requests for small comforts and cheap benefactions.

Prayer is the ultimate act of hope in a world where we choke so easily on the acrid smoke of despair. Every moment of prayer is eschatological: a combat against death and nothingness, so that our youth is renewed and life really lived.

There is new interest in prayer today, but in prayer unconnected with liturgy, Scripture, and theology; a prayer that does not meet or interrelate significantly on all levels of human engagement. The personal and central aspect of prayer is missing.

Karl Barth was the quintessential biblical theologian. Anxious to ground prayer in the biblical tradition, he suggested beginning with the doctrine of the Holy Spirit, but in today's academic religious circles the emphasis is not on the Holy Spirit but on the world spirit or human spirit or simply the spirit of brotherhood. So theologians today recognize no meeting with God but with oneself in a new way. Most definitions are a version of Paul Tillich's "Meditation on the Ground of Being." When asked if he prayed to the "Ground" he said: "I meditate." Me too. Until God comes.

The closest theologians (or novelists) have ever come to describing the humanizing process is in terms of our spousal relationship to God. God is love. Praying is fanning the flames of love so that it becomes a consuming fire.

DISCIPLINED WILDNESS

God is so infinitely lovable that once we get to know Him, we come to love Him, and once we love Him, though we enjoy a vibrant tranquility of being, we suffer an existential anxiety that God's name be hallowed, His will be done, and God's Kingdom come throughout the whole world.

Neurotic anxiety robs us of creativity. But existential anxiety keeps us close to the vital center of the human adventure. St. Paul went running toward that center, trying to sweep everyone into the race: "I am in anxiety until Christ be formed in you." Paul was racing toward the Christian goal: transformation into Christ which means *freedom.*

For the liberated Christian there is no law except *love.* As St. Bernard said: "To Love God is to love Him without measure." Such boundless love makes us wild. That is why the Christian, or at least the saint, the really live Christian, must be a *disciplined wild man or woman.* Conformation to Christ, thinking, loving, and acting like Him, require a rugged, unflinching discipline; but when the Spirit of God irrupts in us as it irrupted in Jesus, a christening transformation occurs, fire is ignited. When we blaze with the incandescent presence of God, no law is needed because the law has been fulfilled.

God's mysterious and momentous secret is not wrested by intellectual acumen or willful determination; nor is it stolen by the clandestine night raids of aggressive occultism or the Promethean pilfering of esoteric spiritual technique. Neither is formidable self-control or flawless psychophysical development. According to the New Testament, it is only those of contrite and humble heart whom God will not resist. It is up to God to reveal Himself, and He has never done so except to a man or woman or child of prayer. People of prayer live by faith. Without faith there is no prayer, and without prayer there is no faith; at least there is not enough faith to keep us alive to God and open to the graceful possibilities of our own deification.

CRY OF THE HEART

Faith is the response of the whole person to the Word of God ("I love you") and its reverberations in all creature and all human events. Prayer is a spontaneous cry of the heart, sometimes in jubilant exultation, sometimes poignant anguish, often in the stunned silence of adoration or the transforming union of love.

Just as faith is a human response to divine initiative, so prayer is a human response to the dialogic overtures of God. Prayer is the most personal act possible. Making prayer to God is more intimate than making love to a spouse. There is a part of a woman so personally and privately inscrutable that even her husband may not trespass. This is equally true of the husband. The inner sanctuary of every human being is exposed only to God's holy scrutiny. It is precisely then, when we are most transparently exposed and radically embarrassed in the presence of God, that we are most human.

How can you plan on sharing that kind of prayer? Apart from the liturgy, it is hard to imagine shared prayer being a spontaneous cry of the heart at all. Prayer is often profaned and desecrated by rigid, static structures as well as by cozy, informal, "anything goes" shared prayer groups. Such groups often end up in therapy rather than prayer. But since the conscious motive for getting together is prayer, the group ordinarily becomes unctuously and vociferously *prayer-conscious* instead of self-obliviously and worshipfully *God-conscious*.

Jesus never got together with His friends for the express purpose of sharing prayer. He prayed in the temple, of course, and He prayed on prayerful occasions when others happened to be around; but He was never involved in any prayer programs or groups. Even when His disciples asked him to teach them to pray, Christ taught them the Our Father but did not pray with them. He did what the evangelists said He always did: He went off by himself to pray (cf. Matt. 14:23). He practiced what He preached in Matthew 6:6: "When you pray, go into your room, shut the door and pray to your Father in secret." The Spirit of Christ, and therefore His prayer, was too wild to be corralled.

Prayer is such a free, spontaneous human act that it cannot even be taught. Some words that serve as vehicles of prayer may be taught, but not the veritable acts of prayer. All we can do is set the stage as humanly as possible, immerse ourselves fully in life, and hope that God will sanctify us.

God came into the world "that we might have life and have it more abundantly" (John 10:10). God empowers us and challenges us to live fully and for this reason commands us to pray. Every decade the world will come up with reasons why we should or should not pray. It does not matter. Each one of us is commanded not by the law, but by the Lord "to watch and pray...to pray without ceasing" (Matt. 26:41; 1 Thess. 5:17). Even when there seems to be reason to pray no success at prayer, the faithful pray out of obedience. Every time they pray, their lives are enhanced and the world enlivened. Live men and women, perhaps devoid of any religious feeling but responsibly in touch with God through prayer, are to be reckoned with. They alone can break through the social, political and religious barriers and become transparent instruments of God's power and peace in the world.

We are all required to venture forth as humanly as possible. The absence of prayer in the modern world, as well as the bizarre forms of pseudo-prayer, is due to our dehumanized and denatured condition. We need to learn to be human again in order to pray. We need to become less crowded, less rushed, less dispersed, less victimized by the tyranny of diversion. We need to simplify our lives. We need to "collect" ourselves in periods of silence and places of solitude, not in order to withdraw or isolate ourselves from others, but in order to relate more thoughtfully and lovingly to some of the others. *We need to lean to meditate.*

Prayer can best be appreciated once we have learned how natural it is to meditate, how congenial and indispensable if we are to live a fully human life. Meditating liberates us from the compulsive drive of our desires; it evokes the deepest and most real dimensions of the authentic self; it *re-collects* the scattered forces of our fragmented lives so that we can discover the basic rhythm of human existence. In meditation, properly understood and perseveringly practiced, the whole person is actualized and the center of our being awakened. The right thoughts, words, and deeds come to us when we are truly awake.

Meditation collects, unifies, and integrates a human being. Prayer raises the mind and heart to God. What's the use of coming into possession of myself, gaining mastery of my human instrument, if I cannot then put my beautiful "I" into relationship with the "Thou" of God? Why all this cold-blooded dutifulness if I cannot ultimately give my life away? Why prowl around in the fathomless and dark abysses of my soul if I cannot find the roots that become routes into a fuller life?

St. John Damascene's eighth-century definition of prayer as a raising of the mind and heart to God is a good one. From beginning to end the life of prayer is open ended; and that is why the life of the person of prayer is characterized by wildness. Men and women of prayer are men and women of God. God is wild. He is not a tame God. He does not fit into our world, our Church, or our plans. So people of prayer, the mystics, passionately devoted to this untamable God, must be, though gentle and humble, irrepressibly wild.

OCCUPATIONAL PRAYER

We can talk about prayer in a hundred different ways. I love to emphasize two dimensions: "occupational" prayer and "spousal" prayer. *Occupation*, according to the dictionary, is our chief business, our vocation. When we respond to the sovereign claim of God with unconditional seriousness, we certainly will not dissociate God from our chief business. We will not relegate God and divine things to a separate compartment called religion. Since God holds the central place in our lives and reveals Himself to some degree in every other place, we live all day in the presence of God. The divine presence is dynamic rather than static, and so it flows into all our thinking and activity. Our whole life is the spiritual life. *Occupational prayer* gives quality and power to that pedestrian life.

Everything in this world is either a sign, sample, or symbol of God. The universe is diaphanous. The world is crammed with God. In every person or event met prayerfully, there is an overriding, transcendent, unconditional character captured in the words of the prophet, "Thus saith the Lord." In every situation men and women of prayer are aware of being addressed, claimed, and sustained. And although this presence comes from *within*, there is something emphatically *Wholly Other* about it. This immanent-transcendent convergence at the deep, prayerful level of our perception is the ineffable mystery at the heart of all experience. "The beyond" is found in our midst.

Occupational prayer is possible, indeed inevitable, once we decide to live deliberately, because of our human nature and the nature of God. "We cannot rest until we rest in God," said St. Augustine. There is only one final love affair, the one with God, and our multilevel lives comprise one exploration into the Godhead. God's Being is in all beings. God penetrates the whole universe. So the anonymous author of *The Cloud of Unknowing* says: "He is the being of all....He is thy being but thou art not His." And Teilhard de Chardin speaks of "that which in everything is above everything...shining forth from the depths of every event, every element," for those with eyes to see. As Gerard Manley Hopkins writes so vividly in his poem "God's Grandeur":

> *The world is charged with the grandeur of God.*
> *It will flame out, like shining from shook foil;*
> *It gathers to a greatness, like the ooze of oil*
> *Crushed.*

Because of grace, the diffusive nature of God in the world, we are able to worship all day long at work and at play, in sickness and in health. We are in touch with the All—God who is more real than we are, closer to us than we are to ourselves. God makes love to us in wonderfully surprising ways. Worship is our response to the One who is "above all and through all and in all" (Eph. 4:4-6). Worship is seeing all in God and God in all. Anything that discloses or penetrates through to this level of reality, whether in community or in solitude, whether in talk, action, or silence, is prayer. In occupational prayer we discover God incognito: At one moment God is a cup of fresh water, the next a child bouncing on our knee, or a beautiful grandmother, a morning walk, or a nude swim in the moonlight.

I know a priest, a monk, who prays best sitting on the porch with his dog. He either talks to the dog about God or to God about the dog. And he gathers the whole world into that uplifting dialogue. I know a great big fat man who makes his best prayer floating in the ocean. With no one around to disturb him, the blue sky and brilliant sun above him, and the rollicking, rolling surf below him, he prays best. I know a college girl who makes her best prayer lying aimlessly on the beach, utterly drenched in the delicious sunshine of God's presence.

That was good prayer for the wee boy who came into church and right there at the door, intuiting God's holy, awesome presence, sank on his knees, bowed his head, and prayed: "O Lord, my name is mud." In that brief moment of humble prayer and posture of adoration, his soul was quieted and his being deeply and divinely touched, as he felt in the marrow of his boyish bones and ebullience of his youthful heart the Sonship of Christ and Fatherhood of God. There you have a mystic, one of God's wild ones. The boy has only to remain faithful.

I know a woman who makes her best prayer lying in the arms of her husband. Naked, exposed, and vulnerable, she surrenders herself unequivocally to the Beloved through her spousal self-giving. Those who see sex simply as carnal knowledge will never realize the reverent and holy affirmation of Being, the deep and adoring worship, or the profound prayer possible in conjugal celebration.

SPOUSAL PRAYER

God will never be the occupational center of our lives if we do not enjoy daily periods of *spousal prayer*. "Enjoy" is the right word, even though getting to prayer and staying there, despite a dozen good reasons to do something else, may often require a fierce determination of will. (Every time I swim I am thoroughly pleased and refreshed, but I often have to drag myself into the lake!) Enjoyment of God in daily spousal prayer is the doorway into the Kingdom, into the realization of divine union. "Knock and it shall be opened unto you," Jesus said (Luke 11:9). Knocking is the fierce and unflagging persistence of the lover who is always there.

We go to prayer because God is there. We want and need to be with Him. If God is real and we are alive to Him, then He must absorb us all by Himself a good part of every day. If God is real, and we take Him seriously, then He will draw us magnetically into prolonged periods of silence and solitude. Whether we have big jobs to do or children to feed does not matter. No other responsibilities compete with this one: to be with God, not indirectly and vicariously as we often are during occupational prayer, but directly and immediately, through intimate spousal encounter. All the apostolic or prayerful work in the world cannot

take the place of these intense and uninterrupted periods of leisurely lovemaking with God. To work is not
to pray. Strictly speaking, these two terrific human
activities are opposites. Work is the most useful human action, whereas prayer, at least on the highest
levels, is the most useless. At these higher levels of
prayer we would never think of using God; instead, all
our energy is spent loving, praising, and celebrating
God.

The man who says he believes in God but is too
busy to spend any time alone with Him in concentrated forms of prayer is like the man who claims he
loves his wife but is too busy ever to be with her. He
provides for her opulently, giving her all she could
possibly need—house, car, clothes, swimming pool,
pony—all, that is, except himself.

Without spousal prayer, occupational prayer is
impossible; so is any worthwhile kind of apostolate,
social or political action, liturgical or family renewal,
governmental or ecclesiastical reform. We cannot be
humanized unless we are divinized by the spark of
faith that is fanned into a blazing fire of love during
silent and solitary periods of prayer.

TIME AND PLACE

Once the decision has been made to spend some
time every day in holy leisure or spousal prayer, we
need to experiment with variations in time and place
until we discover the right time and the right place.
Prayer will never be confined to then and there; it will
simply be a favorite and most conducive time and
place.

One of the good results of secularization is the
breakaway from an artificial and rigid dichotomy
between sacred and profane. We are now prepared to
discover the sacred in the profane. But we still need

specially sacred places and specially sacred times. On the religious level, for instance, I have noticed with remarkable regularity how those convents and monasteries that have abandoned solitude and silence, specially sacred times and places for prayer, have been reduced to shambles. I do not see how we can discern the revelation of God everywhere unless we find it, first of all, in the historical Christ and reenacted in the Eucharist. We need a symbol of the sacred in the midst of the secular to remind us that all is scared and that we all have souls. The Church is a symbol of celebration and joy and leisure and privacy, a sign of transcendence and a point of silence and tranquility; a church is sacred space, symbolizing to us the sacredness of all space.

A favorite place for prayer may be on the roof, at the shore, on a mountaintop, in the woods, by the fireplace, in the bedroom, or the chapel. But the best of all places for prayer will always be in front of the tabernacle with the Blessed Sacrament because this is a focalizing center where the personal, embodied presence of Christ may be experienced with peculiar intensity. At our monastic retreat centers in Colorado and Ireland, both monks and guests make all-night vigils before the Blessed Sacrament in preparation for Sundays and feasts. This has not only heightened our prayer life immensely but deepened our perspective on the whole world.

Finding the right time is just as important as locating the right place. Variations in both time and place are helpful. But there will always be a particular time more conducive than others. Most people never explore nighttime as high time for prayer. We live such routine lives that even on a full-moon night the majority of us will be found in the same old condition in the same old place: sound asleep in bed. I do believe, however, that the best time of all for prayer is early in the morning. I would almost say that a good prayer life depends on getting up early in the morning.

A somewhat prolonged period of uninterrupted time is imperative. Trying to squeeze God into a busy schedule does more harm than good. Whenever I emphasize prolonged periods of prayer, even to priests, ministers, and nuns, I am asked the same question, "How do you fit it all in?" The answer is, "You don't." We all must rearrange our lives so that we fit into God's plan; so that, first of all, there is time to relax in His presence. Prayer can be as refreshing as sleep. If we would learn to pray well, we could sleep less.

One final word on the subject of time: I suggest that we stop doing half the work that presently consumes us. Then let us attend to the remaining half wholeheartedly, with contemplative vision and creative love. I stake the authenticity of our lives and the effectiveness of our work on this radical shift.

REMOTE AND PROXIMATE PREPARATION

Let us assume that we have chosen a specially sacred time and place for spousal prayer and decided there every day with unflinching regularity. What next? The wise men and women of prayer tell us that preparation is key. And they ordinarily designate two kinds of preparation: remote and proximate.

Remote preparation, first of all, is the way we think about God with our everyday minds. Prayer is primarily influenced by our general attitude toward God; and that attitude itself is shaped by our basic concepts and images of Him. If we have poor concepts and puerile images of God, our prayer is necessarily impoverished. There is one attitude in particular that prevails today and spoils prayer, and that is our casual relationship to God. If God is merely a three-letter word, another being, or just another object, then prayer will never erupt from the depths of our being. We cannot be casual with God and prayer. According to Archbishop Anthony Bloom, Russian author of excellent books on prayer, every time we move into prayer we enter the cave of a tiger, and at that moment we are either condemned or saved.

God is terrible and delightful. Only a dreadful experience of God readies us for a joyful one. We must be faithful and humble servants before we become intimate and ecstatic friends. We cannot bulldoze our way into God's presence; we cannot even work our way meritoriously into His favor; we must be seduced. We do not choose God; God chooses us. "And this is charity, not as though we have first loved God, but that He has first loved us" (1 John 3:10).

Here is a basic rule: Be slow to pray. Be sure to pray but slow to pray. God is not nice; He is not a buddy or an uncle or a mascot; He is an earthquake. We must approach Him with fear and trembling. If we preserve in prayer without spiritual pride or greed, without skipping the humble steps of an obedient servant, we will end up enlightened and intimate friends of God. According to the Bible, the beginning of wisdom is fear. This fear is ontological fear, a wonderful, awesome sense of the Numinous, the Holy One. It is very different from the psychological fear that has turned so many religious men and women either into scrupulous, frightened neurotics or pious prigs.

We need to recapture the metaphysical awe of the "pagans" and the serious vigilance of the Jews. The encounter with God in prayer is like the momentous encounter with God in death. Here are the words of a great Jewish man of prayer, the Rabbi Shlomo of Karlin, one of the Hasidim of the eighteenth century. When he was asked to promise to visit a friend, he answered: "How can you ask such a promise? Tonight I will have to pray, and when I pronounce the 'Hear

O Israel,' my soul steps out unto the very edge of life; then comes the darkness of sleep: and in the morning the great Morning Prayer that is a striding through the whole universe; and finally when I fall on my face, my soul bends over the edge of life. Maybe this one more time I will not die as yet, but how could I make any promise for after prayer?" Every time we pray we jeopardize our safety. It is a life-or-death situation. Without this attitude of holy fear, there is no prayer.

Remote preparation is also the way we think of prayer. If we regard prayer as a duty, mortification, or chore, we will never pray well. If we identify prayer with meditation, our prayer life will be stunted and our laborious lives will not be refreshed the way they need to be. Meditation is the way we ready ourselves for prayer. When we really learn to pray, we seldom meditate. We need to meditate only when we are indisposed, out of touch with God.

If we think of prayer as nothing more than a means to an end, one of the ways by which we can manage to have a good day, we may be partially empowered but never wholesomely pleasured; and we end up using God, which is deplorable. To pray in order to have a good day is not entirely wrong; as a secondary motivation it may even be good. A properly human perspective reverses this order of things: we see to it that we have a good day by living deliberately and recollectedly, so that when it is time to pray, we are ready. Here we have a reversal of values based on the Gospels. The way we spend the day is the means; prayer is the end. We accept full responsibility for the quality of the day and look forward to the privileged periods of prayer when we can *do* nothing because God is.

"The Father has uttered one Word: that Word is His Son, and He utters Him forever in everlasting silence; and in silence the soul must hear that Word," said St. John of the Cross. This *wise passiveness,* not contrived by us but induced by God is us, turns out to be the most active and important part of our life. Without any fussing or fuming, our consciousness is altered and our life radically changed. In other words, *life fully lived* is the best remote preparation for prayer; and prayer is the best part of the day and our highest human activity.

A peasant asked Giles, the Swiss hermit, what prayer was like. He said: "It's like going off to war or to a dance." Prayer is combat with and for God. We will often be wounded like Jacob. But in the combat we will be remade and renamed like Jacob if like him "who wrestled with God," we refuse "to let him go" (Gen. 32:24). Prayer is also a dance with God; and that is why men and women of prayer are always tragic—merry, robust warriors who defend the rights of God and dwell with God festively, serving him "wittily in the tangle of [their] mind[s]," as St. Thomas More put it.

Proximate preparation for prayer is the particular way we choose to calm down and tune up immediately prior to a period of spousal prayer. This *centering down* ordinarily takes time, which introduces another reason for a lengthy, uninterrupted period of prayer. In the West the traditional way of achieving this serene and focused attention, a way proved eminently successful, is meditative reading, or *lectio divina*.

In order to be effective, this kind of reading must serve the purposes of prayer. Books must be chosen with discriminating taste and read meditatively. We cannot afford to read what is good for prayer but only the *best*. In a lifetime most of us will not find more than a handful of such books. The least helpful are "meditation books." The most helpful are almost impossible to predict. Caryll Houselander's *The Reed of God* took me by surprise when I was a novice; it kept me going all year and compensated handsomely for the dour dictates of the novice master and the lugubrious colloquies of St. Alphonsus Liguori. Some of the best books are not "religious" or "spiritual" at all, but have what it takes to shake off our lethargy, pierce our mental rigidities, and open us up to the transcendent dimension of life. *Mr. Blue* by Myles Connolly did this for me; so did *The Little Prince* by Antoine de Saint-Exupéry; *Report to Greco* by Nikos Kazantzakis; *Dr. Zhivago* by Boris Pasternak; *The Chronicles of Narnia* by C. S. Lewis; and some of the poetry of E.E. Cummings, T. S. Eliot, Gerard Manley Hopkins, Mary Oliver, and Rainer Maria Rilke.

Meditative reading is probably still the best proximate preparation for the typical Westerner but is by no means the only method. An exceptional film—*Rapture, Cool Hand Luke, Women in Love, A Man for All Seasons, Romeo and Juliet, A Little Romance, The Black Stallion*—or even a television program could do it, but certainly not as regular fare. Good music would be more likely; or perhaps a deep, quiet human encounter, a solitary walk, a bracing swim, or a romp in the autumn leaves or the winter snow. We tend to be so cerebral that Eastern techniques such as yoga can be very helpful preparing us for prayer.

RHYTHMS AND GROWTH

In the Western tradition a fairly consistent rhythm unfolds during a period as well as lifetime of prayer. St. Teresa of Avila defines prayer as "an intimate encounter with God, our Father, who we know loves us." Why do we talk in our sleep? Because an image in our imagination is so vivid it evokes a conversational response. So we begin with imagination in prayer. The world may be in a mess and seem like a gigantic dump, but the imagination is a good dump-picker. And with the help of an enlightened mind, it becomes progressively better. But the positively reliable storehouse for the imagination is the life of Christ with a thousand possible images. We need favorite images to pray with or to help us get started on our way toward prayer. One of St. Teresa's favorite images was Christ being scourged at the pillar. Mother Tessa's favorite image is Christ cooking fish for His apostles on the beach in the early morning hours after the Resurrection.

The second noticeable feature of the ordinary pattern of prayer occurs when we begin to *reflect* on the Christ-image or biblical passage. This is *meditation*; and it should be obvious now that it is not identical with prayer but a step toward prayer. This involves far more than a private visit with Jesus. This is where and how we make our political and social as well as our religious judgments, decisions, and commitments in terms of Christ. The whole purpose of imagination and reflection is to draw us into loving awareness of God. This is prayer. Everything else is preparation.

Growth in prayer is growth in simplicity. There will be less need for imaginative and meditative activities as the loving awareness becomes more intensive and extensive. We learn to pray the way we learned to read. At first we needed a constant supply of pictures. But if we were never weaned away from the pictures, we would never have learned to cope with a page of words. In learning to pray, if God does not detach us from the baby food of the spiritual life, the images, pictures, and even concepts of God, we will never grow up into mature men and women of prayer, who cope no longer with graphic messengers and verbal ambassadors of God, but with God Himself. Nothing but God, that is the heart of prayer. "And if you're lost enough to find yourself," writes Robert Frost in his poem Directive, "by now, pull in your ladder rope behind you and put a sign up *closed* to all but me" [meaning God].

To reach this utter simplicity, this pure human

condition of *enlightened* openness, we must with courage and alacrity pass through the Dark Night of sense and spirit. The Dark Night has been brilliantly outlined by St. John of the Cross. The mystic doctor of the Church indicates how we may recognize the beginning of the Dark Night when God summons us into deeper realms of faith. There are three signs:

1. We are unable to meditate—that is, to use reason and imagination in the things of God. God is communicating Himself no longer by way of sense but transforming the strength of the senses to the Spirit.

2. There is no consolation from God, but neither is there from any creature. Imagination is restless. But there is no desire to fix the senses on the world.

3. The mind is centered obscurely but lovingly on God. There is a certain deep-seated pleasure in being alone with God. A vague, loving, general knowledge or quiet peace alternates with painful aridity and distraction until it finally becomes habitual.

We must recognize the Dark Night in the many secular forms it takes these days as we move from superficial levels of love and understanding into the depths. Many married people I know began to discuss divorce just when they were on the brink of a new and deeper dimension of love they never dreamed of. But they did not see the transitional nature of their Dark Night, with all its painful confusions and disabilities, which would lead them bound faithfully together into nuptial splendor.

So many priests and nuns quit religious life just when they are ready to be led by the Spirit. They don't discern the positive features of the Dark Night and are frightened by the darkness, the wilderness, the desert, so they part with Christ in order to bask in the bright and shiny shallows of a mediocre existence. College students leave the Church just when they are ready to move into dark but deep, pure dimensions of faith precisely because they cannot live on religious formulas and articles of the creed. No one is there to tell them that this Dark Night is the entry into the real realm of faith, into a passionately personal relationship with the living God.

No wonder John of the Cross calls this desert experience a happy night, a "night more lovely than the dawn!" This night unites "the Lover with His beloved, transforming the beloved in her Lover." It is the only way out of our present crisis of faith. All the livelier forms of faith and more fiery degrees of love and higher forms of prayer are on the other side of the Dark Night. The pattern of growth in prayer delineated by John of the Cross corresponds to the love life of the married couple, the vowed life of the religious, and the intellectual life of the college student.

What the mystics call the *prayer of recollection* or *simple regard* is the result of a simplified and unified process of individuation; what they call the *prayer of quiet* is part of the divinizing process whereby God asserts Himself more manifestly in to our consciousness and occupies the center of our energies. All higher forms of prayer are consequent upon our gradual deification as we no longer follow paths paved by merely human industry, but follow unpaved and untraveled roads, led only by the Spirit into realized union with God, a divine mode of existence. This is the goal of the human adventure.

There are gospel principles but no blueprints for the human adventure. It is a unique and solitary journey. We must suffer life in a total way that is totally new. This can be shared a little. But not death. Death must be undertaken alone. Once we vanquish death, and only then, can we live life fully, exuberantly, divinely. The All that God promises is on the other side of death. The rules for attaining the All are joyful ways of dying.

In the meantime, in the maelstrom, moving toward death with the same madness that impelled Jesus into Jerusalem and onto the cross, we live by flirting with death and embracing it. People of prayer are professional lovers of the world. Their vocation is to love. Where there is no love they put love, and they find love. As G.K. Chesterton wrote, they know that they can "make nothing beautiful until they love it in all its ugliness." That is why Christ's yoke is sweet and His burden light to them. That is why, in the throes of death, their laughter rings 'round the world and their prayer is always a spontaneous cry of the heart, as John Donne expressed in His Holy Sonnet XIV:

> *Take me to you, imprison me, for I,*
> *Except you enthrall me, never shall be free,*
> *Nor ever chaste except you ravish me.*

Mystical Passion

The life of any outstanding person is borne forward on the wings of great passion. This is also true of a religious or civic community, a family, or a nation. Modern civilization has lost its strength because of its remarkably low level of affectivity, particularly of passion. Every time I read a newspaper or magazine, every time I go into a college campus or into a coffee shop or typical downtown office, every time I hear confessions or go to church, see a movie or watch television, visit friends or even examine my own conscience, I come to the same conclusion: What we all desperately need in gargantuan measures is an irrepressible zest for life, with an overruling, specific, personal, and passionate objective.

This objective need not be pellucidly clear and it may, undoubtedly should, change its form as we go on putting one foot in front of the other. En route disillusions, disappointments, and contradictions should be expected and transcended. We need to integrate all contradictory elements into a higher synthesis, but this is possible only through total surrender to something greater than all these contradictions. It takes a humorous and stubborn individual to overcome the inevitable obstacles from within and without.

It took me ten years to begin to achieve what I set out to do in 1960 with the Spiritual Life Institute. Monumental problems had to be overcome. The biggest roadblocks, or at least the most heartrending, were created by friends rather than enemies: suspicions, fears, slanders, betrayals, robberies, legalisms. I could go on; it would be a long and lugubrious list. The point is that one stout and sturdy passion turns that entire heap of unhappy obstacles into an inconsequential comedy of human foolishness. Such comedy does not drive us into depression; nor does it elicit a whimper or a snicker; it touches us at the pit of our being and evokes a belly laugh. And there is hardly anything more salubrious to the soul than uproarious belly laughter!

Passion for God has got to be fleshed out in concrete, specific life-projects. Mine, an unflinching determination since 1960, was to glorify God according to the authentic spirit of my apostolic vocation and minister to the deepest and direst needs of humanity. I hope and pray that this concretely specified God-passion will never be snuffed out by the sins of my life but will burn on in my heart until my heart burns out for God.

To be laid waste by one pure passion is to achieve simplicity and purity of heart. The Danish Philosopher Soren Kierkegaard wrote a book called *Purity of Heart* and subtitled it *To Will One Thing*. In his *Report to Greco*, Nikos Kazantzakis wrote about a thirsty Moslem who came upon a well in the desert. He dropped a bucket into the well and pulled it up. It was full of silver. Emptying it, he dumped it into the well again and pulled it up full of gold. The Moslem protested, "My Lord God, I know how powerful you are and what marvels you are capable of! But all I want is a cup of water." He emptied the bucket of gold, lowered it into the well, and retrieved it. It was full of water. He drank and quenched his thirst. That is purity of heart!

Instead of the totally untenable concept of a "pure heart" that allegedly never harbors any aggressive, sensuous, or sexual thought, this term signifies the ability to feel life in all its depth, in joy as well as sorrow. The "pure of heart" are those redoubtable champions who are willing to sense life in its total polarity. They are more like century plants or saguaro cactuses than drooping violets; more like roaring lions than bleating sheep. Such a broad-minded vision and wide range of feeling issuing in a profound experience of polarity are the true significance of the biblical search for "purity of heart" and the emotional foundation of all spirituality.

MOUNTAIN SPIRITUALITY

The stellar moments of human excellence were celebrated by mountain men and women who climbed to the pinnacle of passion, the mountaintop, and were there transfigured. These were giants who matched their mountains. There are many such mountains; some fare famous: Horeb, Tabor, Calvary, Alverna, and Carmel.

Those who scaled these mountaintops and enjoyed such peak human experiences were, like the mountains themselves, ethereal and earthy, eerie and erotic. I mean erotic in the radical sense of that word: a reaching and stretching with every fiber of our body-person for the fullness of life. The phallic symbol seems to be an appropriate, though very partial, embodiment of this erotic thrust toward utmost.

Climbing the mountain, not reaching the top, is the important element. In fact, as the Buddhists say, when you reach the top, keep climbing. Seeking is up to us. Finding is up to God. The ascent is our responsibility. The quality of our ascent depends upon the *mounting of our passion*. The climax depends upon God. St. John of Cross's *The Ascent of Mount Carmel* was originally a passionate poem and subsequently a masterful commentary on mounting passion.

The Ascent of Mount Carmel is very difficult. Our dehumanized condition, our habitual torpor, and the debilitating pressures of our schizoid society are not conducive to mountain climbing and militate against the human vocation: a persevering ascent toward the perfection of love. That is why I must add one more famous mountain, a mythical one, to my list of celebrated pinnacles of passion: Mount Sisyphus.

We must not only deal with the external conditions and extrinsic pressures that impinge upon us but face up to our own internal possibilities. Albert Camus, the French existentialist, was exceptionally good at this and enjoyed the gift of expressing it truthfully and shockingly. Camus was at home with fate. By fate I do not mean the misfortunes that befall us, but the inevitable pain, anguish, and weakness of our human condition. The myth of Sisyphus presents our fate in as stark a form as could be imagined. Just as Sisyphus reaches the top of mountain, the rock he has arduously pushed ahead of him rolls to the bottom, and he must begin the struggle all over again. Camus find in that fate, for those who are brave and honest enough to accept the consciousness of it, something which evokes our passion for life, our struggle for value and meaning, our undying effort of love:

> *I leave Sisyphus at the foot of the mountain....*
> *This universe without a master seems to him*
> *neither sterile nor futile. Each atom of that stone,*
> *each mineral flake of that night-filled mountain, in*
> *itself forms a world. The struggle itself toward the*
> *heights is enough to fill a man's heart. One must*
> *imagine Sisyphus happy.*

What matters is not vast achievement or triumphant victory, but endless effort. St. Teresa of Avila said, "Strive and strive and strive; we were meant for nothing else." There is such a thing as the triumph of failure—a failure of results. The triumph consists in persevering effort. God sanctifies us through our efforts, not our successes. Sisyphus represents the faithful commitment to nothing but God.

FROM RED HEAT TO WHITE HEAT

There is great passion in Shakespeare's *Romeo and Juliet*, Emily Bronti's *Wuthering Heights*, and Wagner's *Tristan and Isolde*. But somehow it is never enough. These romantic classics come close to describing the fire that Christ came to cast upon the Earth. But they don't quite make it. After all is said and done, after all the agony and ecstasy of romantic love, there is something dismal and dissatisfying about these great love stories. They are not mystical and luminous enough. Passion never really takes off; it is stymied and stunted by inevitable human limitations. It reminds me of those faulty firecrackers and rockets we ignite on the Fourth of July; they fill us with wondrous expectation as they hiss, crackle, and fume, but never explode, filling the sky with a riot of sparkle and color.

The passion of St. John of the Cross, on the other hand, broke through every barrier. There was both an explosion and take-off. We find in this towering mountain man of pure passion a luminosity that outshines all the great love-lights of romantic literature. The power and life of John's mystical poetry are a white heat of spiritual passion. That heat molds his imagery and burns through it. Every detail is ablaze with it, even "the breeze from the turret," "the lilies," and the "fanning cedars."

This passion of the mystic is significantly termed "white heat" in contradistinction to the "red heat" of a merely earthly and physical passion. The white heat of a man or woman in love with God is far more intense than romantic red heat. The fire of the classical romantics, or of any great secular lover, may be more expansive and brilliant, but it pales before the concentrated intensity of St. John of the Cross's "living flame of love."

The singular coruscation of even romantic love is due to the erotic effort to transcend sensual love. It tends to pass over into the spiritual passion of an infinite love. Eros almost turns into *agape*. It cannot, however, free itself from subjection to its finite object, from bondage to its sensual conditions. And so the love affair, typified in the great episodes of romantic literature as well as in the more fragile instances of contemporary art forms, however promising, ends in tragedy, a tragedy not really due to its external circumstances, but inherent in its very nature. The mystics leap beyond boundaries into the Mystery. Having exhausted the powers of eros, they are lifted by the Inexhaustible Spirit into *agape* and in that divine realm begin to envision and inhale the impossible possibilities or the possible impossibilities of love.

It takes someone of St. John of the Cross's stature, a superb poet and supernal mystic, to unite so intimately the earthly type and the spiritual antitype, to fuse so completely the most vehement passion with perfect purity. The purity of John's blazing passion is only obtainable by total mortification and a relentless crucifixion of the flesh and its desires. St. John scaled the summit of Mount Carmel not on his own steam, but on the power of the Spirit of God in him *(agape)*, a Spirit rooted in and embodied by His own natural and unstinting quest for supreme value *(eros)*.

As St. John points out, there is only one entrance into the mystical life. That entry is the Dark Night. In the Dark Night passion flames forth unchecked by any barrier because it is perfectly pure, and purity is essentially freedom from limits. That is why mystics who plow through the tumultuous upheavals and torrential storms of the Dark Nights are the most passionate of all people, exploring the terrible uncharted regions of human evolution.

Passion is simply life in its most intense vigor. But people are afraid of passion because they are afraid of life. They blame passion for the limits they refuse to vault. Passion is the breakthrough virtue. If passion remains unspent, our limits remain unleveled. In this way, passionlessly, apathetically, we permit the natural boundaries of our life to enclose and enslave us. We allow finite structures themselves to distort and sully life in fallen sense-bound humanity.

The Incarnation, the life of Christ, was the passion of God breaking through decisively. Human boundaries were pushed back *ad infinitum*. All things were made new. If I have a spiritual life, that means that I am immersed in the life of the wild and insuppressible Spirit transcending all the bastions of the empirical, separative, and lamentably limited ego.

We slink away from the challenge of the spiritual life. We take refuge in a cold and uninspired moralism and in an artificially closed circle of thought and practice. So the stream of life leaves us behind in its backwaters as it sweeps onwards, a turbid, muddy, often destructive, but always swirling force. The result: a mediocre world of nice people. We lack the capacity to purify and spiritualize passion and therefore must avoid it entirely. So what help can we be to those who will and must live with the fullness of life and must love passionately? They are the ones who need to be fed, helped, and directed, led irrevocably all the way up the mountain. But we would rather dally in the meager foothills, pandering to the tiny passions of inert and lukewarm people.

The saints are the bold ones, daring enough to be different, humble enough to make mistakes, wild enough to be burnt in the fire of love, real enough to make the rest of us see how enormously phony we are. They transform the strictures of sense. They are passionate pilgrims of the Absolute, restless until they rest in an infinite love that is the intense passion of pure Spirit. If they seem to withdraw, it is only for the sake of a fuller life from which the limits of that lower life would have debarred them.

The spiritual passion of the Dark Night exceeds the passion of earthly love as the fire of the sun exceeds the fire of the candle. Life is love, passionate and intense. Only in such love is reality touched; the rest is deception, bondage, and spiritual death. Such love draws upwards, ever more persistently, to the mountain peaks. The fulfilled passion of St. John passes into the peace of perfect satisfaction, its energy spent in ecstatic absorption rather than sporadic desire. In this mystic marriage all knowledge and art, all striving and desire, all love and all life are fulfilled. This spousal union is the limitless Being of God eternally filling the virginal emptiness of the soul. It is harmony without striving, love without longing, yes without no, and life without death.

PASSION, THE BREAKTHROUGH VIRTUE

Passion paves the way for the transformation of our lives by the power of the Spirit. Passion is not the exclusive quest of egotistic pleasure but an intense psychological sum of energy that focuses our sensibility and fuses all our faculties into a unified drive toward a supreme value and to particular values that seem to connect with that ultimate prize. If we are passionate enough, all our human potentialities are activated and integrated into a free and lively personality, moving us gracefully from conversion, to completion, into communion: from romance to mysticism.

   Passion is not merely one emotion, or even the sum
of all emotions, but rather a psycho-physical thrust of
the whole body-person toward the goal of all human
striving. Our loving awareness of what truly satisfies
us has a strong emotional quality that colors a wide
range of deep and daring human relationships, all of
which involve the human adventurer in an unconditional and all-pervasive relationship with God, whom
we must all ultimately choose. At the beginning, we
choose God necessarily and unconsciously; as we become progressively human, we choose Him freely and
consciously. The culminating phases of that humanizing, liberating process are so final and the passion
so totally fulfilling that we can appropriately, as we do
in the case of Jesus, refer to this triumph as the passion. The passion is the pass-over from *eros* to *agape*,
from the quest to all the rest, from the symbols and
the signs to Love itself and the One Signified.
   According to St. Augustine, passion is the power
that drives us toward God, restless until it rests in
God. It may take many romantic forms, but it must
eventually become the living flame of mystical love or
it will flicker out. In other words, if we are not mystics, driven by a transcendental hunger and thirst for
God, we are bound to become playboys or playgirls;
or if we don't have what it takes for that, we become
voyeurs, eking out a quasi-existence on vicarious, ve-
nereal pleasures.
   Passion required a compelling, imaginative symbol
on which to focus its energy, and a way of life that
will provide ample opportunity for the spirit to break
free as it grows in mounting momentum from the animated discoveries of romantic love to the divine disclosures of mystical marriage.
   The unconscious Reality toward which passion is
striving so relentlessly can only be grasped through
a symbol, a symbol that relates more to our needs

than to God's nature. The temptation is to become attached to the symbol, whether it be my concept of God, a vocation, a vacation, a political, religious, or social cause, or another human being. The symbol, somehow or other, suggests the completion of myself and awakens in me a range of emotions that start racing through the symbol toward the *pleroma,* the fulfillment of my being through realization of divine union. When the other person ceases to be merely a symbol and becomes a real person, enjoying an existence outside of his or her function as symbol, that is the beginning of love.

Christ is the most perfect symbol of all. His life and message were both remarkably and incomparably passionate, expressing divine invisibilities and human potentialities. If Christ is our symbol, our passion must harmonize with the gospel demand for total dedication. Christ's "follow me" is ruthless, ignoring convention and disregarding common decencies and the obligations of normal living. "Let the dead bury the dead" (Matt. 8:22), he told the man who wanted to postpone the proclamation of the Kingdom of God because of family duties. "No one who puts his hand to the plow and looks back is fit for the Kingdom of God" (Luke 9:62). We must admittedly live within the reality of the world and manage harmoniously. But when the Spirit makes its demands there is nothing to do but comply.

Real passion can be distinguished from its synthetic substitutes. While mere sentiment cares only about the feeling produced, passion is other-directed. There is also an observable external difference. Genuine passion alters our behavior and endures beyond physical union with, or need for, the beloved, even during the course of a long love affair. Since true passion is part of the search for the authentic self, a highly sexual man or woman can remain marvelously indifferent to persons more richly endowed in every way than his or her own spouse.

Blaise Pascal, one of the illustrious intellectuals in history, was man enough and Christian enough to see and say that there is no true human greatness without passion. Passion breaks down the static equanimity that some questionable spiritual techniques strive for, and breaks through the exceedingly narrow framework in which reason imprisons us. The annihilation of Hiroshima illustrates what happens when the power of intellect is cut loose from morality and love. It is obvious that our sick world today has lost its soul. There is hardly a breath of spirit to quicken the spate of ideologies that have sprung up in the last two centuries; and that is why their existence is so transient. Intellect by itself cannot create the psychic unity of the individual and the social unity of peoples. Only when a singular passion takes hold of us, gathering into its wake all dispersed and contradictory efforts, can we achieve personal unity.

St. Thomas Aquinas insisted that to act with passion was more human and therefore more perfect than to act out of merely rational motivation. To act passionately is to act more humanly, and so it is a supra-rational, not a sub-rational act. Our actions are human to the degree that they are intentional acts of the whole person. We cannot feel our way into whole truth. Neither can we intellectually conceive the mystery of life. Passion must be enlightened by reason and reason must be kindled by passion.

INTEGRATING THE DAEMONIC

The passionate elements in us are natural: sex, eros, anger, rage, buffoonery, the thirst for knowledge or power, a yearning for solitude or community— they stimulate our lives and can be constructive or destructive. In order to be helpful they need to be acknowledged, affirmed, and integrated into our whole personality. Sex, for example, should serve the purposes of personal intimacy, whether celibate or married; eros should be ordered in the service of love; anger and rage should be vented through righteous moral indignation; clowning should never succumb to ridicule but remain corybantic relief or a form of love or education. These forces in us are called daemonic because they have the power to take over completely. When one of them goes awry and controls the entire personality, we have "daemon possession" or psychosis.

The opposite of the daemonic is not rational security or peaceful tranquility but passionlessness, a return to the inanimate. Apathy and delayed explosion are the toll exacted by the repression of the daemonic dimensions of being. We must wholesomely incorporate the daemonic into the service of our major project of existence. Without the daemonic aspect our spiritual lives remain vapid. And if our daemons are not allowed to make a constructive contribution to our humanization and deification, then they will play a destructive role.

Repression has prevailed in the past centuries, and we have witnessed the atrocities of mass murder, unspeakable torture, and senseless war. We all harbor in our hearts the same savage impulses that led to such outlandish crimes. Unheeded, undirected daemons are bound to assert themselves furtively; if not in the heinous crimes of Nazism, then in the respectable corruption of government, business and religion. Repressed daemons drive us to perverted forms of aggression. "Violence is the daimonic gone awry. It is demon possession in its starkest form," says psychologist Rollo May.

We evade the daemonic to our detriment by losing ourselves in the herd, in the mindless armies who kill for the nation or freedom, or in the millions of television watchers who observe for entertainment. Thus, the daemonic is dispensed by impersonality. The anonymous single man secluded in a New York City room turns out to be typical killer. He sees, smiles, knows all the television personalities, but he himself is never known. His smile is unseen, his idiosyncrasies unnoticed. This is the horrible tragedy: he remains unnamed, alien, isolated in the crowd. As Scripture tells us, to be unnamed was the most severe punishment Yahweh could inflict on His people. "Their names shall be wiped out of the books of the living" (Exod. 32:32; Ps. 69:28; Rev. 3:5).

How did the Jews preserve their name and become a fitting vehicle for the revelation of God's passion? How did the Greeks achieve their superb civilization? They made love, killed, and bled with zest. Their strong men cried. Their wise women chose their passions. They were not driven by them. The daemonic will get the upper hand as long as we continue to run from it. Wholeness and, therefore, holiness require the fervent inclusion of these hidden powers, these *evil urges*, into the personal passionate presence of every gracious human being. Only if these untamed sources of energy are at our service, consciously, easily and virtuously available, can we live passionately and serve God vigorously.

Passion out of control—lust, for instance—is undoubtedly one of most destructive forces in the world; but the evil let loose in human life by uncontrolled passion is nothing compared to the passion of love accomplished in the redemption and accessible to all followers of Christ. Love is creative only when it is passionate. Great passions are dangerous and often become excessive, especially when devoted to a mean and mediocre object. But good psychologists today agree with Pascal that it is better to repair the damage done by excess than to eliminate passion altogether. Kierkegaard was certainly right when he said that the one who has lost all in passionate love has lost less than the one who has never known it.

FEAR OF PASSION

The more mature and alive we are, the more passionately we live and love. People who are immature cannot cope with passion. They suffer from aversions but never from moral indignation. They satisfy and pool their needs but are incapable of the vehement passion of love. They are forced to rely on law, routine, custom, whim or rational calculation.

Most of us are terribly afraid of passion precisely because it leads us beyond the measured boundaries of the conscious self, the superficial ego. Our fear leads us to settle for convenient and comfortable substitutions. If we cannot control passion in the neatly systematic way we handle everything else in our technological world, we skip it altogether.

There are a million ways of snuffing out the life of the spirit. But the popular, canonized American way that seems to include most, if not all, of the others is our compulsive pursuit of happiness, The notion of happiness as a birthright did not originate with Thomas Jefferson; it was a dominant theme of both the French Revolution and the Age of Enlightenment, Americanized by Jefferson. It would be a remarkable feat to expunge from our American psyches our high expectations of happiness. "The only orthodox object of the institution of government," according to Jefferson, "is to secure the greatest degree of happiness possible to the general masses of those associated under it." What this highly vaunted happiness finally came to mean was simply "not being pained in body or troubled in mind."

Keep that lifeless, passionless definition in mind while you reexamine our political and social institutions, our military-industrial complex, our technology, hospitals, schools, our churches and our families. Are they making us holy? Or are they merely making us happy?

Happiness is big business these days. We will do anything to be happy: tell lies, cheat, break international alliances, matrimonial bonds, pledges of friendship and love, as well as religious commitments. We will dismiss our old people and kill our unborn infants. We thrash around, in and out of war and in and out of each other's beds, pursuing the shadow of our happiness.

Ultimately we refuse to live because there is no way to live without suffering. Passion (*passio*) literally means the suffering of life, creatively, gloriously. To refuse to suffer or to spend a lifetime trying to avoid it is to refuse to live, to love, to be. Our preoccupation with happiness turns out to be a death wish.

Malcolm Muggeridge wrote a stinging piece on this disgraceful and ironic state of affairs and entitled it "The Great Liberal Death Wish." It is worth quoting at length to sum up how our rabid pursuit of happiness leaves us half alive:

> *I have a recurrent nightmare that somehow or other a lot of contemporary pabulum—video tape of television programs with accompanying advertisements, news footage, copies of newspapers and magazines, stereo tapes of pop groups and other cacophonies, best-selling novels, films and other such material— gets preserved like the Dead Sea Scrolls, in some remote salt cave. Then some centuries, or may be millennia later, when our civilization will long since have joined all others that once were and now can only be patiently reconstructed out of dusty ruins, incomprehensible hieroglyphics and other residuary relics,*

archaeologists discover the cave, and set out sorting out its contents and trying to deduce from them what we were like and how we lived. (That is assuming, of course, that we do not, in the process of working out the great liberal death wish, blow ourselves and our Earth to smithereens—a large assumption.) What will they make of us? I wonder. Materially, so rich and so powerful; spiritually, so impoverished and fear-ridden. Having made such remarkable inroads into the secrets of nature; beginning to explore, and perhaps to colonize, the universe itself; developing the means to produce in more or less unlimited quantities everything we could possibly need or desire, and to transmit swifter than light every thought, smile, or word that could possibly delight, entertain or instruct us. Disposing of treasure beyond calculation, opening up possibilities beyond conception. Yet haunted and obsessed by the fear that we are too numerous; that soon as our numbers go on increasing there will be no room or food for us. On the one hand, a neurotic passion to increase consumption, sustained by every sort of imbecile persuasion; on the other, ever-increasing hunger and penury among the so-called backward or underdeveloped peoples. Never, our archaeologists will surely conclude, was any generation intent upon the pursuit of happiness more advantageously placed to attain it, who yet with seeming deliberation, took the opposite course— toward chaos, not order; toward breakdown, not stability; toward death, destruction and darkness, not life, creativity and light. An ascent that ran downhill; plenty that turned into a wasteland; a cornucopia whose abundance made hungry; a death wish inexorably unfolding.

To suppress a death wish we need to proclaim a corresponding life wish, as Jesus did with the good news, to will one thing; eternal life. The good news involves the existential knowledge of being loved by God, of sharing Christ's own experience of that love. What we do must be an unmistakable witness of our *loving awareness.*

But so many of the things we do have nothing to do with beingfulness and therefore nothing to do with the loving will of God. These feverish activities are then happy and haughty distractions. If we don't have the insight and inscape to do better, then we inevitably succumb to the tyranny of diversion; we become do-gooders in a frenzied effort to compensate for our passion deficiency. We mollify our stricken consciences by plunging into a plethora of prodigious doings, but we almost cease to be. Thus we are duped, deluded, and driven, and consequently lose our grip on life.

Oddly enough, we succeed in being moderately happy; by finding the most apathetic slot from which we participate in life guardedly, if at all. Apathy is a withdrawal of feeling—a-pathos or passionlessness. It is not the most spectacular form of suicide, but it is the most common. It has been eroding our civilization and is about to reach its apogee, all in the name of progress and the pursuit of happiness. Without passion, apathy is inevitable or, at best, a complacent mediocrity. When a community or nation needs to be recreated and invested with verve, administrator and statesmen should be replaced by passionate, mystical leaders.

THE FLIGHT FROM EROS INTO SEX

Sex sought with avid abandon is often seen as the key to our pursuit of happiness. Sex is the powerful production and release of bodily tensions. Eros, in contrast, is the power that deeply personalizes the purpose and significantly grasps the meaning of the act.

Eros, the Greek word for passion, is not synonymous with sexual titillation or what we commonly refer to as "eroticism." The Greeks emphasized eros; that is why that word is so familiar to us. They deemphasized sex; that is why we hardly know what term they used for it. Eros pertains essentially to the art of making love (coming into union—communion). Sex is limited to the manipulation of organs. Eros attracts and lures us into union with everything. Eros is wakeful, vigilant, remembering whatever is true and beautiful, whatever is good. Sex is a need; eros a desire. The sex act is indeed the most potent symbolic and specific celebration of relatedness imaginable. But eros *is* relatedness, excitement accompanies sex. Tenderness dominates the erotic quest.

Eros is the longing to enjoy such wide-ranged and deep dimensions of relatedness, all originating from a critical center and tending toward an ultimate end, that we experience a unitive and beautifying fruition of Being, at least incipiently and intermittently, on this Earth. Although dramatically and supremely important in a good sexual relationship, the same erotic desire for union plays a central part in our rapport with animal and plant life, as well as with aesthetic, philosophical, ethical, scientific, socio-political, and religious forms. Eros relates us not only to other persons whom we love, but to the pig we are raising, the house we are building, the car we are driving, the vocation we are following. If we had been sufficiently charged with eros, for instance, we would have participated in a reverent dialogue with our environment that would have precluded our current ecological disaster.

Eros urges us to be united with the beloved, to prolong delight, to discover deeper dimensions of love's meaning, and to treasure the memory of being together. As Rollo May points out, the most memorable moment of sexual love-making is not the final orgasm but the mutually desired penetrating entrance into the secret caverns of the body-person. Apocalypse, however, is not between a woman's legs. But that incomparably beautiful arch, which Thomas Moore describes as "the realm of the soul par excellence—containing, creating, warming assuring," may be the gateway into the transcendent mystery of the universe. Through that feminine archway man discovers his own anima, the feminine principle within his own being, and realizes simultaneously, if he is fully aware and in tune, that the apocalyptic paradise for which he yearns and toward which the whole universe is spinning, may lie through that gorgeous portal, but infinitely beyond. Woman elevates the reverent man. Eros urges man to transcend himself, soaring into realms of the spirit through symbols of the flesh.

The single-hearted, great-souled thrust of eros, the yearning for wholeness, gives form, vitality, and unity to our lives. If we do not reduce our passion to lust, and that is everyone's temptation, then we enjoy what the Greeks called a pregnant soul. We become creators and artists, collaborating in some little way with the Spirit in the building up of God's Kingdom in the world. Highly cultivated eros helps us understand that there is no separate creature or isolated event. If we are erotic enough we see the connection, the binding element in the universe, the interactive process of being and becoming.

"Eros is the center of vitality of a culture—its heart and soul," wrote Rollo May. "And when release of tension takes the place of creative eros, the downfall of the civilization is assured." Along with May I lament the death of eros in our age. When there is no erotic vitality at the center of a person or culture, decadence sets in. When the release of tension replaces creatively mounting passion, the degradation of humanity and the collapse of civilization are assured.

Sex seems to be an outstanding way for a moribund society of robots to prove that they have some
live animality left in them, David Riesman, in *The
Lonely Crowd*, calls it the "last frontier." Gerald Sykes,
in *The Cool Millennium*, remarks: "In a world gone grey
with market reports, time studies, tax regulations and
path lab analyses, the rebel finds sex to be the one
green thing."

But without the fire of eros the frontier freshness
of sex didn't last long. We have ended up fussing in-
terminably with research and statistics. We reduce
love to sex, sex to genitality, and genitality to technique. Fearful of the dangerous, driving force of eros,
we turn this deep source of love and life into manageable and measurable sex.

Promoters of packaged passion like Hugh Hefner
and Dr. Alex Comfort keep our society pleasant but respectable by distributing a carefully calculated measure of sexual "kicks."

The world is full of pepless playboys but bereft of
passionate lovers. While passionate feeling has de-
creased, coital technique has increased and prepared
the way for one of the monstrosities of modern life: casual copulation. People today would rather be compe-
tent performers of cool sex than raptured contemplatives, surprised by joy and lifted beyond their control
into Olympian orbits of ecstasy. Passion is repressed
for the sake of performance; sensuality is mistaken
for sensitivity. Is it really a liberating leap in sexual
style if our technical prowess, with easy access in and
out of coition, inhibits our feeling and suffocates our
passion?

In our passionless, prosaic world we find a vast
obsessive outpouring of erotica in every shape and
form—in book, film, music, in body, word and deed—
so that there is no escape. Every possible sexual pleasure or perversion is available to everyone: the halt

and the lame, young and old. Anyone can see it or do it at any time or anywhere. Imagination is no longer required. Feeling is irrelevant. No impediments either—the Pill has taken care of that. Now we can have sterile sex and shattering orgasms without a care in the world. Waning happiness calls for another spurt. If topless shows grow dull, try bottomless. If one man or woman becomes tiresome, take another. Or two at a time. Or an orgy. Or jump from rafters and, like swifts copulate in mid-air! It is the flesh that quickens; the spirit profits nothing. If my body can evoke a bodily quiver from another, or vice versa, I call it love and claim that I am alive. An orgasm a day keeps the doctor away! A slight twist of Descartes's famous axiom captures the mood of our sensate culture: *copulo ergo sum*. I copulate, therefore I am.

There is no real sexual revolution, only a copulation explosion. The new sexual "freedom" allows us to perform profusely, which generally means frequently, quickly, and lovelessly. Our flight from eros embarrasses and frustrates us. We attempt to cover our shame with sexual activities of high frequency and low value. Our exploits are flimsy, compulsive, and unrelated to love. The wild and wonderful passion of eros has been replaced by timid sensation of sex. Having repressed passion and stifled love, we have nothing sexual left to celebrate except technique.

Technique promises us everything instantly: virtue without effort, knowledge without discipline, intimacy without love, wisdom without struggle, peace without pain, sex without risk, success without trying, spirituality without religion, mysticism without asceticism, provided that we settle for a passionless existence.

FROM ROMANCE TO MYSTICISM

We have reduced eros to sex because we are afraid to love; and we are afraid to love because love leads to death. Love hungers to be with the beloved other, to become the beloved other. This kind of presence and union come about only through ego-reduction, resulting in ego-death. Once I have reduced egotistic craving to zero I am free to be with and to become the beloved other. Until then I am trapped within the confines of the isolated ego.

The coital act is a sexual symbolic celebration of love and a psycho-physical symbol of death. In any act of genuine intercourse, the lover dies to self and rises not only in the life of the beloved, but in the life of the entirely new entity of two become one. Our preoccupation with sexual prowess distracts us from that awful death which lies at the heart of every love act. Our frequent delirious couplings disguise lifelessness in our sex as well as every other dimension of our lives. The Victorian Age repressed sex. We use sex itself to repress the nearness, necessity, and inevitability of death.

Erotic love hurls us into heights and depths simultaneously. In other words, life is bound to tragic. But what right have professional lovers of the world, Christ-men and Christ-women, to expect anything but a tragic life? Tragedy is not catastrophe. It is what happens to human lives that burst the bounds of rational control and the norms of conventional standards. Think of the great love stories, mythic or historical: Helen and Paris, Tristan and Isolde, Cathy and Heathcliff, Abelard and Heloise, Romeo and Juliet. The life of Christ is the best example.

Love-force, or soul-power, is a tragic gift. It can devastate us like a landslide so that we can never rise again to the heights of God. But even such tragic figures are closer to sanctity and to God than the exemplary citizens who cannot even understand the dangers to which the others have succumbed, who know nothing of that stormy upward sweep of soul, the self-expenditure involved in the suffering of life, with a whole heart rendered and sundered. There is no love without tragedy, only insipid substitutions. The only real catastrophe is the death of love. A broken vow, a collapsed friendship, a love betrayed, a cherished secret divulged are worse than the destruction of the Golden Gate Bridge.

Our greatest erotic responsibility is to keep love alive. It isn't easy. What happens when passion breaks through? A hidden force breaks through the protective layers of our habitual ways of thought and behavior and pushes back the assumed boundaries of the up-to-now stuck-in-the-mud self. After a while the ravages of time take their toll. Our original emotion slackens. The original impetus wanes, although we still prize the value.

At this point our tendency is to resume "business as usual" and return to "normal." Really passionate persons will prevent this regression by freely and deliberately choosing appropriate human activities that will continue to relate them significantly to the same value and all that it progressively stands for, even when the original emotion connected with the value has faded.

Rosemary Haughton points out that pure passion must, if it is not to degenerate, renew itself by contact with its source, by means of action related to the symbol that gave it birth. This is the function of sex in marriage and of the Eucharist in the Christian community. As the life of the Spirit increases it can depend less on the power of the symbol; for instance, a devoted elderly couple depend less on sexual attraction and genitality; a spiritually mature person depends less on Eucharistic celebrations. Both sex and Eucharist remain important, but not in the same way.

Falling in love may be romance, but staying in love is mysticism. Romantic love is a good beginning but a poor end. It takes persistent passion to turn romantic sentiment or aesthetic taste into stubborn and seasoned mystical love. Only mystical love can makes sense out of the indissolubility of the marriage bond or the permanency of a celibate vow.

In mystical love there is always something going on: a deeper exploration into the truth, the inscrutable *thouness* of the beloved, and therefore an unflagging loyalty to his or her uniqueness in whom God is revealed as in no other. If divine revelation is finished, then the lovers are finished. Only thus does God become supremely important; and if God is not supremely important He is not important at all. Only if a man and woman's relationship is supremely important will they remain faithful.

To be unique is not a matter of peculiar differences but of outstanding fidelity. When all is said and done, that is what the spiritual life is all about: *fidelity*—to myself and the God who calls me to become more and more gracefully myself, my very best self; not in isolation but in communion with the whole human race. My passion must go on mounting until I am so faithful that God will look on me with pleasure and say: "This is my beloved" (Matt. 3:17).

At the close of *Purgatorio*, Beatrice says to Dante: "You should have been faithful to my beloved flesh," and in her eyes he sees reflected the two-natured Gryphon of Christ. The only way to be faithful to the flesh is by the quickened penetration and transformation of the flesh by the ardor of the Spirit. No puny passions will do, but the total thrust of our erotic being toward the Absolutely Loving God, and therefore toward full participation in the Christ-life on Earth. This faithful following of Christ into the All will make each of us unique and empower us to respond wholeheartedly to every unique situation.

This was the genius of Christ! And the gist of Christianity at its best. This is the earthy destiny of every person: to be so alive, so completely awakened, that we move in and out of concrete human exigencies at a passionate pitch of loving awareness. Then we can pray with Nikos Kazantzakis:

> *I am a bow in your hands, Lord. Draw me lest I rot.*
> *Do not overdraw me, Lord. I shall break.*
> *Overdraw me Lord, and who cares if I break!*

Epilogue

This book was about "meeting"—not the politically correct, publicly cautious, or chirpily careless kind—oh, no. It was about mindful encounters full of risk and wonder as unique instances of astonishing, mysterious otherness connecting and both discovering and revealing the wild and wonderful drama of being there. Who is the source of life, love, and being? The One who is always there. We are the Holy One's living image. So being there should be our specialty. When we really meet an "other," ego defenses collapse, postures dissolve, and communion happens. "The Kingdom of God is between us." All living is meeting. And only contemplatives, attentive, attuned, and passionately present, are capable of vulnerable, altruistic exchange. They reach the pinnacle of care. The Greek word for care is *eros*. Our greatest and earliest theologians agreed with each other: "Eros is the same as agape except more intense."

Such intensity frightens people. Highly refined moments—or seasons—of erotic energy set the stage for historical breakthroughs for evolutionary mutations, for spiritual transformations—a miraculous deepening of human existence for creaturely deification. But what happens? Fear takes possession of us, panic disrupts the evolutionary process, and resistance to change impedes enlightenment and holiness.

Recently I watched the collapse of a robust religious community faced with this exact challenge. Even though they were trained and prepared for it— they came into existence for this very reason—they botched it. Instead of racing into Jerusalem together, stouthearted and faithful, loving and supporting one another en route, and then plunging through death and resurrection into a deeper order of being, they ran peevishly and petulantly the other way, away from the wild Holy One whom they had vowed to follow and sought security and comfort where debauched dim-wits seek it: in the Empire, resorting to all the Empire's techniques—legal, psychological, moralistic, and the malevolent modes of chicanery.

With this betrayal of eros there followed the detritus of a shallow and misinformed therapy: a sad history of bathos. I intended to include in this book a lengthier discussion of eros but now realize it needs a book-length treatment. If we don't come to understand it and activate it we will perish. The perversion of eros—"erotica"—has permeated our society for so long that it fills the media; and our government tolerates it, indeed, protects it. It is utterly baffled by eros and religion. This confusion and its dehumanizing effect are the unfortunate result of a silly political endeavor to be both permissive and puritanical. It's folly of monumental seriousness.

One of the things that surprised me most in the afore-mentioned religious community's crisis was how instinctively and automatically the frightened group turned for help not to the Kingdom—Christ's revelation and revolution—but to the Empire, the slogans, clichés, addictions, the categories and ideologies that promote power, posture, and prestige. Christ resisted those very temptations—to spiritual, material, and political power. Why can't we? Or why won't we?

This raises an embarrassing question: Whom or what do we take with ultimate seriousness? An honest answer will reveal our true identity.

How desperately we need lovers who are sexually integrated, heroic, and chaste. We need not look for perfect models of erotic holiness. What we expect and encourage is the unflagging effort of a fallible clutch of enlightened, disciplined men and women with a sturdy background and a stouthearted orientation. As in every area of moral struggle mistakes are inevitable. Careless mistakes with tragic consequences must, indeed, be resolutely avoided. And yet who is righteous enough, arrogant enough to condemn even such a hapless lover? Ironically, we are even more inclined to denounce lovers—celibate or married—who enrich their God-centered commitment and their undivided and undistracted community life by personal encounters. Such meetings are profound and prayerful but unstudied, unarranged, and unsought but immensely enjoyable, including unself-conscious, other-centered mischievous conviviality. Three signs indicate how healthy and holy these relationships are: reverent humor, lightheartedness, and unself-consciousness.

Now that doesn't sound very exciting, does it? No cutting edge here! No alarming, challenging mode of existence. No stunning revelation. But hold on. At the heart of this serene encounter, this disarming, vulnerable self-presentation, this moral audacity, this reckless gift, this gigantic risk—at the center of this delicious lunacy lies an infinite force, super-personal transerotic, whom the first great theologians, Origen and Gregory of Nyssa, liked to call Eros and whom we, more pedestrian and less forthrightly concrete or visceral, choose, quite property, to refer to as God.

God could care less about connubial capers or capricious cupidity, but he loves intimacy, celebration, and festivity. Otherwise, why Cana? And why so much Dionysian exhilaration connected with blessedness and glory? It's an atmosphere charged with divine intimations—precarious, of course: so many openings to sanctity and calamity. For centuries ascetic Celtic monks excelled at Dionysian delight that issued from God intoxication. For forty years the apostolic hermits of the Spiritual Life Institute, with their Carmelite-Celtic spirit, gracefully achieved the same exuberant, festive lifestyle. After a brief hiatus I feel sure the regularity and hilarity that characterized them and attracted so many followers will be revived.

The point I want to make here, though, is this: In this divine milieu—the meeting—a sexual element is not only appropriate, but essential. Eros in a relational act of intellectual love is by no means a pest, but the source of zest that brings to fruition the whole human aspiration for living intimately in touch with the universe by total attention to and care of this particular, unrepeatable instance of being.

It is this specific, concrete thing that I must cherish now, each one as common and as singular as a stone or a star. When I prize each body as hallowed by God and precious to the Earth I remain grounded in the hurly-burly of substantial existence. Detached from fantasies and pseudo-events I can then wed the real and enjoy the human experience of awareness of life's endless vitality and beauty.

Mary Oliver, a favorite poet, says it with such pungent eloquence in her poem "When Death Comes":

> *When it's over, I want to say all my life*
> *I was a bride married to amazement.*
> *I was the bridegroom, taking the world into my*
> *   arms.*
>
> *When it's over, I don't want to wonder*
> *If I have made of my life something particular,*
> *   and real.*
>
> *I don't want to find myself sighing and*
> *   frightened, or full of argument.*
> *I don't want to end up simply having visited the*
> *   world.*

See how we clobber our way through life: fastening down everything, making it fit. By idealizing, symbolizing, and categorizing, we reduce everything to the meager size of our mind. Even if we had a brain the size of Immanuel Kant's, we would violate things by forcing our meaning on them. As a logotherapist I value meaning very highly. Still, I love how life's rich-textured otherness will not be tamed or domesticated and simply defy our categories. We usually face this fact in animals, wind, and water but how about disciplined wild men and women? Shall we let God direct them or not? Shall we ask them to share their outstanding human experience—the way they stand forth with no support except the Ground of Being? We used to burn them at the stake. Now we send them into exile.

What should we be doing? We need to wonder. We need to pay attention. This can't be done unless we relinquish our obsessive compulsion to symbolize, to impose meaning on everything we see and instead, let all be in their unassimilated otherness. Only then, with eros liberated, are we free to love.

The erotic energy that unites lovers and binds them so freely and felicitously into oneness and wholeness is by nature infectious, and so the whole family or community experiences, as a result, solidarity and fidelity. If eros is ever abandoned or even neglected—certainly if spurned—the family or community will be sundered with division and infidelity. Why and how does this catastrophe assail such good people?

After seventy years of study, an examined life, multiple experiences of love, a constant scrutiny of multifarious levels of society, and my own agony and ecstasy over my failure and success in this labor of love—to offer God a pure heart—after all this, I have an answer: a soft spirituality, which I abhor, cultivates a pretty poison that I detest, and paves the bland, broad way to perfidy, an act so horrifying, I tremble at the thought of it.

Drenched in divine mercy and sustained by a fierce and fiery eros, I pledge allegiance to the One I love. Overwhelm me, Lord, or I perish.

The Principles of Christian Humanism

1. TRANSCENDENCE AND IMMANENCE

   The final goal of human existence is transcendent: Every person, place, thing, and event lures us into the Holy, evoking an irrepressible desire for communion with the Living God. But this Living God is also immanent, the Beyond-in-our-midst, more "we" than we are, more "here" than we are. Transcendence and immanence must never be polarized but held together in creative tension.

2. GRACE AND RESPONSE

   Grace is the deepest dimension in nature, in the whole wide world, inviting all into the One. This summons evokes an exquisitely human response, self-obvious acts of worship, always graceful and reverent: to be still, to behold the manifold in the One, to understand, to love and laugh, we weep and make something beautiful: a bed, a salad, a song, a friend. Such actions, prompted by the Holy Spirit, embody the pure act of the Numinous and purify all human passion.

3. THE REALITY OF JESUS

The awe implicit in our createdness becomes gloriously explicit in Jesus Christ, who is the ontic-existential response to God the Father's passionate love. In His lifestance of pure passion, Jesus introduces into human history the centrality of personal experience and the uniqueness of normalcy. *Ecce homo.* In Jesus we see human reality in essence. Jesus is the apotheosis of humanness; His normalcy makes him unique.

4. DIVINIZATION

Jesus was divinely infected. He became the salient clue to the mystery of God and the meaning of our humanity. His divine nature was contagious. We are all divinized. We are scorched by the Fire, branded by the Holy One. We belong to God and take good care of His world or else we are perfidious.

5. ACTION AND CONTEMPLATION

We cannot take care of our own souls and let the world go hang. We cannot become perfect by seeking perfection directly, but as a by-product of our human effort to glorify God by human work well done. Well-done work depends entirely on the quality of contemplation. The nub of contemplation is mindfulness.

6. CONTEMPLATION AND CONSECRATION

From the most pedestrian instances of falling in love to the Beatific Vision of God, contemplation is taking a long, loving look at the real. Contemplatives, lovers of God and *all* His creation, never want to escape them courageously. Contemplatives do not ignore secularization but examine and judge it in terms of the Gospel, human nature, and the centrality of the sacred. They hate to reject anything and love to affirm the intrinsic goodness of everything, consecrating all that is to the One in whom they "live and move and have their being."

7. SILENCE, SOLITUDE, AND CELBRATION

We cannot live mindfully in the world, keep love alive, glorify, and enjoy God without prayerful silence and solitude, without careful public celebration of a worship that unites us all at the deepest level of being, whatever our religion, in, for example, the Mass, the Jewish Seder, or Buddhist meditation.

8. BROAD-MINDEDNESS AND HUMOR

We cannot afford to be parochial, provincial, or insular. Narrow-mindedness, humorlessness, moralism, and grumpy rectitude are an affront to the amplitude of Christ's mind and the openness of His Sacred Heart. Why do we insist on fencing off the great wild scope of our human nature? Because we are created, we are indebted; because we are graced, we are grateful; because we sin, we are repentant; because we participate in the Godhead, the future is open, and *now* is a momentous moment, an opening door into eternal life, into the kingdom of God.

9. THE LONG VIEW AND CREATIVITY

The *long view* of reality, based on scripture, tradition, and our own invaluable, personal, mystical experience, should arm us sufficiently to take a stand against the technobarbaric juggernaut and our mindless modern stampede into torrential trivia. Living in the heart of the Church, being the body of Christ, we have the stuff we need to bear this responsibility effectively, creatively, and humbly.

10. FREEDOM AND DETACHMENT

Human authenticity means freedom. Freedom does not mean we can do anything we want. It means we really want to do what we must in order to become the unique persons God requires us to be, free to become our best selves. There is no freedom without detachment from all that is not God. Detachment is not a flight from the world, nor a disinclination to creatures, nor a safe noncommitalism. Detachment is a daring, solicitous, warmhearted, unselfish love of everything. Detachment does not mean that we love nothing but God; it means that we love everything in God: the manifold in the One. It does not mean that we love things less and less, it means that we love them more and more, but selflessly, as part of our vast, undivided love of God.

11. DISCIPLINED LIFE

Freedom is impossible without a disciplined life, a "rule" of life that we harness all our scattered energies for the one thing necessary: enlightened love; a way of life that will enable us to resist the pressures of society to become numb, inane, and indifferent, letting far too many things happen to us.

12. RELATEDNESS AND REVERENCE

A person is one in search of another. The whole human adventure is an I-Thou relationship. The one question is: How significantly and sapiently are we related to all the others and, through this self-transcending endeavor, to the Wholly Other? What characterizes this relatedness to mineral, animals and persons? Reverence, the key virtue, because it incites and protects love. These are principles of sanctity, not safety, guidelines to a human life divinized, not a secure life routinized. Christ came that we all might live fully and enjoy building the Kingdom of God on Earth with unavoidable pain and unflagging panache.

Selected Readings

The selected bibliography that follows highlights, but does not exhaust, the many writings I mention and/or quote in this volume. I have chosen to cite here those I consider most important to the thoughts I present here, and they represent a wide swath of writings that I have appreciated over my lifetime. In most cases, I cite the original edition (or the original publication date) of a book, but readers who wish to explore further may find that newer editions—and sometimes, different translations—will satisfy their curiosity.

Agee, James. *A Death in the Family*. New York: McDowell, Obolensky, 1957.

Bielecki, Tessa. *Teresa of Avila: Ecstasy and Common Sense*. Boston: Shambhala, 1996.

Buber, Martin. I and Thou. Trans. Walter Kaufmann. New York: Scribner, 1970.

Camus, Albert. *The Myth of Sisyphus: And Other Essays*. New York: Knopf, 1955.

Chesterton, G. K. *Orthodoxy*. San Francisco: Ignatius Press, 1995 (1908).

Commission for Children at Risk. "Hardwired to Connect: The New Scientific Evidence for Authoritative Communities." New York: Institute for American Values, 2003.

Connoly, Myles. *Mr. Blue.* New York: Scribher, 1928.

De la Mare, Walter. "Hi!" In *The Complete Poems of Walter de la Mare.* New York: Knopf, 1976.

Donne, John. "Holy Sonnets" in *John Donne: The Major Works, including Songs and Sonnets and Sermons.* Oxford World's Classics. Ed. John Carey. New York: Oxford University Press, 1990.

Dostoyevsky, Fyodor. *The Brothers Karamazov.* Trans. Konstantin Mochulski. New York: Bantam, 1970 (1880).

Eliot, George. *Silas Marner.* New York: Bantam, 1981 (1861).

Eliot, T. S. "The Waste Land" (1922). In *Collected Poems, 1909-1962.* New York: Harcourt Brace, 1963.

Ellul, Jacques. *The Humiliation of the Word.* Trans. Joyce Main Hughes. Grand Rapids, Mich.: Wm. B. Eerdmans, 1985.

Farb, Peter: *Word Play: What Happens When People Talk.* New York: Random House, 1974.

Frankl, Viktor E. *Man's Search for Meaning.* Trans. Ilselasch. Boston: Beacon Press, 1959.

Frost, Robert. "Directive." In *The Poetry of Robert Frost: The Collected Poems, Complete and Unabridged.* New York: Henry Holt, 1979.

Fry, Christopher. "A Sleep of Prisoners." In *Three Plays: First Born, Thor, Sleep of Prisoners.* New York: Oxford University Press, 1965.

Hammarskjöld, Dag. *Markings.* Trans. Leif Sjöberg and W. H. Auden. New York: Knopf, 1964.

Heschel, Abraham. *A Passion for Truth.* New York: Farrar, Straus, and Giroux, 1973.

Hopkins, Gerard Manley. "God Grandeur." In *Gerard Manley Hopkins: The Major Works.* Oxford World's Classics. Ed. Catherine Phillips. New York: Oxford University Press, 1986.

Houselander, Caryll. *The Reed of God*. London: Sheed & Ward, 1944.

Von Hugel, Friedrich. *The Mystical Element of Religion, as Studied in Saint Catherine of Genoa and Her Friends*. Milestones in the Study of Mysticism and Spirituality. London: Herder & Herder, 1999 (1908).

Huxley, Aldous. *Grey Eminence: A study in Religion and Politics*. New York: Harper, 1941.

Kazantzakis, Nikos. *The Last Temptation of Christ*. Trans. Peter A. Bien. New York: Simon & Schuster, 1960.

———. *Report to Greco*. Trans. Peter A. Bien. New York: Bantam, 1961.

———. *Zorba the Greek*. Trans. Carl Wildman. New York: Simon & Schuster, 1953.

Kerr, Walter. *The Decline of Pleasure*. New York: Simon & Schuster, 1962.

Kierkegaard, Søren. *Purity of Heart Is to Will One Thing*. Trans. Douglas V. Steere. New York: Harper & Row, 1956 (1846).

Kittel, Gerard. *Love* (from *Bible Key Words from Gerhard Kittel's* Theologisches Wörterbuch zum Neuen Testament). Trans. G. Quell and E. Stauffer. London: Adam and Charles Black, 1949.

Krakauer, Jon. *Under the Banner of Heaven: A Story of Violent Faith*. New York: Doubleday, 2003.

Lallemant, Louis, S. J. *The Spiritual Doctrine of Father Louis Lallemant of the Company of Jesus, Preceded by an Account of His Life by Father Champion, S. J.* Ed. A.C. McDougall, London: Burns, Oates and Washbourne, 1928.

L'Engle, Madeleine. *Walking on Water: Reflections on Faith and Art*. Wheaton. Ill.: Harold Shaw Publishers, 1980.

May, Rollo. *Love and Will*. New York: W.W. Norton, 1969. Menninger, Karl A. *Whatever Became of Sin?* New York: E. P. Dutton, 1973.

Merton, Thomas. *Contemplation in a World of Action.*
Notre Dame, Ind.: University of Notre Dame
Press, 1999 (1971).

Moore, Brian. *Catholics.* New York: Holt, Rinehart &
Winston, 1972.

Muggeridge, Malcolm. "Albion Agonistes." *The
Alternative* (Feb. 1976). Pp. 10-11.

———. "The Great Liberal Death Wish." *Imprimis* 8,
no. 5 (May 1979).

O'Donoghue, Noel Dermot. "The Paradox of Prayer."
Doctrine and Life 24 (Jan. 1974). Pp.36-37.

Oliver, Mary. "When Death Comes" In *New and
Selected Poems.* Boston: Beacon Press, 1992.

Percy, Walker. *Lost in the Cosmos: The Last Self-Help
Book.* New York: Farrar Straus Girous, 1983.

Pieper, Joseph. *Leisure: The Basis of Culture.* Trans.
Alexander Dru. New York: Pantheon Books,
1964 (1938).

Raines, Robert A. *Creative Brooding: Readings to
Provoke Thought and Trigger Action.* New
York: Collier, 1977.

Riesman, David, with Nathan Glazer and Reuel
Denney. *The Lonely Crowd: A Study of the
Changing American Character.* New Haven: Yale
University Press, 1961.

Rilke, Rainer Maria. *The Book of Hours: Prayers to a
Lowly God.* Trans. Annemarie S. Kidder.
Evanston, Ill: Northwestern University Press,
2002.

Salinger, J. D. *The Catcher in the Rye.* New York:
Little, Brown, 1951.

Seeliger, Wes. "Western Theology: Are You a Settler or
a Pioneer?" *Desert Call* (Spring 1981).

Soelle, Dorothee. *The Strength of the Weak: Toward
a Christian Feminist Identity.* Philadelphia:
Westminster, 1984.

Spangler, David. *The Call.* New York: Riverhead,
1996.

Spengler, Oswald. *The Decline of the West.* Trans.
Charles Francis Atkinson. New York: Oxford
University Press, 1991 (1926, 1928).

St. John of the Cross. *The Ascent of Mount
Carmel.* Orleans, Mass.: Paraclete Press, 2002.

———. *The Dark Night of the Soul.* Trans. F. Allison
Peers. New York: Image Books, 1959.

St. Thërîse of Lisieux, *Story of a Soul: The
Autobiography of St. Thërîse of Lisieux.* Third
Edition. Washington, D.C.: ICS Publications,
1999.

Styron, William. *Sophie's Choice.* New York: Random
House, 1979.

Suzuki-roshi, Shunryu. *Zen Mind, Beginner's Mind.*
Trumble, Conn.:Weatherhill, 1973.

Swami, Vivekananda, The Complete Works of Swami
Vivekananda, Vol. 1 (Mayavati: Advaita Ashrama,
1955), pp. 324-325

Sykes, Gerald. *The Cool Millennium.* New York:
Prentice-Hall, 1973.

Tibbetts, A.M., and Charlene Tibbetts. *What's
Happening to American English?* New York:
Scribner, 1978.

Tolkein, J. R. R. *The Lord of the Rings.* 3 Volumes.
London: Allen & Unwin, 1954-1955.

Vann, Gerald. *The Heart of Man.* New York: Image
Books, 1962.

Watkin, E. I. *The Bow in the Clouds: An Essay
Towards the Integration of Experience* London:
Sheed & Ward, 1931.

Wilde, Oscar. *The Soul of Man Under Socialism and
Selected Critical Prose.* Ed. Linda Downing. New
York: Penguin, 2001.

William McNamara, or Abba Willie, as his friends call him, has been a monk all his life. Blessed and directed personally by good Pope John, he became the first ecclesial hermit in the United States. Subsequently, he founded the Spiritual Life Institute, established four communities of apostolic hermits, and now lives alone in a fifth hermitage located in New Pine Creek, Oregon. He is the author of several previous books, including *The Art of Being Human* and *The Human Adventure*.

CPSIA information can be obtained at www.ICGtesting.com
Printed in the USA
LVOW091712181211

259992LV00001B/66/P